Data Warehousing Web Sites

The following World Wide Web sites can provide you with comprehensive, up-to-date information about data warehousing (Chapter 29 describes these sites and lists others):

    www.dw-institute.com/

    pwp.starnetinc.com/larryg/
    index.html/

    www.olapreport.com/

    www.datawarehousing.com/

    www.idwa.org/

    www.ctp.com/

What to Do with a Data Warehouse

Why build a data warehouse? Here are four different classes of what you can do:

- ✔ **Basic querying and reporting:** "Tell me what happened."

- ✔ **OLAP:** "Tell me what happened and why."

- ✔ **Data mining:** "Tell me what may happen" or "Tell me something interesting."

- ✔ **EIS:** "Tell me lots of things, but don't make me work too hard."

Major Trends in Data Warehousing

Behold, a new generation of data warehousing technology will soon become mainstream! Here's what's new and exciting:

- ✔ **Operational data store (ODS):** An environment in which updates to operational data in various source systems are reflected almost immediately in a consolidated informational environment rather than in the traditional batch-oriented manner.

- ✔ **Virtual data warehousing:** An environment in which distributed components, rather than a single centralized data warehouse, are used to store contents and desktop tools can access data from these multiple locations.

- ✔ **Multimedia data warehousing:** A data warehousing environment that has not only traditional data types (numeric, character, and date information) but also images, video, audio, and other complex objects.

Hungry Minds™

For Dummies: Bestselling Book Series for Beginners

Data Warehousing For Dummies®

Cheat Sheet

Three Levels of Data Warehousing Complexity

Not all data warehouses are created equal. The following three-level classification can help you figure out the characteristics of your particular environment and then choose appropriate technologies, products, and architectural options:

- **Data warehousing lite:** A relatively straightforward implementation of a modest scope, based on "safe" technology. (The term *data mart* is often synonymous with *data warehouse lite* and is more commonly used.)

- **Data warehousing deluxe:** A standard data warehouse implementation that makes use of advanced technologies to solve complex business information and analytical needs.

- **Data warehousing supreme:** The data warehouse of the future, with leading-edge technologies, large-scale distribution of data, and other unconventional characteristics.

A Guide through the Maze of OLAP Acronyms and Terminology

You most likely will want to perform online analytical processing (OLAP) after you have built your data warehouse. Here's a guide through the maze of OLAP acronyms and terminology:

- **ROLAP, or relational OLAP:** An environment in which OLAP functionality is performed with data stored in a relational database.

- **MOLAP, or multidimensional OLAP:** An environment in which a specialized multi-dimensional database (MDDB) is used to store data for OLAP functionality.

- **HOLAP, or hybrid OLAP:** An environment with a combination of MOLAP and ROLAP data storage. Summarized information is typically stored in an MDDB, and detailed data is stored in a relational database.

- **DOLAP, or desktop OLAP:** An environment in which the client tool (a desktop or laptop computer) can operate in a self-contained manner, usually after downloading information from an OLAP database server.

- **Drill-down:** A method in which the results of a query are manipulated to see increasing levels of detail without having to rerun the query.

- **Drill-up:** (The opposite of drill-down.) A method in which results are manipulated to consolidate detailed data to a higher level of summarization without having to rerun the query.

- **Drill-across:** A method in which increased levels of detail about data are displayed across the top of a report.

- **Drill-through, or reach-through:** In this method, part of a HOLAP solution, increased levels of detail are displayed by moving from one database environment (an MDDB with summa-rized data, for example) to another (a relational database with detailed data, for example).

- **Pivoting:** A method in which a report is rearranged on-screen to provide a different view of its contents.

 ™

References for the Rest of Us! ®

BESTSELLING BOOK SERIES

Are you intimidated and confused by computers? Do you find that traditional manuals are overloaded with technical details you'll never use? Do your friends and family always call you to fix simple problems on their PCs? Then the For Dummies® computer book series from Hungry Minds, Inc. is for you.

For Dummies books are written for those frustrated computer users who know they aren't really dumb but find that PC hardware, software, and indeed the unique vocabulary of computing make them feel helpless. For Dummies books use a lighthearted approach, a down-to-earth style, and even cartoons and humorous icons to dispel computer novices' fears and build their confidence. Lighthearted but not lightweight, these books are a perfect survival guide for anyone forced to use a computer.

> *"I like my copy so much I told friends; now they bought copies."*
> — Irene C., Orwell, Ohio

> *"Quick, concise, nontechnical, and humorous."*
> — Jay A., Elburn, Illinois

> *"Thanks, I needed this book. Now I can sleep at night."*
> — Robin F., British Columbia, Canada

Already, millions of satisfied readers agree. They have made For Dummies books the #1 introductory level computer book series and have written asking for more. So, if you're looking for the most fun and easy way to learn about computers, look to *For Dummies* books to give you a helping hand.

Hungry Minds™

DATA WAREHOUSING FOR DUMMIES®

DATA WAREHOUSING FOR DUMMIES®

by Alan R. Simon

Hungry Minds™

Best-Selling Books • Digital Downloads • e-Books • Answer Networks • e-Newsletters • Branded Web Sites • e-Learning

New York, NY ◆ Cleveland, OH ◆ Indianapolis, IN

Data Warehousing For Dummies®

Published by
Hungry Minds, Inc.
909 Third Avenue
New York, NY 10022
www.hungryminds.com
www.dummies.com

Library of Congress Catalog Card No.: 97-80741

ISBN: 0-7645-0170-4

Printed in the United States of America

10 9 8 7 6 5

1O/RY/RQ/QR/IN

Distributed in the United States by Hungry Minds, Inc.

Distributed by CDG Books Canada Inc. for Canada; by Transworld Publishers Limited in the United Kingdom; by IDG Norge Books for Norway; by IDG Sweden Books for Sweden; by IDG Books Australia Publishing Corporation Pty. Ltd. for Australia and New Zealand; by TransQuest Publishers Pte Ltd. for Singapore, Malaysia, Thailand, Indonesia, and Hong Kong; by Gotop Information Inc. for Taiwan; by ICG Muse, Inc. for Japan; by Intersoft for South Africa; by Eyrolles for France; by International Thomson Publishing for Germany, Austria and Switzerland; by Distribuidora Cuspide for Argentina; by LR International for Brazil; by Galileo Libros for Chile; by Ediciones ZETA S.C.R. Ltda. for Peru; by WS Computer Publishing Corporation, Inc., for the Philippines; by Contemporanea de Ediciones for Venezuela; by Express Computer Distributors for the Caribbean and West Indies; by Micronesia Media Distributor, Inc. for Micronesia; by Chips Computadoras S.A. de C.V. for Mexico; by Editorial Norma de Panama S.A. for Panama; by American Bookshops for Finland.

For general information on Hungry Minds' products and services please contact our Customer Care Department within the U.S. at 800-762-2974, outside the U.S. at 317-572-3993 or fax 317-572-4002.

For sales inquiries and reseller information, including discounts, premium and bulk quantity sales, and foreign-language translations, please contact our Customer Care Department at 800-434-3422, fax 317-572-4002, or write to Hungry Minds, Inc., Attn: Customer Care Department, 10475 Crosspoint Boulevard, Indianapolis, IN 46256.

For information on licensing foreign or domestic rights, please contact our Sub-Rights Customer Care Department at 212-884-5000.

For authorization to photocopy items for corporate, personal, or educational use, please contact Copyright Clearance Center, 222 Rosewood Drive, Danvers, MA 01923, or fax 978-750-4470.

For information on using Hungry Minds' products and services in the classroom or for ordering examination copies, please contact our Educational Sales Department at 800-434-2086 or fax 317-572-4005.

For press review copies, author interviews, or other publicity information, please contact our Public Relations department at 317-572-3168 or fax 317-572-4168.

Hungry Minds™ is a trademark of Hungry Minds, Inc.

About the Author

Alan R. Simon is the director of worldwide data warehousing at Cambridge Technology Partners, a leading international consulting firm. His information technology career began in the late 1970s, when, as a senior at Arizona State University, he was responsible for maintaining a data warehouse for the Arizona attorney general's office.

After earning a master's degree in management information systems from the University of Arizona, Alan spent four years as a U.S. Air Force officer. During that time, he also founded and ran a small consultancy that developed PC-based management and reporting systems for small businesses in Colorado and Arizona.

He later worked with the Digital Equipment Corporation database systems group, first as a data modeling tool developer and later as a senior product manager for distributed database management systems — the forerunner to today's generation of data warehousing technology. After leaving DEC in late 1991, he turned his efforts back to consulting and book writing.

Alan lives on a farm in northeastern Pennsylvania. Beginning in January 1998, he will write a data warehousing column for *Database Programming & Design* magazine.

Acknowledgments

I'd like to thank the three people most responsible for making this book a reality: Gareth Hancock, acquisitions editor; Rebecca Whitney, project editor; and Matt Wagner, of Waterside Productions, my agent.

Publisher's Acknowledgments

We're proud of this book; please register your comments through our Hungry Minds Online Registration Form, located at www.dummies.com.

Some of the people who helped bring this book to market include the following:

Acquisitions, Development, and Editorial

Project Editor: Rebecca Whitney

Acquisitions Editor: Gareth Hancock

Technical Editor: Bill Karow

Editorial Manager: Mary C. Corder

Editorial Assistant: Darren Meiss

Production

Project Coordinator: Valery Bourke

Layout and Graphics: Kelly Hardesty, Angela F. Hunckler, Brent Savage, Cameron Booker

Proofreaders: Michael Bolinger, Kelli Botta, Michelle Croninger, Rachel Garvey, Rebecca Senninger, Rashell Smith, Janet M. Withers

Indexer: Liz Cunningham

Special Help: Suzanne Thomas

General and Administrative

Hungry Minds, Inc.: John Kilcullen, CEO; Bill Barry, President and COO; John Ball, Executive VP, Operations & Administration; John Harris, Executive VP and CFO

Hungry Minds Technology Publishing Group: Richard Swadley, Senior Vice President and Publisher; Mary Bednarek, Vice President and Publisher, Networking; Joseph Wikert, Vice President and Publisher, Web Development Group; Mary C. Corder, Editorial Director, Dummies Technology; Andy Cummings, Publishing Director, Dummies Technology; Barry Pruett, Publishing Director, Visual/Graphic Design

Hungry Minds Manufacturing: Ivor Parker, Vice President, Manufacturing

Hungry Minds Marketing: John Helmus, Assistant Vice President, Director of Marketing

Hungry Minds Production for Branded Press: Debbie Stailey, Production Director

Hungry Minds Sales: Michael Violano, Vice President, International Sales and Sub Rights

Contents at Glance

Cartoons at a Glance

By Rich Tennant

page 7

page 99

page 143

page 183

page 239

page 265

page 63

Fax: 978-546-7747
E-mail: richtennant@the5thwave.com
World Wide Web: www.the5thwave.com

Table of Contents

· ·

Part III: Business Intelligence and Data Warehousing 99

Chapter 8: An Intelligent Look at Business Intelligence 101

Chapter 9: Simple Database Querying and Reporting 109

Introduction

*T*he data warehouse is coming! The data warehouse is coming!

The data warehousing revolution is sweeping corporate information technology (IT) departments around the world. If you're an IT professional or you're fashionably referred to as a *knowledge worker* (someone who regularly uses computer technology in the course of your day-to-day business operations), data warehousing is for you! If you haven't come face-to-face with this phenomenon, you soon will. *Data Warehousing For Dummies* guides you through the overwhelming amount of hype about this subject to help you get the most from data warehousing.

If you're an IT professional (a software developer, database administrator, software development manager, or data-processing executive), this book provides you with a clear, no-hype description of data warehousing technology and methodology — what works, what doesn't work, and why.

If you regularly use computers in your job to find information and facts as a contracts analyst, researcher, district sales manager, or any one of thousands of other jobs in which data is a key asset to you and your organization, this book has in-depth information about the *real* business value (again, without the hype) you can gain from data warehousing.

Why I Wrote This Book

Although data warehousing can be an incredibly powerful weapon for you and others in your organization, pitfalls (lots of them!) are scattered along your path, from thinking about data warehousing to implementing it. The path to data warehousing is similar to the yellow brick road in *The Wizard of Oz:* Even though the journey seems relatively straightforward, you have to watch out for certain obstacles along the way, such as which technology path to take when you have a choice and all kinds of things you don't expect. Although you don't have to figure out how to handle winged monkeys and apple-throwing trees, you do have to deal with products that don't work as advertised and unanticipated database performance problems.

I've been working with data warehousing since the beginning of my career in the late 1970s. Though the current data warehousing revolution began in the early 1990s and we now have a much broader array of technologies and tools, the principle of data warehousing isn't all that new (as mentioned in Chapter 1), even though the term *is* relatively new.

What is new, however, is the intense, almost universal interest in data warehousing among medium-size and large organizations. Nearly every study done since 1994 to survey interest in data warehousing shows more than 90 percent of Fortune 2000-size organizations having at least one data warehousing initiative under way or on the drawing board. It seems that *everyone* wants a data warehouse!

This broad interest in data warehousing has, unfortunately, led to confusion about these issues:

- ✔ **Terminology:** For example, because no *official* definitions exist for the terms *data warehouse, data mart,* or *data mining,* product vendors declare definitions that are best suited to the products they sell.

- ✔ **How to successfully implement a large data warehousing system:** Should you build one large database of information and then parcel off smaller portions to different organizations, or should you build a bunch of smaller-scale databases and then integrate them later?

- ✔ **Advances in technology:** Issues such as the Internet are having an effect on data warehousing.

This book is, in many ways, a consolidation of my down-to-earth, no-hype conversations with and presentations to clients, IT professionals, and many others in recent years about what data warehousing means to business organizations: today *and* tomorrow.

How to Use This Book

You can read *Data Warehousing For Dummies* in either of these ways:

- ✔ **Read each chapter in sequential order, from cover to cover.** If this book is your first real exposure to data warehousing terminology, concepts, and technology, this method is probably the way to go.

- ✔ **Read selected chapters that are of particular interest to you and in any order you want.** The chapters have been written to stand on their own, with little dependency on any other chapter.

To give you a sense of what awaits you in *Data Warehousing For Dummies,* this section describes the contents of the book, which is divided into seven parts.

Part I: The Data Warehouse: Home for Your Secondhand Data

Part I gets down to the basics of data warehousing: concepts, terminology, roots of the discipline, and what to do with a data warehouse after you build it.

Chapter 1 gets right to the point about a data warehouse: what you can expect to find there, how and where its content is formed, and some early cautions to help you avoid pitfalls that await you during your first data warehousing project.

Chapter 2 describes in business-oriented terms exactly what a data warehouse can do for you.

The different types of data warehouses you can build (small, medium, or way big!) and the circumstances in which each one is appropriate are described in Chapter 3.

Chapter 4 describes the phenomenon of data marts (small-scale data warehouses) and just what the big deal is about them.

Part II: Data Warehousing Technology

In Part II, you go beyond basic concepts to find out about the technology behind data warehousing, particularly database technology.

Chapter 5 talks about relational databases (if you're an IT professional, you're probably familiar with them) and how these products are used for data warehousing. Chapter 6 describes multidimensional databases, the other type of databases used for data warehousing, and explains whether they're still a viable option for your data warehousing project.

Data warehousing middleware — software products and tools used to extract data from source applications and do all the necessary functions to move it into a data warehouse — is the focus of Chapter 7, along with the issues you have to watch out for in this area.

Part III: Business Intelligence and Data Warehousing: Not a Contradiction in Terms

Part III discusses the concept of *business intelligence:* the different categories of processing you can perform on the contents of a data warehouse. From "tell me what happened" processing to "Tell me what *may* happen" processing, it's all here!

See Chapter 8 for an overview of business intelligence and what it means to data warehousing.

Chapters 9 through 12 each describe in detail one major area of business intelligence (querying and reporting, analytical processing, data mining, and executive information systems, respectively). These chapters present you with ready-to-use advice about products in each of these areas.

Part IV: Data Warehousing Projects: How to Do Them Right

Knowing about data warehousing is one thing; being able to implement a data warehouse successfully is another. Part IV discusses project methodology, management techniques, the analysis of data sources, and how to work with users.

Chapter 13 describes data warehouse development (methodology) and the similarities to and differences from the methodologies you use for other types of applications.

Find out in Chapter 14 the right way to manage a data warehouse project to maximize your chances for success.

Chapters 15 and 16 each discuss an important part of a data warehouse project (analyzing data sources and working with users, respectively) and give you lots of tips and tricks to use in each of these critical areas.

Part V: Data Warehousing: The Big Picture

This part of the book discusses the big picture: data warehousing in the context of all the other organizations and people in your IT organization (and even outside consultants) and your other information systems.

Find out in Chapter 17 how to acquire external data (information about competing companies' sales of products, for example). You can also read about how to use that information in your data warehouse.

To understand how a data warehouse fits into your overall computing environment with the rest of your applications and information systems, see Chapter 18.

For an executive boardroom view of data warehousing, check out Chapter 19. Is this discipline as high a priority to the corporate bigwigs as you may imagine, considering its popularity?

Chapter 20 describes how to deal with data warehousing product vendors and the best ways to acquire information at the numerous data warehousing trade shows.

For advice about what to do in systems that are already in place that are sort of (but not really) like a data warehouse and used for simple querying and reporting, read Chapter 21. To replace those systems or upgrade them to a data warehouse, that is the question.

You may have to deal with data warehousing consultants (or maybe you are one). Chapter 22 fills you in on the tricks of the trade.

Part VI: Data Warehousing in the Not-Too-Distant Future

Every area of technology is constantly changing, and data warehousing is no exception. Because data warehousing is on the brink of a new generation of technologies, the chapters in this part of the book detail some of the most significant trends.

Chapter 23 describes operational data stores, or ODSs, which are data-warehouse-like environments in which updates occur much more quickly than in a typical data warehouse. When are ODSs appropriate? How do you go about implementing one of them? The answers are here.

Data warehouses typically include only a few different types of data: numbers, dates, and character-based information, such as names and addresses and product descriptions and codes. Chapter 24 fills you in on the next wave of data warehousing, in which multimedia data (pictures, images, videos, audio, and documents) are included as part of a data warehouse.

Chapter 25 talks about the idea of implementing a virtual data warehouse: one that doesn't feature all the typical copying of data back and forth. When is virtual data warehousing a good idea? What are the restrictions and limitations you must overcome to implement a virtual data warehouse? Read Chapter 25 to find out!

Part VII: The Part of Tens

Last, but certainly not least, is the ...*For Dummies* institution: The Part of Tens. This part of the book has eight chapters chock-full of data warehousing hints and advice. Could you ask for anything more to close out this book?

Icons Used in This Book

This icon denotes tips and tricks of the trade that make your projects go more smoothly and otherwise ease your foray into data warehousing.

Beware! Data warehousing traps, hype, and other potentially unpleasant experiences are pointed out.

Data warehousing is all about computer technology. When you see this icon, the accompanying explanation digs into the underlying technology and processes, in case you want to get behind the scenes, under the hood, or beneath the covers.

We're on the brink of a new generation of data warehousing! This icon tells you about a major trend in technology (or a way of implementing data warehousing) that's likely to become important to you *soon*.

Some things about data warehousing are just so darned important that they bear repeating. This icon lets you know that I'm repeating something on purpose, not because I was experiencing déjà vu.

A Word about the Product References in This Book

(Consider this icon a test run.) In Parts II and III, I mention a number of products and list the Web sites where you can find information about them. The brief product descriptions are paraphrased from the respective vendors' Web sites and were up-to-date at the time this book was written. I mention the products in those chapters as *examples* of products in the chapter rather than as a recommendation. (How's that for a disclaimer?)

Part I

The Data Warehouse: Home for Your Secondhand Data

The 5th Wave   By Rich Tennant

"THIS SECURITY PROGRAM WILL RESPOND TO THREE THINGS:
AN INCORRECT ACCESS CODE, AN INAPPROPRIATE FILE REQUEST,
OR SOMETIMES A CRAZY HUNCH THAT MAYBE YOU'RE JUST
ANOTHER SLIME-BALL WITH MISAPPROPRIATION OF SECURED
DATA ON HIS MIND."

In this part . . .

This part of the book explains, in absolutely no-hype terms, the basics of data warehousing: what a data warehouse is, where its contents come from and why, what you use it for after you've built it, and options you have for choosing its level of complexity.

The chapter about data marts (the latest hot topic in the data warehousing world) can help you understand what they really are in relation to a data warehouse.

Chapter 1

What's in a Data Warehouse?

*I*f you gather in a room 100 computer consultants experienced in data warehousing and give them this single-question written quiz, "Define a data warehouse in 20 words or fewer," at least 95 of the consultants will turn in their paper with a one- or two-sentence definition that includes the terms *subject-oriented, time-variant,* and *read-only.* The other 5 replies will likely focus more on business than on technology and use a phrase such as "improve corporate decision-making through more timely access to information."

Forget all that. The following section gives you a no-nonsense definition guaranteed to be free of both technical and business-school jargon.

The Data Warehouse: A Place for Your Used Data

A *data warehouse* is a home for "secondhand" data that originates in either other corporate applications, such as the one your company uses to fill customer orders for its products, or some data source external to your company, such as a public database that contains sales information gathered from all your competitors.

If your company's data warehouse were advertised as a used car, for example, it may be described this way: "Contains late-model, previously owned data, all of which has undergone a 25-point quality check and is offered to you with a brand-new warranty to guarantee hassle-free ownership."

Most organizations build a data warehouse in a relatively straightforward manner:

1. The data warehousing team selects a *focus area,* such as tracking and reporting the company's product sales activity against that of its competitors.

2. The team in charge of building the data warehouse assigns a group of business users and other key individuals within the company to play the role of Subject-Matter Experts. Together, these people compile a list of different types of data that enable them to use the data warehouse to help track sales activity (or whatever the focus is for the project).

3. The group then goes through the list of data, item by item, and figures out where it can obtain that particular piece of information. In most cases, the group can get it from at least one internal (within the company) database or file, such as the one the application uses to process orders by mail or the master database of all customers and their current addresses. In other cases, a piece of information is not available from within the company's computer applications but could be obtained by purchasing it from some other company. Although the credit ratings and total outstanding debt for all of a bank's customers, for example, aren't known internally, that information can be purchased from a credit bureau.

4. After completing the details of where each piece of data comes from, the data warehousing team (usually computer analysts and programmers) create *extraction programs*. These programs collect data from various internal databases and files, copy certain data to a *staging area* (a work area outside the data warehouse), ensure that the data has no errors, and then copy it all into the data warehouse. Extraction programs are created either by hand (custom-coded) or by using specialized data warehousing products.

That's it! The most successful data warehouses are built by spending adequate time on the first two steps (analyzing the need for a data warehouse and how it should be used), which makes the next two steps (designing and implementing the warehouse to make it ready to use) much smoother.

Interestingly, the analysis steps (determining the focus of the data warehouse and working closely with business users to figure out what information is important) are *nearly identical* to the steps for any other type of computer application. Most computer applications create data as a result of something happening while the application is being used to conduct business, such as filling a customer's order. The primary difference in a data warehouse is that it relies exclusively on data obtained from other places. Figure 1-1 shows the difference between these two types of environments.

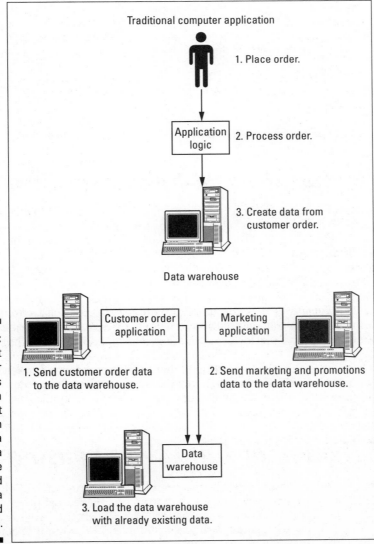

Figure 1-1: Most computer applications create data as a result of an activity; a data warehouse instead swipes data created elsewhere.

Traditional computer application

1. Place order.

Application logic — 2. Process order.

3. Create data from customer order.

Data warehouse

Customer order application — 1. Send customer order data to the data warehouse.

Marketing application — 2. Send marketing and promotions data to the data warehouse.

Data warehouse

3. Load the data warehouse with already existing data.

More Formal Definitions

If you cringe at the thought of defining the concept of secondhand data in your data warehouse projects to your executive sponsors, this section gives you two definitions (more formal, more traditional, yet still hypefree) that you can use instead.

Today's data warehousing defined

Data warehousing is the coordinated, architected, and periodic copying of data from various sources, both inside and outside the enterprise, into an environment optimized for analytical and informational processing.

The keys to this definition for computer professionals are that the data is copied (duplicated) in a *controlled* manner and is copied *periodically* (batch-oriented processing).

Note: This definition is *still* hypefree.

A broader, forward-looking definition

The definition in the preceding section is adequate for what I call *first-generation* data warehousing. As new technologies and models of data access come into play, however (as discussed in Part VI of this book), a broader definition is necessary. This definition, which isn't constrained by the one-way, batch-oriented copying of data, still emphasizes that information from many different sources is necessary.

Data warehousing is also, therefore, the process of creating an architected information-management solution to enable analytical and informational processing despite platform, application, organizational, and other barriers.

The key concept in this definition is that barriers are being broken and distributed information is being consolidated, although no preconceived notion exists for the exact means of doing so, such as duplicating data.

A Brief History of Data Warehousing

Many people, when they first learn about the basic principles of data warehousing, particularly copying data from one place to another, think (or even say), "That doesn't make any sense! Why waste time copying and moving data and storing it in a different database? Why not just get it directly from its original location when someone needs it?"

To better understand the "why we do what we do" aspect of data warehousing, it's important to look at its historical roots — how data warehousing became what it is today.

The 1970s

The 1970s. Disco and leisure suits were in. So were platform shoes. And the computing world was dominated by the mainframe. Real data-processing applications, the ones run on the corporate mainframe, almost always had a complicated set of files or early-generation databases (not the table-oriented relational databases most applications use today) in which data was stored.

Although the applications did a fairly good job of performing routine data-processing functions, data created as a result of these functions (such as information about customers, the products they ordered, and how much money they spent) was locked away in the depths of the files and databases. It was almost impossible, for example, to see how retail stores in the eastern region were doing against stores in the western region, against their competitors, or even against their own performance in some earlier period. At best, you could have written up a report request and sent it to the data-processing department, where it was put on a waiting list with a couple thousand other report requests, and you may have had an answer in a few months — or not.

Some enterprising, forward-thinking people decided to take another approach to the data access problem. During the 1970s, as minicomputers were becoming popular, the thinking went like this: Rather than make requests to the data-processing department every time data from an application's files or databases is needed, why not identify a few key data elements (for example, a customer's ID number, total units purchased in the most recent month, and total dollars spent) and have the data-processing folks copy this data to a tape each month during a slow period, such as over a weekend or during the midnight shift? The data from the tape could then be loaded into another file on the minicomputer, and the business users could use decision-support tools and report writers (products that allowed access to data without having to write separate programs) to get answers to their business questions and avoid continually bothering the data-processing department.

Although this approach worked (sort of) in helping to reduce the backlog of requests the data-processing department had to deal with, the usefulness of the extracted and copied data usually didn't live up to the vision of the people who put the systems in place. Suppose that a company had *three* separate systems to handle customer sales: one for the eastern U.S. region, one for the western U.S. region, and one for all stores in Europe. Also, each of these three systems was different from the others. Although data copied from the system that processed sales for the western U.S. region was helpful in analyzing western region activity for each month and maybe on a historical basis (if previous batches of data were retained), questions about trends across the entire United States or the world couldn't be answered easily without copying more data from *each* of the systems. People typically gave up at this point because answering the questions was usually too time-consuming.

The 1980s

The 1980s: the era of yuppies. PCs, PCs, and more PCs suddenly appeared everywhere you looked — and more and more minicomputers too. Before anyone knew it, "real computer applications" were no longer only on mainframes; they were all over the place — everywhere you looked in an organization. The problem called "islands of data" was beginning to look ominous: How could an organization hope to compete if its data was scattered all over the place on different computer systems that weren't even all under the control of the centralized data-processing department? (Never mind that even when the data was all stored on mainframes, it was still isolated in different files and databases and was just as inaccessible.)

The group of enterprising, forward-thinking people, freed from the delirium of 1970s disco and leisure suits, came up with a new idea: Because data is located all over the place, why not create special software to enable people to sit at a PC or a terminal and make a request, such as "Show per-store sales in all worldwide regions, ranked in descending order by improvement over sales in the same period a year earlier"? This new type of software, called a *distributed database management system* (distributed DBMS, or DDBMS), would magically pull the requested data from databases across the organization, bring all the data back to the same place, and then consolidate it and sort it and do whatever else was necessary to answer the user's question. (This process also was supposed to happen pretty darned quickly.)

To make a long story short, although the concept of DDBMSs was a good one and early results from research were promising, the results were plain and simple: They just didn't work in the real world. Also, the "islands of data" problem still existed.

The 1990s

Now, during the 1990s, disco is back. (Luckily, no one has spotted any leisure suits yet, except at retro-'70s parties.) At the beginning of the decade, some 20 years after computing "went mainstream," business computer users were still no closer to being able to use the trillions of bytes of data locked away in databases all over the place to make better business decisions.

The original group of enterprising, forward-thinking people has now retired (or perhaps switched to doing Web site development). Using the time-honored concept of "something old, something new" (the "something borrowed, something blue" part doesn't quite fit), a new approach to solving the "islands of data" problem has surfaced. If the 1980s approach of reaching out and accessing data directly from the files and databases didn't work, the philosophy this time is to go back to the 1970s method in which data from those places was copied to another location — and do it right this time.

And data warehousing was born.

The current trend is not to go after data from just one place, such as a single application, but rather to go after everything that's needed, regardless of how many different applications and computers are used in the organization. Client/server technology can be used to put the data on servers and give users new and improved analysis tools on their PCs.

Most important, have a plan in place before you begin this process. Know the focus of what you're trying to do and the questions you're likely to be asking. Will you be asking mostly about sales activity? If so, put plans in place for regular monthly (or weekly or even daily) extractions of data about customers, the products they buy, and money spent. If you work at a bank and your business focus is managing the risk across loan portfolios, for example, get information from the bank's applications that handle loan payments, delinquencies, and other data you need; then add in data from the credit bureau about your customers' respective overall financial profiles.

Is a Bigger Data Warehouse a Better Data Warehouse?

A common misconception that many data warehouse aficionados hold is that the only good data warehouse is a big data warehouse — an enormously big data warehouse. Many people even take the stance that unless some astronomically large number of bytes is stored, it isn't truly a data warehouse! "Five hundred gigabytes? Okay, that's a *real* data warehouse; it would be a better data warehouse, however, if it had at least a terabyte (1 trillion bytes) of data. Twenty-five gigabytes? Sorry, that's a data mart, not a data warehouse." (Data marts are described in Chapter 4.)

I often use a somewhat off-color rebuttal in response to the bigger-is-better philosophy about data warehousing, but the editors won't let me mention it in a family-rated book. (Feel free to send me an e-mail message, though, at 70714.2517@compuserve.com, and I'll forward a copy to you.)

Instead, you can look at this issue in another way. Imagine that Crocodile Dundee, the famed Australian pub regular from the 1986 movie, is now a data warehousing consultant. He and Sue Charlton (the journalist who travels to Australia to interview him and brings him back to New York City) are standing on a corner in Winslow, Arizona, when they're approached by another computer consultant. Their dialogue goes something like this (if you haven't seen the movie, you have to rent the video or watch it on cable so that it makes sense):

Other consultant (sneers and then menacingly pulls out a specification sheet and starts reading): Half a terabyte of data, 35 database tables —

Sue Charlton: Look out! He's got a data warehouse!

Crocodile Dundee (with Australian accent!): That's not a data warehouse. . . .

Crocodile Dundee (pulls out his own specification sheet and starts reading): Two terabytes of data, 76 tables — *this* is a data warehouse!

Okay, back to being (sort of) serious. The point is simply this: The size of a data warehouse is a *characteristic,* almost a by-product, of a data warehouse; it's not an objective. *No one* should ever set out with a mission to "build a 500-gigabyte data warehouse that contains (whatever)."

The path to determining the size of a data warehouse looks like this:

1. **Determine the *mission,* or the business objectives, of the data warehouse.**

   Ask the question, "Why bother creating this warehouse?"

2. **Determine the *functionality* the data warehouse should have.**

   Figure out what types of questions users will ask and what types of answers they will seek.

3. **Determine what *contents* (types of data) should be in the data warehouse to support its functionality.**

4. **Determine, based on the content (which is based on the functionality, which in turn is based on the mission), how big your data warehouse should be.**

Realizing That a Data Warehouse (Usually) Has a Historical Perspective

In almost all situations, a data warehouse has a historical perspective. Some amount of time lag occurs between the time something happens in one of the data sources (a new record is added or an existing one is modified, for example) and the time the results of that event are available in the data warehouse.

The reason for the time lag is that you usually *bulk-load* data into a data warehouse in large batches. Figure 1-2 illustrates a model of bulk-loading data.

Bulk-loading is giving way to *messaging,* the process of sending a small number of updates, perhaps only one at a time, much more frequently from the data source to a target — in this case, the data warehouse. With messaging, you will have a much more up-to-date picture of your data warehouse's subject areas than you do today because you're putting information into an operational data store (described in Chapter 23) rather than into a traditional data warehouse.

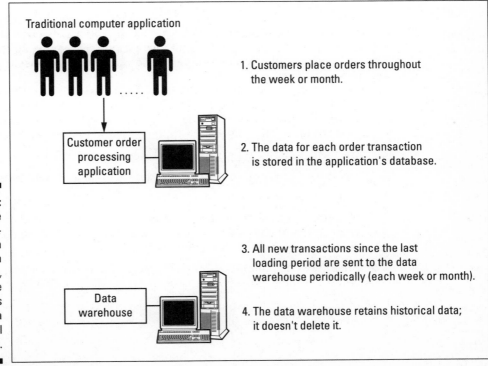

Traditional computer application

1. Customers place orders throughout the week or month.

Customer order processing application

2. The data for each order transaction is stored in the application's database.

3. All new transactions since the last loading period are sent to the data warehouse periodically (each week or month).

Data warehouse

4. The data warehouse retains historical data; it doesn't delete it.

Figure 1-2: Because you bulk-load data into a data warehouse, the time delay gives you a historical perspective.

It's Data Warehouse, Not Data Dump

An often-heard argument about what should be stored in a data warehouse goes something like this: "If I have to take the trouble to pull out data from all these different applications, why not just get as much as I possibly can? If I don't get everything, or as much as possible, I won't be able to ask all the business questions I might want to."

In a commonly related story about knowledge gained from a successful data warehouse implementation, a grocery-store chain discovered an unusually high correlation of disposable baby diapers and beer sales during a two- or three-hour period early every Friday evening and found out that a significant number of people on their way home from work were buying both these items. The store then began stocking display shelves with beer and disposable diapers next to one another, and sales increased significantly.

Although I don't know whether this story is true (it certainly has been told often enough), I believe that it confuses the issue when you have to figure out what should — and should not be — in your data warehouse. The moral of this story is usually mistaken as, "Put as much data as possible in the warehouse." In reality, the data warehouse just described was probably one that focused exclusively on sales activity. Remember that although disposable diapers and beer are dramatically different products, they are members of the same *type* of data (products).

The following example emphasizes why you should be selective about what goes in your data warehouse and not just assume that you should be able to ask any possible question and therefore have to get every possible type of data from all the sources.

Suppose that you're creating a data warehouse for a cruise ship company. As shown in Figure 1-3, the Tucson Desert Cruise Ship Company (its motto is "Who needs an ocean?") uses four applications that handle different tasks:

- Reservations and cancellations
- Food-and-beverage service for all cruises
- All trip itineraries and after-the-fact information about the weather, unusual events, and all onboard entertainment scheduling (movies, gambling, and all the events that used to be shown on *The Love Boat*, such as singles-night limbo contests)
- All crew assignments

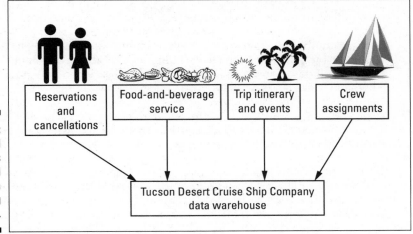

Figure 1-3:
A fictional company's proposed data warehousing environment.

Figure 1-4 shows one possible environment for your data warehouse if you were to pursue the philosophy of "Go get everything you possibly can," or what I call the *data dump* approach.

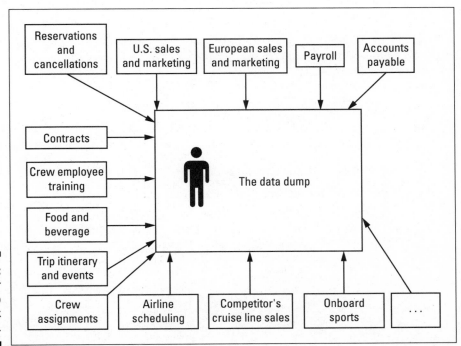

Figure 1-4:
What your data dump can look like.

So what's the problem? By having the information shown in Figure 1-4 in your data warehouse, you — and every other person who uses the warehouse — can ask questions and make report requests, such as "What is the average number of room-service vegetarian meals ordered by passengers who were on their third cruise with Captain Grumby in command and in which a half-day stop was made in Grand Cayman when its temperature was between 75 and 80 degrees?"

What is the *real business value,* however, of asking this type of question? Assuming that you receive an answer to the question, what would you do as a result that could have a positive business effect?

Look at it this way: For some types of data, you can analyze, analyze, and analyze some more and still find out little of value that could positively affect your business. Although you can put this data in your warehouse, you probably won't get much for your trouble. Other types of data, though, have significant value "locked away" and therefore *do* belong in your warehouse. Concentrate on the latter, and ignore the former!

Chapter 2

What Should You Expect from Your Data Warehouse?

In This Chapter

▶ Making business decisions based on facts, not on intuition

▶ Knowing whether "data at your fingertips" is *truly* valuable

▶ Looking at cross-organization communications and your data warehouse

▶ Bringing different business organizations closer together

*A*ll too often, the members of a data warehouse development team proudly unveil their creation, get a few "oohs" and "aahs" from their user community, and then find out that "if you build it, they won't necessarily come." The data warehouse just sits there, quietly being restocked every week or every month and supporting only a few random user information requests until plans eventually are drafted for its replacement.

Many, or perhaps most, of these unfortunate situations can be avoided if everyone, from the executive sponsors to the technicians and developers, focus their efforts on a single question: "What do you do with a data warehouse?"

It's not the contents of the warehouse (the data) that's important; rather, it's how the data is used in everyday business life.

Using the Data Warehouse to Make Better Business Decisions

Suppose that John is a district manager at MegaRetroMania, Ltd., a national chain of video-rental stores that specializes in movies from the 1950s and earlier. Mary is John's counterpart in another district. Both excitedly awaited the rollout of MegaRetroMania's brand-new data warehouse, an event that finally occurred a month ago. John and Mary both attended the data warehousing orientation class in which they learned how to run reports and make information requests using the contents of the warehouse. Each person received a handsome, ready-for-framing certificate indicating successful completion of the course.

On July 20, the day after June's results had been finalized and loaded into the data warehouse, John sits down at his PC, clicks the icon that enables him to access the data warehouse, and makes this request:

> Show me, for each of my stores, a breakdown of second-quarter sales compared to first-quarter sales, each store's second-quarter sales from a year earlier, and the sales of all competitors within two square miles of each store's location.

As John watches the little "Working, please wait" hourglass icon twirl for a few seconds on-screen, he thinks, "It's fascinating how they can make it seem like the sand is really sifting from top to bottom like that." After the results of his request are displayed on-screen directly in front of him, he prints the report, walks over to the printer to retrieve the five printed pages, flips through them for a few moments, and then thinks, "That's really neat!"

Then he slips the report into the middle drawer on the left side of his desk before leaving for lunch.

And he never looks at it again.

Mary runs the same identical report for her district; after printing the report and flipping through the pages, however, she (unlike John) has a pen in hand and circles one number, underlines another, and writes "Uh-oh!" next to the line containing the information for a store that she knows is having problems.

Then Mary returns to her desk, report in hand, and picks up the telephone. First, she calls her problem-child store. After the manager comes to the phone, Mary spends the next half-hour making follow-on information requests from the data warehouse, discussing the result of each request with the store manager, and considering various options, such as sales promotions.

After Mary takes her regular two-mile lunchtime walk, she calls the manager of another store in Madison County, Iowa, whose second-quarter sales were relatively flat after experiencing at least 15 percent growth every quarter for the past three years, a fact she obtained from the data warehouse when she noted the lack of growth in the second quarter. While the store manager is on the phone, Mary gets a week-by-week sales breakdown from the warehouse and is surprised to see that the first three weeks of the quarter had been fairly good, with sales during each week slightly ahead of the preceding one. During the fourth week of April, however, a large dip occurred, followed by an even larger dip the following week and yet another drop the week after that (the worst week any store had ever had, it turns out, in the long, distinguished history of MegaRetroMania) before sales began picking up in mid-May.

Suddenly, the store manager has an idea — maybe the Olympic Games were causing the problem! The Olympics had been held in Madison County for the first time ever, and *everyone* had attended. Even that store's primary customer base, the legions of photographers who usually come to Madison County to take pictures of covered bridges during a four-day period and rent movies to watch in their motel rooms at night, were preoccupied for those three weeks by the Olympics.

Satisfied that no burgeoning problem is waiting in the Madison County store — just a once-in-a-lifetime anomaly, most likely — Mary turns her attention to the other annotations on her printout. By the end of the day, five stores have action plans in place for special promotional campaigns to combat competition that has opened in the past few months near those MegaRetroMania locations.

Here's a quiz. True or false: Mary and John both used the data warehouse today.

The answer: False.

You may be thinking, "What? Of course, John used the data warehouse today. He ran a report and looked it over."

No! Although John *accessed* the data warehouse, he did not *use* it. He looked over a printout and stuffed it away forever, and then it was business as usual. When you compare his action to Mary's, the differences are obvious.

(Remember the philosophical question about the tree falling in the forest? Here's a potential technology-age successor to that question: If a user accesses information from a data warehouse but does nothing with that information, is that person really a user?)

No matter what else appears on a data warehousing project's mission statement and no matter what words are used to convey the project's merits to the people who control the money as the data warehousing project's sponsors seek funding, the primary purpose of a data warehouse is to help people make better business decisions. Data warehousing isn't about simply accessing data and then doing nothing with it; it's about *really using* data.

Here's one way to make sure that data warehouse users act more like Mary than like John: When you conduct training sessions before users are turned loose on the new data warehouse, be sure to not only teach them how to access data (which types of queries and reports they can run or which types of data are available, for example) but also feature real-world examples of how to use the results of their warehouse access.

The training session for MegaRetroMania district managers (and other warehouse users), for example, may feature end-to-end hands-on training that explains how to get sales reports and what the reports will look like. To make sure that users understand the usefulness of the data warehouse, the instruction could also feature role-playing or some other type of training in what to do with those reports to improve the stores' performance.

Finding Data at Your Fingertips

So what's the big deal about linking data warehousing to better business decision-making? Everyone has heard the phrase "information (or knowledge) is power," and a long-accepted maxim says that the more skillfully people use information in the course of their jobs, the greater their chances for success.

The process of gathering data from many different sources (if it's even attainable) has traditionally been tedious, particularly before computers became commonplace, and it has remained that way during the information age. Some novels and movies would have us believe that after we press just a few keystrokes, vast amounts of data are automatically accessible from anywhere in the world regardless of, for example, the platform we're using, the structure of the data (how it's organized), or different ways the data is encoded or keyed.

The real world isn't quite that orderly, and anyone who has struggled to perform what should be simple tasks (merging Pacific Rim sales data from one system with North American sales data from another, for example) is probably aware of the difficulties.

Suppose that Steve is a district sales manager at BlackAndWhiteVideos, Inc., MegaRetroMania's upstart archrival. Unlike John and Mary, though, Steve has no data warehouse from which to make requests, such as "Show me the top 20 BlackAndWhiteVideos stores across the district in which monthly total comedy video rentals are at least double those of action videos." Instead, Steve has to get the answer to this question the old-fashioned way, as shown in Figure 2-1:

1. Write and distribute to all store managers in the district a memo stating that no later than the fifth day of each month, he wants a report sent to him, based on transaction records from each store's point-of-sale (POS) computer system, of rental dollars by category (such as comedy, action, and icky romantic movies that his kids hate to watch).

2. On the fifth day of each month, look through the reports received and note each store from which a report has not been received.

3. Spend most of the next two days calling store managers who haven't sent reports and hearing something like, "Oh, wow, I totally forgot all about that; what do you want me to send you again?"

4. While waiting for each of the missing reports, begin entering into a spreadsheet the numbers from the reports that have been received.

   Each month, it occurs to Steve that he should send a new memo asking managers to mail him a disk with each store's data on it (already in spreadsheet format) so that he doesn't have to reenter the information. He never quite gets around to that request because he assumes that it takes several months to train someone in each store to be able to extract data from the POS application into a spreadsheet.

5. By the 12th of each month, make another round of phone calls to the stores that still haven't submitted their reports, and this time threaten to — well, you get the idea.

6. Finally, by the 20th of each month, after the spreadsheet program has all the necessary information, run a few simple sorting routines to get the necessary reports.

7. Before he knows it, prepare to start all over for the next month's data.

I have four questions about Mary at MegaRetroMania and Steve at BlackAndWhiteVideos (forget about John at MegaRetroMania — he's a loser):

1. Who is making more effective use of technology?

2. Who is likely to be more productive in a district manager's role?

3. Who will likely make more timely business decisions with (using business-school talk) a more positive impact on short-term and long-term revenues?

4. Who is more likely to be frustrated and look for another job where much less time is wasted?

(Answers: 1. Mary, 2. Mary, 3. Mary, 4. Steve)

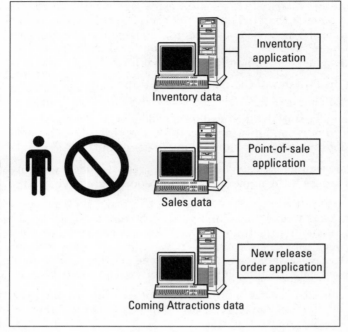

Figure 2-1:
Without
a data
warehouse,
data isn't at
a user's
fingertips
— it's
usually out
of reach!

What's important is that both Mary and Steve *could* have access to the same information and in the same way because both MegaRetroMania and BlackAndWhiteVideos have similar computer systems with similar data. The difference is that because MegaRetroMania has chosen to invest in data warehousing technology, Mary and her counterparts (even that loser John, if he would only get with the program) can make business decisions that are both information-based and timely.

Here are two more questions to consider:

1. Does your current job more closely resemble Steve's or Mary's in how you're able to get access to information you need?

2. Regardless of how you answered the first question, would you prefer that your job were more like the others?

(Answers: Either 1. Steve and 2. Of course!, or 1. Mary and 2. No way.)

Facilitating Communications with Data Warehousing

A "softer" benefit of data warehousing, one that's much less tangible than having information for better business decisions but nonetheless real, is that it often facilitates better communications across a company than what existed before the warehouse project began:

1. The *information technology (IT) organization* — the centralized organization that handles infrastructure (hardware and software platforms, networking, and communications, for example) — begins working more cooperatively with its customers in the business organizations.

2. Business organizations that are drawn together as part of a data warehousing project often gain more appreciation for each other's missions and challenges.

Part of the better communications picture occurs (usually) between applications development and customers in the organization's business units.

Data warehousing can also promote increased levels of communication across different business units.

IT-to-business-organization communications

If you're a veteran of an IT-organization-versus-business-organization war in your company, you may have won some battles and lost others. Make no mistake about it, though: The other side is the enemy!

If you're on the IT side, you may grumble about these issues:

- ✔ Business users make unrealistic requests for new applications and enhancements to existing applications, and they don't participate during application development and testing.

- ✔ Users are so technology-challenged that they require hand-holding for the simplest application functions.

On the other side, business users commonly make these types of complaints:

- ✔ IT application developers have no idea about how the company's business is run and usually don't even bother to ask. They just put whatever features they want into the applications, regardless of whether those features are even applicable to the business processes.

> ✔ IT is too slow in responding to requests for support. (All together now: "How slow are they?")

Particularly since the early 1980s, when the then-new personal computer and local-area network permitted business organizations to take direct responsibility for part of their information management and application capabilities, many companies have experienced an era of mistrust and lack of communications between IT and business.

Data warehousing projects often give organizations a chance to mend the rift between IT and business users. The nature of data warehousing (for example, the focus on business questions and the data necessary to answer those questions) gives people from both sides an opportunity to better understand the other group's roles and concerns.

The result of increased IT–business organization communications is often more effective and efficient working relationships, as a degree of trust is developed. A successful project or two usually can do wonders in achieving increased cooperation.

Better communications between IT and business organizations is not necessarily a given just because they jointly embark on a data warehousing effort. For example, if you use the word *dysfunctional* in response to a request to describe in a single word the relationship between IT and the business community in your company, you may want to look at some team-building workshops or other remedial training before proceeding with a data warehousing project.

Communications across business organizations

Data warehousing involves, in many ways, the use of technology to break down barriers that are inherent in large companies, such as different computer systems performing similar functions for different groups of users or different databases with information that, if the company were to start over, would be better kept in a single database. A sales-and-marketing organization responsible for one of its company's products naturally wants to help integrate its data (performance results) with that of another sales-and-marketing organization, responsible for a different product, that uses a different computer system (possibly as a result of a corporate acquisition), right?

Hah! Corporate intrigue and turf wars are the hallmark of business. Business executives and their staff members usually think of information not as a *corporate* strategic asset but rather as a *personal* one.

The breaking-through-barriers nature of data warehousing usually takes a top-level mandate from a chief executive officer (CEO) or chief operating officer (COO): "Thou shalt all cooperate, or thou shalt look for another job." That type of mandate, however, is probably a corporation's best chance for overcoming detrimental corporate politics and "kingdom building."

Suppose that you're a senior company executive at a consumer products company, with an environment that looks like the one shown in Figure 2-2. You decide that it's worth paying a million dollars to enable your managers and analysts to get timely access to data so that they can — remember what I discussed first in this chapter? — *make better business decisions.*

Using the cooperate-or-else mandate, you can ask — and receive answers to — the barrier-busting questions that present you with a consolidated picture of your sales, regardless of how many source systems the data comes from. In addition, after the first successful collaborative, cross-organization data warehousing effort, people are likely to feel less territorial and work more closely together for the common good of the company.

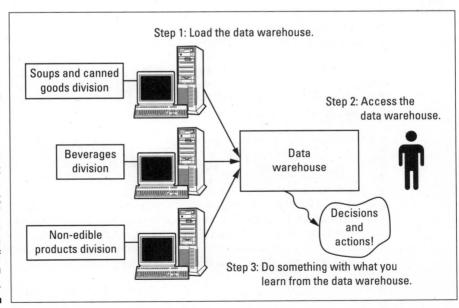

Figure 2-2: A typical data warehousing environment with different products' sales data stored on a variety of application systems.

Or they may not. Any lack of cooperation on the part of the leaders and members of a particular business organization, however, will be *extremely* apparent because their data either won't be in the warehouse (often called a *data gap*) or, worse, the data warehouse project will probably fail — and it will be obvious who's at fault.

I don't mean to imply that finger-pointing and blame-casting should be an inherent part of your data warehousing project; rather, you should implement, from the beginning, a clear directive for cooperating with peers that everyone is expected to follow.

Facilitating Business Change with Data Warehousing

Data warehousing also involves facilitating change in business processes. In addition to being able to make better, information-driven operational and tactical decisions, you gain insight into key areas that can help you make strategic decisions about the fundamental aspects of your business.

Your data warehouse can act as an early-warning system to let you know that major business change may be necessary. Imagine that it's 1981 and you have just gotten into the video-rental business. You're the part owner and purchasing manager for a regional chain of retail stores that sells LPs, 45s, cassettes, and 8-tracks. If you had a data warehouse then, one that gathered information from the point-of-sale computers in all your stores and external data about your competitors' sales activity (purchased from an external source), you probably would have noticed a couple of interesting trends as you looked at product revenues over time:

✔ **Sales of both 8-tracks and 45s has dropped off remarkably.** Because your competitors' sales for those items are also way off, you may decide that you don't need to devote the shelf space to stock these types of items anymore.

✔ **Films on VHS-format tape are rented much more frequently than the same films in Beta format.** Because the video business is somewhat new (remember that it's 1981), your rental numbers may be declaring that VHS is the winner and that Beta-format tapes are another item probably not worth ordering and putting on the shelves.

Both these decisions are, for the most part, tactical because they involve product-stocking decisions. Neither decision fundamentally changes the way your company does business, but rather helps you decide which products are the better ones to keep in stock.

Suppose, though, that trend-line information coming back from the data warehouse shows relatively flat sales of all types of music and dramatically increasing revenues from video rentals. The future of your chain may lie not in sales of LPs and cassettes (and, eventually, CDs) but rather in video rentals. Rather than have to rely on a gut feeling, you can make data-driven strategic decisions about how your business should change.

Imagine having to make the same type of decision in the mid-1990s. Video-rental numbers are probably decreasing because of price pressure from large megastores, and the CD music business is under the same type of pressure. The highly positive growth curve from your little foray into the sale of music CDs and computer CD-ROMs over the Internet, however, is almost identical to your in-store retail video boom from back in the early days of the Reagan administration. Again, your data warehouse provides the analytical capability for you to make data-based decisions rather than have to rely on hunches or, at best, bits and pieces of data gathered from various computer systems (don't forget Steve at BlackAndWhiteVideos).

Chapter 3

Have It Your Way: The Structure of a Data Warehouse

In This Chapter

▶ Constructing your data warehouse to *always* fit your unique business needs

▶ Classifying data warehouse architectures to help you plan your own implementation

▶ Deciding whether your data warehouse should be centralized or distributed (and accepting the trade-offs)

Although I generally dislike trite sayings, I have to make an exception: "No two data warehouse implementations are exactly alike."

One of the worst data warehousing mistakes you can make is to try to force your business analysis and reporting needs to fit into an environment you copied from somewhere else.

You *should* leverage the knowledge and experience of other people by studying their experiences with data warehousing products; asking questions about the most difficult problems they encountered during product development and after their data warehouse was put into use; and determining how effective their users have been in making better, information-based business decisions.

You *should not* automatically assume, however, that every aspect of someone else's data warehousing environment is exactly right for you.

Ensuring That Your Implementations Are Unique

A data warehouse is composed of many different components, each of which can be implemented in several (perhaps *many*) different ways. These components include

✔ The breadth (the number of different subjects and focus points, for example, or the number of different organizations that will use it)

✔ The number of sources that will provide data

✔ The databases in which data is stored

✔ The data (the elements and the level of detail and how much history is being maintained, for example)

✔ The front-end tool used to access data

✔ The means by which data is moved from source applications into the data warehouse and loaded

✔ The overall architectural complexity of the environment

The odds are overwhelming that no two data warehouse implementations (neither those now in existence nor all those to be completed during the next ten years) will be identical in each of the preceding seven categories.

Two companies in the same industry, for example, each may have a sales-and-marketing data warehouse that supports 300 users across four different business organizations, allows access using the same online analytical processing (OLAP) product (OLAP is described in Chapter 10), and uses the same database management system in which to store approximately 50 gigabytes of data.

The two companies are likely to have these differences, however:

✔ Different data sources, unique to each respective company

✔ Different data, as a result of the different sources

✔ The use of different source-to-warehouse movement techniques

If one of those companies, therefore, tried to adapt the other's data warehousing solution in its entirety, it would be making a *big* mistake. (Or, as your schoolteachers used to tell you, "Do your own work — no copying!")

Classifying the Data Warehouse

Although you must ensure that your data warehouse fits your own unique needs, some guidelines can help you determine the probable complexity of its environment and structure. I use a three-tier classification for planning a data warehouse; by determining a likely category for an implementation, I have *early in the project* some specific guidelines for its complexity, development schedule, and cost.

Here are my classifications:

- ✓ **Data warehouse lite:** A relatively straightforward implementation of a modest scope and one in which you don't go out on any technological limbs (it's almost a low-tech implementation)

- ✓ **Data warehouse deluxe:** A standard data warehouse implementation that makes use of advanced technologies to solve complex business information and analytical needs

- ✓ **Data warehouse supreme:** The data warehouse of the future (not quite ready for prime time, but close), with leading-edge technologies, large-scale data distribution, and other unconventional characteristics

The data warehouse lite

A *data warehouse lite* is a no-frills, bare-bones, low-tech approach to providing data to help with some of your business decision-making. *No-frills* means that proven capabilities and tools already within your organization are, wherever possible, put together to build your system.

Is it a data warehouse lite or a data mart?

I coined the term *data warehouse lite* for an article I wrote for *Database Programming & Design* magazine in December 1995. Since then, the term *data mart* has been commonly used to refer to the same thing. A *data mart* should be, in its purest sense (as described in Chapter 4), an environment that receives a portion of a data warehouse's content, providing easier access to this information subset for a select group of users. As often happens in information technology (IT) areas in which vendors jockey for market share, however, many people now think of a data mart as little more than a small-scale data warehousing environment.

Don't be confused by the terminology! I prefer my lite–deluxe–supreme classification because it's easy to remember and helps me visualize the complexity of the environment I'm setting out to build. When I discuss project opportunities with clients, however, and they mention that they want to build a data mart, they're usually referring to what I call a data warehouse lite. It's not the wording that matters, because all these definitions are continually being revised anyway. If you concentrate on the seven different aspects of the environment — breadth, sources, database, data content, tools, extraction and movement, and architecture — you won't be confused.

Subject areas

A data warehouse lite is focused on the analysis of only one or two subject areas. Suppose that in your job at a telephone company, you analyze the sales of services such as call waiting, caller ID, and voice mail to consumer households. If you build a data warehouse lite exclusively for this purpose, you have all the necessary information to support your analysis and reporting for the consumer market. You wouldn't have any information about business users' long-distance usage and payment history, however, because it's part of a different subject area, as shown in Figure 3-1.

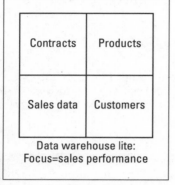

Figure 3-1:
A data warehouse lite has a narrow subject-area focus.

Contracts	Products
Sales data	Customers

Data warehouse lite:
Focus=sales performance

Data sources

A data warehouse lite has only a handful of data sources — and sometimes only one. As part of an overall single-application environment, for example, it acts as the restructuring agent for the application's data to make it more report-friendly.

The most common means of restructuring a single application's data is to denormalize the contents of the application's relational database tables to eliminate as many relational *join operations* (the process of bringing together data from more than one database table) as possible when users run reports or do simple querying. *Denormalization* is the opposite of the relational database concept of *normalization,* a somewhat complex set of guidelines that tells you which data elements should be in which tables in a database (as explained in Chapter 5). For purposes of data warehousing, denormalization is the important concept to understand, and, fortunately, it's a simple one. When you denormalize a database, you don't worry about duplicated data; you try to create rows of data in a single table that most likely will mirror the reports and queries users run. Figure 3-2 shows an example of a single-source data warehouse lite built on denormalization.

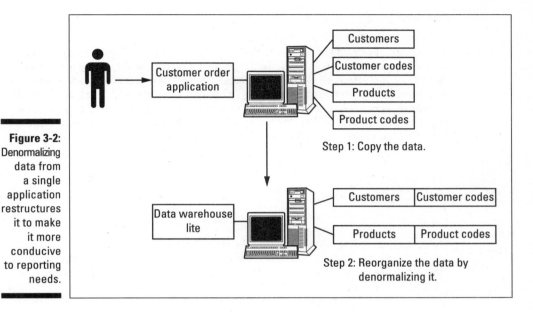

Figure 3-2:
Denormalizing
data from
a single
application
restructures
it to make
it more
conducive
to reporting
needs.

Although externally provided data (as explained in Chapter 17) may be used in a data warehouse lite implementation, the data is rarely newly acquired. You're more likely to incorporate external data you already use for analysis (perhaps in a stand-alone manner).

Database

The primary reason that a data warehouse lite is *usually* built on a standard, general-purpose relational database management system (RDBMSs are described in Chapter 5) is your organization's general familiarity with RDBMSs, particularly the easy-to-use structure built around tables and columns.

In some situations, though, a multidimensional database (MDB) is used, as described in Chapter 6.

For a data warehouse lite implementation, either a general-purpose RDBMS or MDB product usually suffices. Because of relatively modest data volumes (discussed in the following section) and the narrow subject-area focus, technical barriers that would drive your database platform decision one way or the other are unlikely to be reached.

Data content

A data warehouse lite has limited content — just enough to satisfy the primary purpose of the environment but not enough for many unstructured what-if scenarios by its users. You must choose carefully, therefore, from among the set of all possible data elements and select a manageable subset, elements that — without a doubt — are important to have. This process is the same as for any data warehouse implementation, except that you must be more disciplined than ever when you're making decisions about what content to include.

Use standard reports, particularly those that now require a great deal of manual preparation, as one of your primary guides to determine data content in a data warehouse lite.

Tools

The users of a data warehouse lite usually ask questions and create reports that reflect a "Tell me what happened" perspective, as described in Chapter 9. Because those users don't do much heavy-duty analytical processing, the products they use to access the data warehouse should be easy to use. Although some power users may use more advanced tools to access the data warehouse for more complicated processing, they're a minority of the user community.

Data extraction, movement, and loading

Simplicity is the name of the game in a data warehouse lite. The process of extracting data from sources and performing all the functions necessary to prepare that data for loading into the data warehouse should therefore be as straightforward as possible, with these two elements:

✔ Either simple file transfers or (believe it or not) tape used as the means for moving data from its sources to the data warehouse

✔ Straightforward custom code (or perhaps an easy-to-use tool) used for the extraction and movement of the data

If the data source for your data warehouse lite is built on a relational database and you're planning to use the same DBMS product for your data warehouse, one of the easiest ways to handle data extraction and movement is to use SQL. The following steps — as shown in Figure 3-3, they're easier to understand than SQL code! — provide a standard procedure for this process (tailor them to your particular environment, of course):

1. **On the system that houses your warehouse, use the SQL CREATE TABLE statement to create the definition for each table in your data warehouse lite.**

2. **Create a database backup tape containing copies of all tables from the source that provides data to the warehouse, and then reload those tables into a staging area on the system where your data warehouse will be located.**

   Although you could, alternatively, use a file-transfer program to copy all the source tables to the system, you must ensure that the network bandwidth and time window are adequate to do it that way. For a single source to your data warehouse and the same DBMS on both systems, you're better off using a backup tape.

3. **Use the SQL INSERT statement, with a nested SELECT statement specifying the source tables and their respective columns that will be used to populate the data warehouse table — and how the tables will be joined — to load the data into your data warehouse lite.**

4. **Run a series of quality assurance (QA) routines to verify that all data has been loaded properly.**

   Check row counts, numeric totals, and whatever else you can.

That's it!

Architecture

The *architecture* of a data warehouse lite is composed of the DBMS used to store the data, the front-end tools used to access the data, the way the data is moved, and the number of subject areas. The watchword of this environment is *minimalist:* no bells, no whistles, nothing fancy — just enough technology applied to the environment to give users access to data they need.

Figure 3-3: The low-tech approach to moving data into a data warehouse lite: database backup tapes.

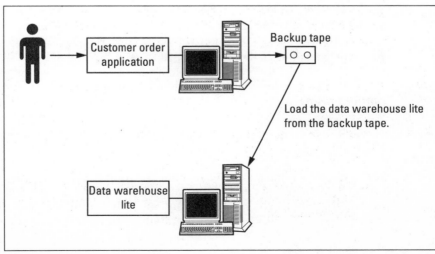

The three-tier architecture of a data warehouse lite, shown in Figure 3-4, isn't the same one that describes a client/server environment based on middleware and distributed computing services. Rather, a data warehouse lite contains these major component types:

1. A single database contains the warehouse's data.

2. That database is fed directly from each of the sources providing data to the warehouse.

3. Users access data directly from the warehouse.

Figure 3-4:
The architecture of a data warehouse lite is built around straight-line movement of data.

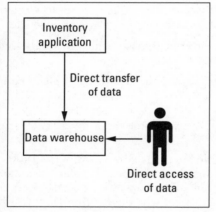

The data warehouse deluxe

You most likely will focus most of your data warehousing-related activities on the *data warehouse deluxe* environment, as shown in Figure 3-5. Data from many different sources converges in these "real" data warehouses, which make available a wealth of architectural options you can tailor to meet your specific needs.

Subject areas

A data warehouse deluxe contains a broad range of *related* subject areas — everything (or most things) that would follow a natural way of thinking about and analyzing information.

Recall the telephone-company example mentioned earlier in this chapter, in the "Subject areas" section of the data warehouse lite description. In a data warehouse deluxe, you're likely to find not only the subject area of consumer add-on services (among other items) but also these elements:

- Business add-on services
- Consumer basic calling revenues and volumes
- Consumer long-distance calling revenues and volumes
- Business basic calling revenues and volumes
- Business long-distance calling revenues and volumes

The subject range is broader for a data warehouse deluxe, for these two reasons:

- The user base is broader (more organizations are having their people use the data warehouse).
- The scope of any given user's queries and reports is broader than just one or two subject areas. For example, a user may run reports comparing trends in add-on services for businesses *and* consumers to see where to concentrate future sales-and-marketing efforts.

Figure 3-5:
A data warehouse deluxe has a broader subject-area focus than a data warehouse lite.

Contracts	Products	Economic data	Returns	Customer credit data
Sales data	Customers	Competitor sales	Inventory levels	Sales territories and wholesalers

Data warehouse deluxe:
Broadening the horizon

Data sources

You won't be lucky enough to find any single-source environments when you're building a data warehouse deluxe. Although the exact number of data sources depends on the specifics of your implementation, it isn't uncommon to find an average of eight to ten applications and external databases that provide data to the warehouse.

Now you have a whole new set of — I have to use the word — problems you must deal with, including the ones in this list:

- **Different encodings for similar information:** Different sets of customer numbers come from different sources, for example.
- **Data integrity problems across multiple sources:** The information in one source is different from the information in another when it should be the same.

✔ **Different source platforms:** As an example, an IBM mainframe with DB2/MVS may contain the data in one of the sources, another IBM mainframe with VSAM files may have another set of source data, and the rest of the source data may all be stored in SQL Server databases on Windows NT servers.

Database

Data warehouse deluxe implementations are big — and getting bigger all the time. Implementations involving hundreds of gigabytes (a gigabyte equals 1 billion bytes) and even a terabyte (1 trillion bytes) are increasingly being built.

A relational database management system is usually used for larger data volumes (more than 50 gigabytes); smaller implementations use either relational or multidimensional products.

Data content

When you implement a data warehouse deluxe, you almost always need (unlike with a data warehouse lite) access capabilities in addition to simple results reporting. Therefore, although you may be able to use standard reports as a starting point when you're deciding what should be in your warehouse, that's rarely enough. You must do the following:

1. Take a complete inventory of available information, known as a *source systems analysis,* as discussed in Chapter 15.

2. In what is one of the most severe tests of how well the IT people and business users will get along throughout the data warehousing project, review each candidate source element and figure out

   • What should be in the data warehouse and what should be left out.

   • What should be summarized and what should be left at the detailed level.

   • What should remain in the data warehouse forever and what should be purged.

   • Whatever else you need to know.

Tools

The broad range of subject areas, and the wealth of data, means that you usually have several different ways of looking at the contents of a data warehouse deluxe. This list shows the different ways of using a data warehouse (Part III discusses them in-depth):

✔ **Simple reporting and querying:** As with a data warehouse lite, the purpose of the warehouse is to "tell me what happened."

✔ **Online analytical processing (OLAP):** You use the warehouse to "tell me what happened — *and why.*"

✔ **Executive information system (EIS):** In this model, a variety of information is gathered from the data warehouse and made available to users who don't want to mess around with the data warehouse — they want to see snapshots of many different things. Its purpose is "tell me lots of things, but don't make me work too hard to get the answers."

✔ **Data mining:** In this relatively new area, statistical, artificial intelligence, and related techniques are used to "mine" through large volumes of data and provide knowledge even without users having to ask specific questions. Its purpose is "tell me something interesting, even though I don't know what questions to ask, and also tell me what *may* happen."

You're likely to employ at least three — and perhaps all four — of these types of data warehouse access when you use a data warehouse deluxe, *and no single product supports all of them.* Although tool vendors increasingly try to provide suites of products to handle as many of these different functions as possible, you *will* deal with different products — and so will your user community.

Do *not* assume that you can simply select a single vendor whose products will satisfy all the business intelligence capabilities your users need. Make sure that you carefully check out the vendors' products — all of them — because you have no guarantee that a top-notch OLAP tool vendor's data mining tool is equally as good, for example. Don't be afraid to mix and match; you have no reason to shortchange your data warehouse users simply to avoid having to deal with one more vendor.

Data extraction, movement, and loading

Prepare for the challenge! Whereas with a data warehouse lite you can usually handle source-to-warehouse movement of data in a straightforward, low-tech manner, you're now entering the Difficulty Zone, where many data warehousing projects meet their Waterloo.

You're likely to experience difficulty in this domain for several reasons:

✔ **You're dealing with many different data sources, some of which may contain overlapping data.** For example, suppliers' information may come from two different purchasing systems and some of your suppliers have entries in both systems. You may run into different sets of identifiers you have to converge (for example, six alphanumeric characters as the SUPPLIER_ID in one of the systems and a unique integer known as SUP_NUM in the other).

✔ **If your data warehouse is large (measuring more than about 50 gigabytes), you're likely to experience difficulties in extracting, moving, and loading your windows — the time frames in which updates are made to the warehouse.** The time window is complicated by the number of data sources you have to handle.

✔ **Call it "Simon's rule of exponential warehouse complexity": The chances of having a messed-up extraction–movement–loading process are exponentially related to the number of data elements to be loaded into the data warehouse.** (I always wanted to have one of these tech-nology guidelines named after me, even if I have to do it myself!)

If you could assign some difficulty factor (an integer, for example) to the process of getting data into the warehouse, the following measures would hold true: You have n data elements to be included in the data warehouse with a difficulty factor of x. If you now have $2n$ data elements, your difficulty factor is not $2x$; rather, it's x *squared*.

(Confused? Hey, I wasn't good at this stuff in school, either. I'm still working on the problem where you have to determine where two trains traveling in different directions and at different speeds will meet. Who cares?)

Back to the rule I named after myself. To make it easier to understand, assign some numbers to n and x. If your data warehouse will have 100 elements in (n), suppose that the difficulty factor (x) is 5 and that you double the number of elements ($n = 200$). Your difficulty factor is 25 (5 squared), not 10.

✔ **The process of dealing with so many data sources, all headed toward one place (your data warehouse deluxe), has all the elements of too many cooks in the kitchen, or whatever that saying is.** To make the extraction–movement–loading process go smoothly, you may deal with many different application owners, official keepers of the database, and other people from a variety of different organizations, all of whom have to cooperate as though they're part of a professional symphony orchestra. The reality, though, is that they perform more similarly to a group of kindergarten students who each picked a musical instrument from the toy bin and were told, "Now play something!" Although the process isn't necessarily doomed to failure, expect a number of iterations until the data warehouse deluxe is loaded just right.

Architecture

It's time for a pop quiz: How many tiers are in the architecture for a data warehouse lite? If your answer is three, you're right!

A data warehouse deluxe can have three tiers also. The architecture was shown earlier, in Figure 3-4, except with more data sources and perhaps more than one type of user tool used to access the warehouse. Chances are, however, that it will look more like Figure 3-6. In addition to other "way stations" as necessary for *your particular environment,* your environment may have these elements:

✔ **Data mart:** Receives subsets of information from the data warehouse deluxe and serves as the primary access point for users (data marts are discussed in-depth in Chapter 4)

✔ **Interim transformation station:** An area in which sets of data extracted from some of the sources undergo some type of transformation process before moving down the pipeline toward the warehouse's database

✔ **Quality assurance station:** An area in which groups of data undergo intensive quality assurance checks before you let them move into the data warehouse

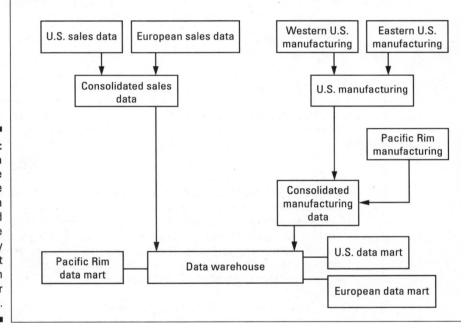

Figure 3-6: A data warehouse deluxe often has a complicated architecture with many different collection points for data.

The data warehouse supreme

I have to make a confession: I've never seen a data warehouse supreme; you've probably never seen one either. Why? Because I don't think that one exists yet!

They will, however, and soon. Although today's state-of-the-art data warehouse typically looks like a complicated data warehouse deluxe, after you read this section, you'll know what the data warehouse of tomorrow will look like. (Sounds like an exhibit at a World's Fair, doesn't it?)

Subject areas

The number of subject areas in a data warehouse supreme is unlimited! Why? Because the data warehouse is *virtual;* it isn't all contained in a single database or even within multiple databases you personally load and maintain. Instead, only part of your warehouse (probably a small part) is physically located on some data warehouse server; the rest is out there in cyberspace somewhere, accessible through networking capabilities as though it were all part of some physically centralized data warehouse. Now your warehouse users have an infinite number of subject-area possibilities — anything that could possibly be of interest to them.

Think of how you use the Internet today to access Web sites all over the world — sites that someone else creates and maintains. Imagine that each of those sites contains (rather than advertising, job ads, electronic storefronts, and whatever else you spend your time surfing the Internet trying to find) information about some specific area of interest to you. Suppose also that you can query and run reports using the contents of one *or more* of these sites as your input. That is the model of the data warehouse supreme: opening up an unlimited number of possibilities to users.

Data sources

Because of the wide breadth of subject areas in a data warehouse supreme, it has numerous data sources. The good news: Because many of the sources are external to your own warehousing environment, you aren't personally responsible for all the extraction, transformation, and loading to get them into your warehouse. The bad news: Someone has to perform those tasks, and you have little or no control over such elements as quality assurance processes or how frequently the data is refreshed.

I have more good news, though: Because the most critical part of a data warehouse supreme is still internally acquired data (the data coming from your internal applications), from that aspect, the things you do today to make the data warehouse-ready will still be done in the future.

Because you populate your data warehouse supreme with multimedia information — in addition to traditional data, such as numeric, alphabetic, and dates — the types of data sources broaden from traditional applications to video servers, Web sites, and databases that store documents and text.

Database

A data warehouse supreme most likely consists of a database environment that meets these requirements:

✔ It's distributed across many different platforms.

✔ It operates in a *location-transparent* manner: Users make queries that access data from the appropriate platform without their having to know the physical location (in much the same way as Internet Web sites are accessed today by name rather than by network address).

✔ It has *object-oriented* capabilities to store images, videos, and text in addition to the traditional data, such as numeric and date information.

✔ Because of dramatically faster performance, it increasingly permits you to access data directly from transactional databases without having to copy the information to a separate data warehouse database.

Data content

Not to belabor the point, but look at the way you access the Internet today, with seamless convergence of different types of data: narrative documents, videos and other images, and ordinary data, such as numbers and character information. A data warehouse supreme has all this — all the different types of data you need to support better business decision-making. (Chapter 24 describes the details of how you use the multimedia aspects of a data warehouse supreme.)

In terms of total capacity, a data warehouse supreme is huge; it surpasses today's limits (a few terabytes). The causes of this capacity expansion are the distribution of the information across many different platforms, much faster and higher-performance networking infrastructure, and increasingly "smarter" database management systems — in addition to, of course, steadily increasing disk storage capacities.

Tools

As far as I can tell, the Big Four types of business intelligence discussed earlier in this chapter — basic reporting and querying, OLAP, EIS, and data mining — are all part of the data warehouse supreme environment. Of the four, the most significant advances and improvements during the next few years probably will occur with data mining, as vendors push enhancements into their products.

The biggest difference between today's state-of-the-art data warehouses and the data warehouse supreme, however, is the dramatically increased use of push technology, as described in Chapter 23. Using *intelligent agents* ("assistants" you program to perform certain functions for you), you can have information fed back to you from the far ends of the Internet-based universe, not to mention from your own large data warehouse servers within your own company. Figure 3-7 illustrates some of the ways in which intelligent agents can help you make much more efficient use of data warehousing.

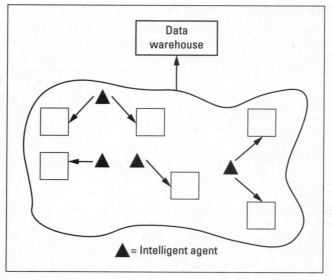

Figure 3-7:
Intelligent
agents
are an
important
part of the
push-
technology
architecture
of a data
warehouse
supreme.

Data extraction, movement, and loading

Here's how the extraction, movement, and loading of data occurs in a data warehouse supreme:

1. Data that is moved (copied) from a source application's database or file system into a separate database in the data warehouse is handled almost identically to how you perform those tasks in a data warehouse deluxe.

2. The increasing use of *operational data stores,* or ODSs (real-time availability of analytical data instead of having to deal with delayed access) means that more messaging occurs between your data sources and your warehouse database. (See Chapter 23 for information about ODSs.) The data source determines that data should be moved into the warehouse environment rather than the warehouse having the responsibility to request updates and additions. When new data is inserted into the source database (or existing data is modified or deleted), the appropriate instructions and accompanying data are sent to the warehouse.

Architecture

Figure 3-8 shows an example of what the architecture of a data warehouse supreme may look like. Keep this thought in mind, though: With all the upcoming technology trends and improvements discussed in this section, your data warehouse supreme can look like (almost) anything you want.

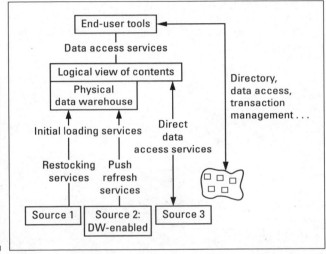

Figure 3-8: Sample architecture from a data warehouse supreme (although it can look like anything).

Double data warehouse with cheese

Just kidding! I wanted to see whether you're paying attention.

To Centralize or Distribute, That Is the Question

Traditional data warehousing — creating a data warehouse lite or data warehouse deluxe — usually involves copying data from one or more different source databases and files into a *single* warehouse-owned database. Whether that database is relational or multidimensional is irrelevant. The main point is that it's *centralized:* Only one database is on one platform that all users access.

Even when you subsequently copy part of your data warehouse's content into one or more data marts for users, as shown in Figure 3-6, you still have a single, centralized collection point into which all the source data converges.

As data warehouse environments become larger and more complex, though, you should consider *not* funneling all your data into a single database; rather, your data warehouse could be a collection of databases that make up your overall information delivery and analytical environment. Figure 3-9 shows what a brokerage firm's distributed, noncentralized data warehousing environment may look like.

Figure 3-9:
A data warehouse may consist of more than one database, under the control of the overall warehousing environment.

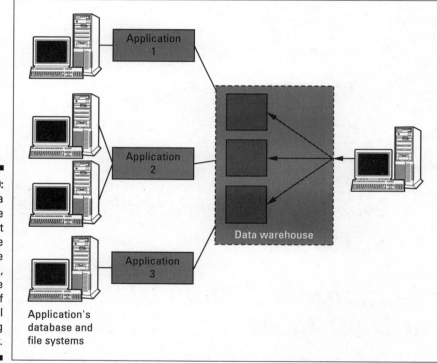

Chapter 4

Data Marts: Your Retail Data Outlet

About two weeks before writing this chapter, I was on a business trip to Los Angeles and driving down the Ventura freeway on a nice summer day. (I always call it the Ventura highway, after the *America* song from the 1970s: "Ventura highway, in the sunshine; where the days are longer. . . ." Oops, I got a little carried away there.) An ad was on the radio for a regional (I think) hardware chain based on this premise: "Shop at our stores because we have *fewer* products than the big warehouse-like competition. It's much easier to get in and out of here more quickly with what you need."

Interestingly, another hardware chain on the east coast ran ads a few years ago with almost the identical theme. This chain used to make fun of the warehouse-size competition by featuring radio ads with helicopter search parties looking for shoppers lost in a distant department and references to shuttle buses having to take shoppers between departments in the warehouse-size stores. The premise was the same: "We have *less* merchandise than the other guy, so shop with us because it's easier."

That's the idea of the data mart.

The Idea behind Data Marts

Forget all the hype. The idea of a data mart is hardly revolutionary, despite what you may read in the computer trade press and hear at conferences and seminars.

A data mart is simply a scaled-down data warehouse, that's all.

No official, standard definition exists for a data mart, just as no official, standard definition exists for a data warehouse or operational data store or data mining or virtually any other concept in this realm of the technology landscape. Vendors do their best to define data marts in the context of their products; consultants and analysts usually define data marts in a way that's advantageous to their particular offerings and specialties. That's the way this business goes, and there's nothing wrong with it; be prepared, however, to ask the tough questions.

Architectural Approaches to Data Marts

You can take one of three main approaches to creating a data mart:

- ✔ Sourced by a data warehouse (most or all of the data mart's contents come from a data warehouse)
- ✔ Tactical, quickly developed, and created from scratch
- ✔ Developed from scratch with an eye toward eventual integration

Data marts sourced by a data warehouse

Many data warehousing experts would argue (and I'm one of them, in this case) that a true data mart is a "retail outlet" with its contents provided from a data warehouse, as shown in Figure 4-1.

In an environment like the one shown in Figure 4-1, look at the relationship between the data sources, the data warehouse, the data mart, and the user in this way:

1. The data sources, acting as suppliers of raw materials, send data into the data warehouse.

2. The data warehouse then serves as a consolidation and distribution center, collecting the raw materials in much the same way as in any data warehouse.

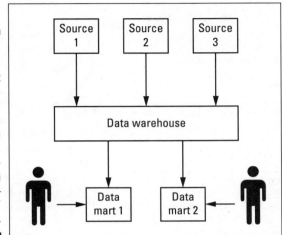

Figure 4-1:
The retail-
outlet
approach to
data marts:
All the data
comes from
a data
ware-
house in
"wholesale—
retail"
mode.

3. Instead of the user (the consumer) going straight to the data warehouse, though, the data warehouse serves as a wholesaler with the premise of "we sell only to retailers, not directly to the public." In this case, the retailers are the data marts.

4. The data marts order data from the warehouse and, after stocking the newly acquired information, make it available to consumers (users).

Before moving on to the next approach, though, I want to show you a variation of the sourced-from-the-warehouse model. Sometimes the data warehouse that serves as the source for the data mart does *not* have all the information the data mart's users need. You can solve this problem in one of two ways:

✔ Supplement the missing information directly into the data warehouse before sending the selected contents to the data mart, as shown in Figure 4-2.

✔ *Don't* touch the data warehouse; instead, add the supplemental information to the data mart in addition to what it receives from the data warehouse, as shown in Figure 4-3.

If your data mart needs data that's not in the data warehouse, which of these two approaches should you choose? If your data mart is the only one within your company that needs that additional data (be sure to ask around), leave the warehouse alone and bring the supplemental data directly into your data mart. If other data marts or other projects served by the data warehouse can use the additional information, you should add it to the data warehouse *first* and then send it, along with the other contents you need, to your data mart.

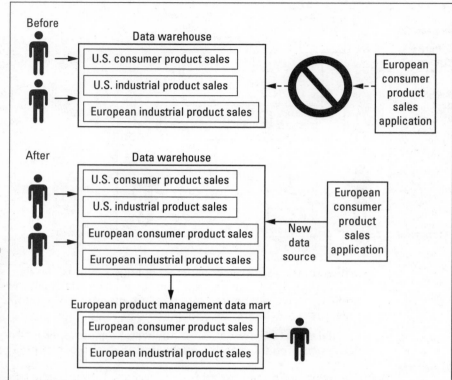

Figure 4-2:
Sprucing up
the data
warehouse's
contents as
part of a
data mart
project.

Tactical, quick-strike data marts

Sometimes you just don't have a data warehouse from which to get data for your data mart, so you have to do it yourself. In many (probably most) of these situations, you create a tactical, quick-strike data mart that is, in effect, a miniature data warehouse. You follow the same methodology and complete the same processes of data extraction, transformation, quality assurance, and loading. The difference is that you're doing it on a smaller scale than with a full-blown data warehouse.

What does a smaller scale mean? As shown in Figure 4-4, data brought into a tactical data mart is often necessary to answer a specific set of business questions within relatively narrow confines. Some examples are a specific region or territory within a company, a subset of a company's overall product line, or some other subsetting model.

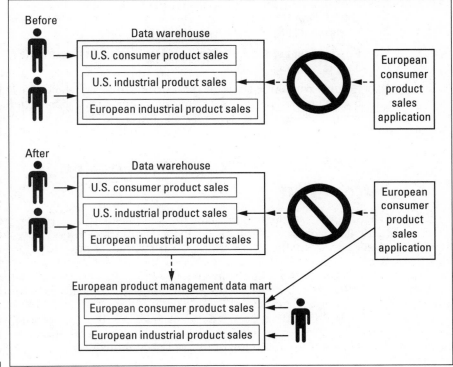

Figure 4-3: Get the majority of the data mart's contents from the data warehouse and supplement it with additional information acquired directly from the missing sources.

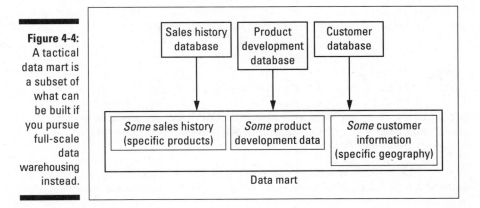

Figure 4-4: A tactical data mart is a subset of what can be built if you pursue full-scale data warehousing instead.

So the question must be asked: If you have to start from scratch and don't have a data warehouse to provide data to your data mart, why not build a full-scale data warehouse instead? Here are three reasons to go the data mart route:

✔ **Speed:** A tactical data mart is typically completed in 90 to 120 days rather than the much longer time required for a full-scale data warehouse.

✔ **Cost:** Doing the job faster means that you spend less money; it's that simple.

✔ **Complexity and risk:** When you work with less data and fewer sources over a shorter period, your environment is likely to be significantly less complex — and have fewer associated risks.

Bottom-up, integration-oriented data marts

What happens, though, if pressing business needs steer you toward a tactical data mart and you have a longer-term vision of its contents being integrated with other data? Have you created an architectural dead end? Will you have to throw away your data mart at some point and start over with a "real" data warehousing effort? Will Batman arrive in time to save Robin from the Riddler? (Sorry about that — the reruns are getting to me.)

Theoretically, you can design data marts so that they're eventually integrated in a bottom-up manner, by building a data warehousing environment (in contrast to a single, monolithic data warehouse).

Pay close attention to the word *theoretically.* Bottom-up integration of data marts isn't for the fainthearted. You can do it, but it's more difficult than creating a tactical data mart that will always remain stand-alone. Can this approach be successful? The answer is a definite maybe.

What Should Be in a Data Mart

If a data mart is a smaller-scale version of a data warehouse, the question comes up again: What does "smaller scale" mean in reference to the contents of a data mart?

This section describes some ways you can select subsets of information for a data mart and the circumstances under which you may want to try each approach.

Geography-bounded data

A data mart may contain only the information relevant to a certain geographical area, such as a region or territory within your company. Figure 4-5 illustrates an example of geography-bounded data.

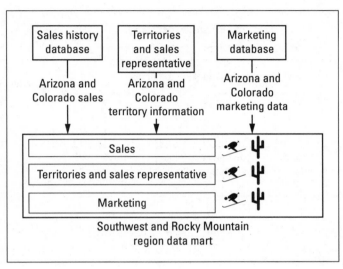

Figure 4-5: A geography-bounded data mart contains only sales information relevant to a specific territory (Arizona and Colorado, in this example).

Although the use of a geography-bounded data mart is technically feasible and relatively straightforward, it's often not such a good idea. Why? Because a cross-geography comparison (for example, "How are our Arizona stores doing versus our Pennsylvania stores?") is a natural use of any data warehouse environment. When you create separate data marts for various geographical reasons, you make it much more difficult to make these types of comparisons.

Organization-bounded data

Another approach to deciding what should be in your data mart is to base decisions on what information a specific organization needs when it's the sole (or at least primary) user of the data mart. As shown in Figure 4-6, a bank may create one data mart for consumer checking-account analysis and another data mart for commercial checking accounts.

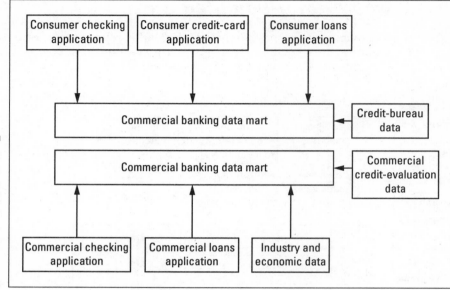

Figure 4-6:
Each organization in this bank gets its own data mart, tuned to its specific needs.

This approach works well when the overwhelming majority of inquiries and reports are organization-oriented. That is, the commercial checking group has *no need whatsoever* to analyze consumer checking accounts and vice versa. It pays to dig into the business needs during the scope phase of a data warehousing or data mart project. Outsiders, for example, may think, "Okay, put all checking-account information, both consumer and commercial, into the same environment because, this way, reports can be run comparing average balances and other information for the entire checking-account portfolio at the bank." After additional analysis, though, you may notice that the bank doesn't do this type of comparison, so why not keep the two areas separate and avoid unnecessary complexity?

Function-bounded data

Using another approach, one that crosses organizational boundaries, you establish a data mart's contents based on a specific function (or set of related functions) within the company. A multinational chemical company, for example, may create a data mart exclusively for the sales and marketing functions across all organizations and across all product lines, as shown in Figure 4-7.

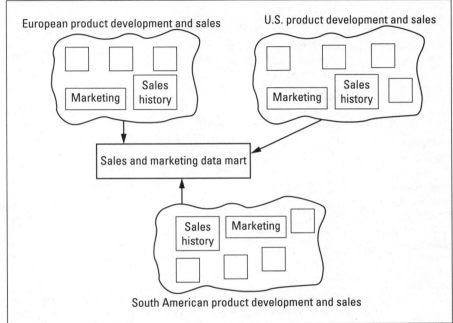

Figure 4-7:
If it relates
to sales and
marketing,
it goes into
the data
mart.

Competitor-bounded data

A company may occasionally be so focused on a specific competitor that it may make sense to create a data mart oriented toward that particular competitor. As shown in Figure 4-8, this type of environment may include competitive sales, all available public information about the competitor (particularly if the information is available over the Internet), and industry analysts' reports, for example.

To truly provide the business intelligence that's necessary in a competitor-driven situation, you should construct the data mart to include multimedia information in addition to the traditional data types typically found in a data warehouse. (Chapter 24 describes multimedia data and data warehousing.)

Answers to specific business questions

An organization's operations occasionally are driven by the answers to a selected number (often a handful) of business questions. Based on the answers, a company may speed up or slow down production lines, start up extra shifts to increase production or initiate layoffs, or, possibly, choose to acquire or not acquire other companies.

Figure 4-8:
The data
mart as a
weapon
of war:
Everything
you can
possibly
learn
about a
competitor,
and how
you match
up goes into
this data
mart.

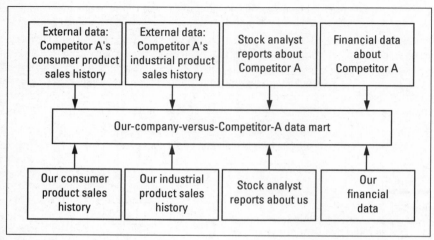

Business questions with this degree of weighty importance have tradition-ally caused nightmares for the in-house employees chartered with digging out data and reports, consolidating and checking the information, and reporting the results to executive management. Sounds like a job for a data warehouse, you say? Before constructing a full-scale data warehouse that can answer these (and many other) business questions, however, it's probably worth considering that the answer may be a small-scale data mart *designed specifically* to answer those high-impact, high-value "How are we doing?" type of questions.

Later, this type of environment may grow into a larger-scale data warehouse. It often makes more sense, however, to concentrate your efforts on support-ing a data mart with *known* business value instead of on supplementing it with volumes of additional data that *may* provide business value (but can also slow response time or significantly complicate the end-to-end architec-ture). Again, the job you do up-front, in the early phases of your project, make a big difference in the direction you take and your level of success.

Anything!

Any set of criteria you can dream up can determine a data mart's contents. Some make sense; others don't. Some take you into an architectural dead end because you get only limited value and have to start all over to expand your capabilities.

Data mart or data warehouse?

Now that you (presumably) have read an entire chapter about the concept of data marts, I want to make one important point. If you start a project from the outset with either of the following premises, you already have two strikes against you:

✔ "We're building a real data warehouse, not a puny little data mart."

✔ "We're building a data mart, not a data warehouse."

By labeling your project as one or the other of these terms, you already have made some preconceived notions about the work you will do, *before* you have even begun to dig into the business problem. Until you understand the following three issues, you have no foundation on which to classify your impending project as either a data mart or a data warehouse:

✔ The volumes and characteristics of data you need

✔ The business problems you're trying to solve and the questions you're trying to answer

✔ The business value you expect to gain when your system is successfully built

As mentioned at the beginning of this chapter, what's more important is that no formal definitions distinguish a data mart from a data warehouse. If you're extracting and rehosting a subset of data from an existing application into another environment, you can accurately deem what you're building as a data mart.

If you're starting from scratch, however, and extracting data from one or more source systems, handling the quality assurance and transformation, and copying that data into a separate environment, what determines whether you're building a data warehouse or a data mart? Although some guidelines exist, such as number of subject areas and volumes of data, it all comes down to this statement: As soon as you start labeling your environment as one or the other, you're adding preconceived notions and beliefs about its characteristics that may not fit your business needs.

Here's the answer: Forget about the terms *data warehouse* and *data mart*. Concentrate instead on your business problem and its possible solution: What data do you need in order to perform certain informational and analytical functions; where is that data now and in what form; and what do you have to do to make it available to your users?

Leave the terminology wars to the vendors and analysts. Don't get caught up in the hype.

Implementing a Data Mart — *Quickly*

No matter how you decide to divide the universe of possible contents into some subset for your data mart, it's important to remember that in order to obtain maximum business value from your data mart, you must implement it *quickly*.

Here are the three keys to speedy implementation:

- ✔ **Follow a phased methodology.** As described in Chapter 13, you spend the majority of your up-front time on the project focusing on the specific business value you want.

- ✔ **Hold to a fixed time for each phase.** If you set aside two weeks for your scope, for example, stick to that window. Don't extend any phase (especially the early ones) unless the project is doomed to failure.

- ✔ **Avoid *scope creep* at all costs.** Though costly and dangerous in any project — data warehousing or otherwise — *scope creep* (when additional feature requests keep creeping in long past the cutoff point) is devastating in a data mart effort. You probably will add complexity with only marginal incremental business value (if any) and do little other than put your project at risk.

Part II
Data Warehousing
Technology

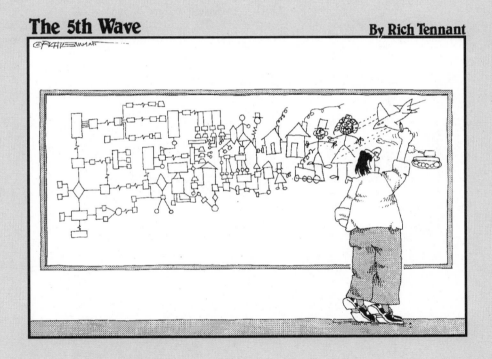

In this part . . .

A data warehouse without a database is like a day without sunshine. But what kind of database?

Whether you're inclined toward a traditional relational database or a somewhat newfangled multidimensional database as the home for your warehouse's data, you have to understand the basics of both options and when each one is appropriate. It's all here!

Chapter 5

Relational Databases and Data Warehousing

*T*he contents of a data warehouse do not, strictly speaking, have to be stored in a database. You could, for example, use a series of files on an IBM mainframe as your primary data warehouse storage and, using custom-developed client/server front-end software, access information from those files.

In nearly all situations, though, your project benefits significantly from the use of a database management system (DBMS) rather than file-based storage, as discussed in this chapter and Chapter 6.

A fundamental question exists, though: What *type* of DBMS is most suitable for data warehousing?

This chapter explains the use of relational database technology (today's overwhelmingly dominant database technology) for your data warehouse, including its benefits and challenges. Chapter 6 discusses an alternative approach you can use: multidimensional databases.

Although the current generation of data warehousing implementations (since the early 1990s) grew up on multidimensional databases, the market-place is now experiencing a clear-cut trend toward using relational data-bases, particularly for large-volume data warehouses (more than about 50 gigabytes of data). Multidimensional databases are *not* dead; rather, they can still provide value to smaller-scale environments (data warehouse lite systems and data marts, as discussed in Chapters 3 and 4, respectively).

The Old Way of Thinking

Jump back to 1995. The data warehousing revolution was picking up steam, and companies all over the country (yours was probably one of them) and the world were captivated by not only the concept of data warehousing but also the principles of online analytical processing (OLAP — discussed in more detail in Chapter 10).

The world of data warehousing and OLAP held the widespread belief in 1995 that you *absolutely* could not successfully build a data warehouse by storing data in a relational database; only a multidimensional database could be used.

This relational-versus-multidimensional war ranked up there with the all-time champion of polarized technology proponents: the Ethernet versus token-ring local-area networking (LAN) wars of the mid-1980s. (Proponents of either LAN technology fervently — and sometimes savagely — argued that their approach was much superior to the other and that only fools would attempt to implement a LAN using the other technology. If you were involved with client/server computing or networking back then, you probably remember the argument well. Relational-versus-multidimensional was a 1990s version of this memorable classic!)

The following section describes what was behind this can't-do-it-with-relational belief.

A technology-based discussion: The roots of relational database technology

Relational database management systems (RDBMSs) have their roots in the relational data model developed by Dr. E.F. Codd, then with IBM, back in 1970. (He first described it in his landmark paper, "A Relational Model of Data for Large Shared Data Banks," published in *Communications of the ACM*, Vol. 13, No. 6, June 1970, pp. 377-387. You can check out the paper on the Web, at www.acm.org/classics/nov95/.) Throughout the 1970s, in an attempt to commercialize relational technology, IBM and a few other organizations worked on prototypes, proof-of-concept systems, and early starts at product development.

What is a relational database management system?

Forget all about the mathematical foundations of the relational model, the principles of normalization, and other highly technical aspects of RDBMSs. If you're interested, consult any one of the many available books that discuss RDBMS principles and technology in detail.

For purposes of this book, an *RDBMS* is a software system that manages relational databases. So what's a relational database?

In a typical spreadsheet program, columns and rows form a series of cells. If each column is headed by a name of a data attribute (CUSTOMER_NUMBER, PRODUCT, and QUANTITY_PURCHASED, for example) and each row has *a single value* for each attribute, you have the basics of a relational database *table,* as shown in this example:

CUSTOMER_ NUMBER	PRODUCT	QUANTITY_ PURCHASED
12345	Vegetable soup	5
45678	Cooking oil	3
42973	Lawn fertilizer	2
81115	Blankets	88
81115	Vegetable soup	33

A relational database typically has many different tables — a CUSTOMER_MASTER_INFORMATION table and a PRODUCT_MASTER_INFORMATION table, for example, in addition to the one just shown, which could be called WHO_ORDERED_WHAT. Information from across the various tables can be constructed by *joining* them (making a match between tables, usually by looking for columns in two or more tables that are the same). For example, CUSTOMER_MASTER_INFORMATION may contain the following rows of data:

CUSTOMER_NUMBER	CUSTOMER_NAME
12345	Mark Jones
45678	Daniel Michaels
42973	Karen Warner
81115	Susan Robinson

If you join these two tables and use CUSTOMER_NUMBER as the common attribute, you can see that customer #81115, named Susan Robinson, ordered 88 blankets and 33 cans of vegetable soup. (She must be going on a camp-out!) From either of the individual tables, you have only bits and pieces of this information: You don't know the customer's name from looking only at the first table, for example, and you don't know what products Susan Robinson ordered from looking only at the second table. The power of the relational database becomes evident when tables are joined.

When tables in a relational database are joined, problems start occurring. Back in the early, pre-relational days of databases, data usually was linked by using pointers, which told the DBMS software the location of the next logical piece of data or the previous piece of data or some other path that made sense. Because it's somewhat complicated, don't worry about the details — the important thing is that old-style databases usually had pointers intermixed among the data.

Relational databases do *not* have pointers in them because one of the fundamental principles of this approach is that you can join any pieces of information in the database. Pointers don't make sense, therefore. (Again, although the principle is somewhat more complicated than that and has to do with set-based operations on the data, just remember that relational databases, unlike their predecessors, don't use pointers.)

Back when pointers were used, accessing logical sequences of data was fairly quick, even on older hardware. Data access went something like this:

1. Go directly to the first record you want (usually from some type of index).

2. After reading the record, read the pointer attached to it that indicates where to go next.

3. Go directly to the record indicated by that pointer.

4. Read that second record, and then read its pointer.

5. Repeat this process until you reach the end of the list or until some-other criteria tells your program to stop.

In a relational database, without pointers, it's up to the RDBMS (remember that the RDBMS is a software program that manages the relational database) to figure out how to *most efficiently* access data and provide the answer you're looking for. If you look at the example in the preceding sidebar, "What is a relational database management system?," you may want to know how many products Susan Robinson ordered and how many of each.

One way that the RDBMS could find this information is by scanning the CUSTOMER_MASTER_INFORMATION table from top to bottom until it finds the customer named Susan Robinson. (To keep this example simple, assume that no two customers have the same name.) After the RDBMS finds that row of data, it gets the customer number and goes to the WHO_ORDERED_WHAT table. The RDBMS then scans that table, from top to bottom, looking for any row of data where CUSTOMER_NUMBER is equal to 81115 (Susan Robinson's customer number). Unlike in the first table, though, the RDBMS doesn't stop when it finds the first row of data that meets this criteria, because the table may have 1 or 100 or 1,000 or any number of rows indicating what Susan Robinson ordered.

A relational database does not store data in any kind of sorted order, though an *index* could be used for sorting to help with the process of locating data. In an official sense, the exact physical order in which data is stored is *implementation-defined:* The DBMS product "decides" (and it's none of your business) how the product works, as long as it does work.

Back to the history of relational databases. (This discussion *is* leading somewhere!) Vendors spent most of the 1970s (the research era of relational databases) *and* the 1990s trying to solve a nasty problem: If a relational database couldn't have pointers to efficiently tell the software how to return data to users, what should be done? An RDBMS product has a subsystem, usually known as a *query optimizer* (or a similar term), that tries to consider many aspects of how the data is organized, such as the ones in this list:

- The number of tables from which you're asking for information as part of the join process
- The size (if it's known) of each of those tables
- Any indices that are available to prevent having to scan each table from end to end
- System characteristics (what type of hardware and how the data is stored on the disks, for example)

Here's the punchline: RDBMS vendors spent about two decades working on their query optimizers to make relational database technology suitable for online transaction processing (OLTP) applications, such as customer order processing, checking-account systems, and zillions of other types of applications that companies use to run their businesses. Finally, near the end of the 1980s, the corporate IT world (most of it, anyway) became convinced that RDBMS products weren't just "for play." RDBMSs began to be used as part of real-world OLTP applications, replacing the old-style databases (the ones with the pointers) or file systems.

And along comes data warehousing. So what's the significance? Here it is, summed up in a few sentences.

OLTP applications typically access a small number of tables (preferably one but usually only two or three) during a given *transaction,* a series of steps that either access data from a database or put data into it. That 20 years' worth of optimization, therefore, was oriented toward making sure that these OLTP-style transactions with a small number of tables in them were as efficient as possible.

Data warehousing applications — the online analytical processing (OLAP) ones, as described in the following section — rarely access one or two or three tables at a time. Rather, the nature of data warehousing (bringing together a great deal of information that, when the pieces of data are related to one another, provides business intelligence capabilities) usually means that a large number of tables must be accessed as part of a single query.

(At the risk of getting ahead of myself, the way you design your relational database plays a large part in the number-of-tables situation you have to deal with.)

When RDBMS products that had evolved over two decades to support OLTP-type database access with reasonable performance were suddenly put to work in OLAP environments, they began performing in a somewhat less-than-desirable manner. It wasn't anyone's fault: The products were just expected to do something that they hadn't been developed to do. That's when the philosophy of not using RDBMSs for data warehousing was developed.

To use an analogy, a four-wheel-drive, off-road vehicle and a sports car both have similar characteristics: an engine, four wheels with tires, and a steering wheel, for example. A sports car, however, has been developed to use the basic common framework of an automobile to go fast; in off-road situations out in the wilderness, the driver of a sports car is probably in trouble.

The OLAP-only fallacy

Because the preceding section says that performance a few years ago was subpar when RDBMSs were used for OLAP purposes, you may think that RDBMSs were therefore deemed unsuitable for data warehousing.

Wrong!

Without going off on a tangent of blaming vendors and their marketing pitches (I do that in Chapter 20), it's absolutely incorrect to make an indelible link between OLAP functionality and a data warehouse. Consider the following points:

- Did OLAP and data warehousing hit the big leagues at the same time? *Yes.*

- Do you almost always perform OLAP functionality with data that has been loaded into a data warehouse? *Yes.*

- Is OLAP the only thing you can do with a data warehouse? *No!*

Part III of this book discusses the area of *business intelligence,* which is the reason you build a data warehouse. Go ahead — take a peek at the table of contents or skim over to those chapters. OLAP is only one of four different classes of business intelligence.

To make a blanket statement that RDBMS technology is unsuitable for data warehousing is to state unequivocally that the only thing you would want to do with a data warehouse is OLAP processing. Again, that's *incorrect.*

The New Way of Thinking

Now it's 1997; what has changed?

Understanding how RDBMSs were enhanced to support data warehousing

RDBMS vendors, at least the ones still in business after surviving the Great Database Wars of the 1980s, are run by smart people. These smart people saw what was going on: the growth of data warehousing, the problems the vendors' respective products were having in supporting the type of processing most commonly done after the data warehouse was built, and the rise of multidimensional database vendors (discussed in Chapter 6). These people figured, "Hey! We have to do something about this situation."

The major problem vendors faced was that, unlike OLTP applications, many data warehousing queries against a database involved database join operations with four, five, six, or even more tables. Checking into the problem (although I'm oversimplifying a little, it gets the point across), it turned out that the typical relational query optimizer would, when faced with a join operation involving a large number of tables, do the programming equivalent of throwing its hands in the air, shaking its head in confusion, and saying, "I dunno — you tell me!" The query optimizer would "give up" and do one large "join the tables all possible ways and then figure it all out afterward" response (known as a *Cartesian product*). This inefficient means of joining tables caused these types of queries to run slowly.

Most RDBMS vendors enhanced their query optimizers to do a *star join* — a different, more efficient way of doing joins when a large number of tables is involved in a query. When a database was designed according to the principles of a star schema (discussed later in this chapter), the problems from having a large number of tables involved in a single query were dramatically reduced.

Handling the very large database (VLDB) problem — and getting the RDBMS answer

In the early days (a few years ago) of the current generation of data warehousing, most data warehouses were rather small, measuring about 50 gigabytes of data or smaller. As technologies mature and IT professionals become more comfortable with data warehousing (and as they become more daring after getting a few successful projects behind them), they commonly need or want increasingly larger amounts of data in a warehouse. These folks want not only larger amounts, though, but also increasing levels of detail (not just summarized information).

The DBMS world has had for years a term that applies to very large databases. The term is *very large database,* or *VLDB.* How's that for descriptive?

VLDB has become increasingly synonymous with data warehousing. And, almost without fail, VLDB data warehouses have been implemented using RDBMS technologies. The combination of warehouse-sensitive query optimization (the star joins mentioned in the preceding section), new types of indices, and *parallel processing* capabilities has permitted RDBMS products to deal with VLDB situations much more effectively than they could only a few years ago.

Parallel processing in the RDBMS world is a relatively complex proposition and another vendor-versus-vendor battlefield because of different ways of doing it. The mechanics of parallel processing (not to mention the arguments used by both sides) don't matter much here. It's important, though, to understand that in parallel database processing, a single database table is divided into multiple *partitions* (different segments of the same table, each containing different rows of data). Furthermore, queries against the database table run in parallel against each of the partitions, effectively reducing the time it takes to get an answer to a query because each parallel query is operating against a smaller amount of data than would be in the entire table if it weren't partitioned.

Designing Your Relational Database for Data Warehouse Usage

The traditional usage of relational databases, to support transaction-processing applications, has meant that certain design principles had to be followed. If you had to deliberately violate one of those principles, you had to handle your own work-arounds.

What's the story behind relational database design and data warehousing? Read on.

Looking at why traditional relational design techniques don't work well

Relational databases are designed, in their purest sense, according to the principles of *normalization*. Without getting into all the mathematical formalities, this section explains what normalization means.

Explaining normalization in plain language (or trying to)

Because a relational database is laid out like a table, it cannot have any *repeating groups* of data (more than one telephone number for a customer, for example) within that row. Although you could have columns called PHONE_NUMBER_1 and PHONE_NUMBER_2, of course, they're technically different pieces of data, even though they relate to the same concept (a telephone number). The official way to handle repeating groups, known in the world of conceptual data modeling as *multivalued attributes,* is to create a separate table with a primary key join column. (In this example, you put the CUSTOMER_ID column in both the master customer table and in the other table with the phone numbers so that a customer's complete record can be reconstructed.)

The reason you go through this seemingly ridiculous, overly complex set of steps is to ensure that a relational database is in *first normal form* (no repeating groups of data).

A relational database can also be designed to include other normal forms. *Second normal form* (no partial-key dependencies) and *third normal form* (no non-key dependencies) are the most commonly used forms in relational database design, though the seldom used *fourth normal form, fifth normal form,* and *Boyce–Codd normal form* are also options. (A database book can give you more information about these terms.)

To get to the point: A relational database is *normalized* (when the rules of normalization are followed or mostly followed) because of the way it is accessed during typical OLTP functions.

More specifically, one of the primary purposes is to prevent *update anomalies,* or the updating of a column in a given row but not updating that column with the same value in another row in that table. Update anomalies are a little complicated and not necessary to understand; just remember that normalization is important for update operations.

A data warehouse, however, (almost) never permits update operations. At least first-generation data warehouses don't permit update operations because data is modified by bulk reloading operations rather than single in-place updates as part of a transaction. One of the main benefits of normalization-based relational design, therefore, doesn't really apply to a data warehouse.

The side effect of normalization

What if update operations don't really apply to a relational database? One of the side effects (results) of a highly normalized database is that it has many tables in it; to create data warehousing facts of information (sales by quarter by territory, for example), many multi-table join operations must occur.

If a highly normalized database has a number of tables because facts are broken down into multiple tables (primarily to prevent update anomalies) and if a data warehouse doesn't support update operations (in the OLTP sense), why normalize?

Why, indeed.

Exploring new ways to design a relational-based data warehouse

You can use one of two main techniques to design your relational database for data warehousing use:

- ✔ **Highly denormalized:** You gleefully throw away the rules of normalization and put data where it makes the most sense, not based on update-oriented restrictions. Denormalization is typically used for relational data warehouses that support basic querying and reporting (as explained in Chapter 9, with examples), *not* for OLAP.

- ✔ **Star schema:** This method mimics the multidimensional structures of facts and dimensions, discussed in Chapter 6, but uses relational fact tables and dimension tables. The star schema is recommended for relational databases used for OLAP (known as ROLAP).

Choose your relational design approach carefully. Although people have a tendency to assume that "data warehousing equals OLAP equals star schema" when a data warehouse is being built primarily to support the generation of specific reports (as explained in Chapter 9), a denormalization-oriented design approach may well work better. Check out both approaches: Run benchmarks, but don't just assume one or the other.

Relational Products and Data Warehousing

This section discusses some leading relational database products you may use for your data warehouse. It also lists URLs to vendors' Internet Web sites.

A major trend that will pick up steam is the convergence of object-oriented databases with relational products. Although the SQL3 standard, now under development, specifies an official language-based approach for relational-object databases, products are already appearing for which nontraditional data types (time-oriented, image-oriented, and video-oriented, for example, rather than character or numeric or date) are available as *plug-ins* (additional database services) to the basic relational database engine. Check them out if you think that your data warehousing environment may have a need for multimedia data, as discussed in Chapter 24.

 Almost all the vendors listed in this section have, during the past few years, acquired OLAP or multidimensional-oriented technology to integrate into their product lines and architectures. It's worth keeping an eye on the whole picture because a data warehousing environment may well have both relational and multidimensional servers. In this type of environment, integration that is as seamless as possible is important.

 Disclaimer: The vendors and their products listed in this section are included because companies use them to build data warehouses. No recommendations or referrals or anything like that are implied.

IBM DB2 family

www.software.ibm.com/data/db2

The IBM DB2 family is an outgrowth of the IBM flagship relational DBMS product for MVS/ESA mainframes. Many organizations with corporate standards and mandates, such as "Thou shalt do all large database processing on the mainframe" or "The AS/400 is our only nonmainframe platform," deploy data warehousing using a version of DB2 for either of those platforms. (I've done both.)

Informix

www.informix.com

Informix is a leading DBMS vendor whose database servers are commonly used for relational-based data warehouses.

Microsoft SQL Server

www.microsoft.com

The Microsoft SQL Server is an institution for many departmental applications in which Microsoft products are dominant. In these organizations, data marts are often built using SQL Server. Microsoft should be interesting to watch as its product line for its data warehousing strategy "scales toward the enterprise" (as its products are increasingly used for applications that formerly were run on a mainframe).

Oracle

www.oracle.com

Oracle is a leading DBMS vendor whose recent product, Oracle 8, is the latest generation of its flagship RDBMS, which dates back to 1980.

Red Brick

www.redbrick.com

Red Brick has, according to its Web site, an "exclusive focus on relational database servers for data warehouse applications." Much of the technology that has gone into standard RDBMS products was pioneered at Red Brick, which was once considered the only viable relational alternative for data warehousing (as contrasted with multidimensional databases).

Sybase

www.sybase.com

Sybase, the third member of the RDBMS Big Three (along with Oracle and Informix), is also retrofitting its OLTP DBMS product suite for data warehousing.

Chapter 6

You're Entering a New Dimension: Multidimensional Databases

*B*efore I describe multidimensional databases, I have to talk about relational databases. Although I realize that it was the topic of Chapter 5, I have to make one more point.

Relational databases have become the steady, general-purpose champion of the data-management world. The straightforward table–row–column structure, not all that different (at least conceptually) from a basic spreadsheet, is a flexible method by which data can be organized for many different purposes.

That's the good news.

The not-so-good news is that the flexibility comes with a price. Specifically, in some areas of data management (not many, but some), the table–row–column structure is inefficient and performs poorly, at least until the relational database management system (RDBMS) is enhanced (or, in some cases, overhauled) to handle these out-of-the-ordinary missions.

One of these areas is *multidimensional analysis,* a way of looking at data as facts organized by dimensions. (All this stuff is covered later in this chapter.) As Chapter 5 points out, RDBMS products have been augmented with specialized, enhanced multi-table query optimization to handle data more efficiently in a multidimensional manner.

This isn't the first time in recent history that new types of database products have emerged and overcome RDBMS inefficiencies. Back in the 1980s, a class of applications was identified in which the data-management needs were ill-handled by RDBMS products (especially the generation available at that time). These applications all needed user-specified data types that would vary among different implementations. For example, computer-aided design/computer-aided manufacturing (CAD/CAM) applications had to be capable of specifying data types that related to product drawings, blueprints, and other related factors. Computer-aided software engineering (CASE) needed data types to represent applications and systems, databases, graphical representations of entities and attributes, process and data flows, and other parts of the application-development process.

What resulted was *object-oriented database management systems (ODBMSs)* that eliminated the table–row–column structures of relational databases and instead introduced, directly into the database engine, the concepts of classes and subclasses (or types and subtypes), objects, properties, methods, and the other parts of object-oriented technology.

Now consider multidimensional analysis. Because RDBMS technology wasn't well-suited to this multidimensional way of looking at data, particularly in terms of performance, vendors set out to develop their own structures tuned and optimized for improved performance.

If you track happenings in the database management world, you're probably familiar with the convergence of relational and object-oriented database technology, as mentioned in Chapter 5. RDBMS products are being equipped with object-oriented extensions. Arguably, this approach to handling complex data types (objects) has won out over nonrelational products ("pure" ODBMSs) primarily because of the large installed base of relational products and applications running on top of them. Will the same thing happen in the data warehousing world — relational technology overtaking and then overwhelming specialized multidimensional products? Stay tuned.

The Idea behind Multidimensional Databases

Multidimensional databases (MDDBs) throw out the conventions of their relational ancestors and organize data in a manner that's highly conducive to multidimensional analysis. To understand multidimensional databases, therefore, you must first understand the basics of the analytical functions performed with the data stored in them.

Multidimensional analysis is built around a few simple data organization concepts, specifically facts and dimensions.

Facts

A *fact* is an instance of some particular occurrence or event and the properties of the event all stored in a database. Did you sell a watch to a customer last Friday afternoon? That's a fact. Did your store receive a shipment of 76 class rings yesterday from a particular supplier? That's another fact.

Dimensions

A *dimension* is an index by which you can access facts according to the value (or values) you want. For example, you may organize your sales data according to these dimensions:

- ✔ Customer
- ✔ Time
- ✔ Product

The basics

In this simple example, you can organize and view your sales data as a three-dimensional array, indexed by these three dimensions:

- ✔ In July 1997 (the time dimension), Customer A (the customer dimension) bought class rings (the product dimension): 79 of them for $8,833 (the rest of the fact, consisting of *attributes*).

- ✔ In 1997 (the time dimension), Customer A (the customer dimension) bought many different products (the product dimension) — a total of 3,333 units for $55,905 (the attributes).

Notice the subtle difference between the way the dimensions are used in these two examples. In the first one, *time* relates to a month; *customer* relates to a specific customer; and *product* is for a specific product.

In the second example, however, *time* is for a year, not a month; *customer* is still the same (an individual customer); and *product* is for the entire product line.

Multidimensional analysis supports the notion of *hierarchies* in dimensions. For example, time may be organized in a hierarchy of year⇨quarter⇨month. You could view facts (or the consolidation of facts) in the database at any one of these levels: by year, quarter, or month.

Similarly, products may be organized in a hierarchy of product family⇨ product type⇨specific products. Class rings may be a product type; "class ring, modern style, onyx stone" may be a specific product. Furthermore, class rings, watches, other rings, and other items all would "roll up" into the *jewelry* product family.

"Is there a limit to the number of dimensions?"

Theoretically (and I do mean theoretically), you can have as many dimensions in your multidimensional model as necessary. The question always exists, however, of whether your multidimensional database product can support them. A more important question, though, is that even if a product allows 15 dimensions, for example, does it make sense to create a model of that size? (You can read more about efficiency and storage-management in a moment.)

You can, for example, add geography to the dimension list in the preceding example so that you can see and organize facts according to sales territories, states, cities, and specific stores.

"How should I choose the levels in a hierarchy?"

Very carefully. The good news is that the levels in a hierarchy enable you to perform *drill-down* functionality, as discussed in Chapter 10. Even better news is that by having multiple levels within a hierarchy, you can quickly get answers to your questions because of the information that has been set up at each of those specified levels that are waiting for your queries.

The bad news, however, is that unless you explicitly determine that you will include a level in a hierarchy, you cannot, using a multidimensional database, see your facts at that particular level. (You may see them at a higher, more summarized level of detail or at a lower level of detail, but not at *that* level.)

Before you create a bunch of levels in each of your dimension hierarchies (just in case you need them), first consider that every one of these predefined levels affects storage requirements for your multidimensional model.

Here's a guideline to follow: Because multidimensional databases have fairly rigid structures built around the *precalculation* of facts (creating and storing aggregates in the database rather than performing report-time aggregation and calculation), the more dimensions you have and the more levels in each dimension you have, the greater your storage requirements.

Physical database structures in an MDDB

Though nearly all MDDB products are built around the concept of facts and dimensions and hierarchies, no such thing as an MDDB standard definition exists. In the relational world, nonstandardization has also been somewhat of a problem, particularly with value-added features, such as constraints and stored procedures. The basic relational table–row–column structure, however, has been fairly easy to export or unload into a flat file of some type and then reload into another RDBMS product.

Don't forget your spreadsheet!

Though MDDB products typically provide data to an OLAP tool, many users are just as happy to use a plain old spreadsheet program as their primary analytical tool. For example, Essbase (an Arbor product) has an add-in interface to Microsoft Excel. You would use the interface to make your data requests and then, after receiving data back into your spreadsheet, manipulate it as you would manipulate any other data.

When you put together a multidimensional analysis component to your business develop-ment environment, don't forget about your spreadsheet users: They may happily receive dimensionally stored data through their spreadsheet product rather than through the interface the underlying MDDB product provides. In the MDDB world, vendors have taken a variety of different approaches to their respective products' physical representations of data. Why? Because they all have been seeking ways to overcome storage and complexity problems caused by overdoing it with dimensions and levels of hierarchies.

MDDB vendors have tried to use, wherever possible, "sparse array-manage-ment techniques" to reduce the amount of wasted space in any data model. (If you're a computer science or MIS major, you may recall this subject from a class in data structures.) They've all taken different paths, and portability from one MDDB product to another hasn't exactly been a high priority for these companies.

When you're evaluating products, don't get caught up in worrying about physical storage techniques: Making sure that your business needs can be met by the logical representations that are provided (such as the hierar-chies, levels, and facts) is much more important. Eliminate products that seem clunky or that have, for example, a hierarchy model that doesn't seem quite right for your data. *Then,* for the products you like, "kick the tires" a little to see how they work inside.

Are Multidimensional Databases Still Worth Looking At?

If relational technology is absorbing the multidimensional world and quickly becoming capable of handling this area of data management, are MDDBs now a dead-end technology?

Not necessarily. This question is much the same ROLAP-versus-MOLAP debate that continues to be waged. Check out the guidelines in Chapter 10 for the style of OLAP you should consider under various circumstances. You may well have specific needs that make MDDBs the sensible answer for your environment.

Other Specialized Database Technology for Data Warehousing

This section describes a couple of other database technologies that may be interesting as you research your data warehousing options.

Sybase IQ

www.sybase.com/products/dataware/iq.html

Several years ago Sybase introduced IQ, a product built on *bit-mapped indexing technology*. The IQ data sheet at the Sybase Web site says that the product supports bit-mapped indexing for both *low-cardinality* and *high-cardinality* data. An example of low-cardinality data is a particular attribute with a small range of values (the colors of an automobile, for example); high-cardinality data consists of "range-oriented" values (for example, sales volumes and unit sales).

IQ is now perceived by data warehousing aficionados as more of a data mart solution (Chapter 4 talks about data marts), as an alternative to MDDB or relational technology for small-scale data warehousing environments.

In-memory databases: Is anything really there?

Another interesting area of advanced database technology is the storage of data in main memory (rather than on disk) for *extremely fast* access.

One of the main drawbacks to the use of in-memory data has been having to deal with system failures. For transactional databases, transactions could be lost unless the content could be reconstructed from a log that was stored on disk, for example. Another drawback was the amount of main memory usually available on a computer system — it was rarely suitable for all except extremely small-scale databases.

Recent advances in very large memory-management technology have done much to overcome the latter problem. With regard to the former problem, though, how about a data warehouse rather than a transactional database? A bulk-loaded data warehouse isn't as susceptible to catastrophic data loss as a transaction processing system. If the system crashes and data is lost, the data warehouse can be reloaded from its sources. Although a little downtime to handle the reloading is necessary, during normal no-problem operations, queries can be handled very quickly.

In-memory database technology is still a little out there on the horizon, and not many organizations seem to be trying it. Still, if mainstream products embrace this approach, it soon could open up a whole new world of data warehousing possibilities.

Chapter 7

Stuck in the Middle with You: Data Warehousing Middleware

- -

In This Chapter
▶ Middleware defined

▶ Middleware services and functionality you should know about

▶ Middleware products to check out

- -

*I*n the world of distributed computing — basically any environment in which data has to move from one system to another — middleware is a key component in making it all work. This chapter discusses data warehousing middleware in detail, from the basics to the specific services that apply to your data warehousing environment. At the end of the chapter is a list of vendors who have middleware products that may be useful in your data warehousing project.

What Is Middleware?

Loosely defined, *middleware* is a set of services that perform various functions in a distributed computing environment, such as a client/server system. Here are some types of middleware services:

- ✔ **Security:** Authenticates a particular client program to some system component to verify, for example, that the client program and its user are really who they say they are

- ✔ **Transaction management:** Ensures *transactional integrity* — that a system or database doesn't get corrupted if problems occur

- ✔ **Directory:** Enables a client program to find other services or servers located in a distributed enterprise

These types of services are typically part of a distributed transaction-processing environment. I don't mean that a data warehousing environment cannot also include these services; it's just that other middleware services are more important to a data warehousing environment, as described in the following section.

Middleware for Data Warehousing

In a data warehousing environment, the middleware services are the set of programs and routines that do the following:

1. Pull data from the source (or sources).
2. Make sure that the data is correct.
3. Move it around the environment from platform to platform, as necessary.
4. Handle any necessary data transformations.
5. Load the data into the data warehouse's database (or databases).

The services

In a more formal sense, the preceding list is handled by these middleware services:

- Data selection and extraction
- Data quality assurance, Part I (at the component level)
- Data movement, Part I (also at the component level)
- Data mapping and transformation
- Data quality assurance, Part II (after transformation has occurred)
- Data movement, Part II (into the data warehouse's platform environment)
- Data loading (into the data warehouse)

Figure 7-1 illustrates how these middleware services flow together in a moderately sized data warehousing environment.

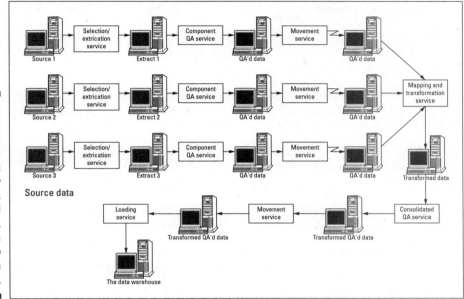

Figure 7-1:
The data
warehousing
middleware
services
flow
together,
from end
to end,
from data
sources to
the data
warehouse.

(Note, though, that your data warehousing environment may differ, particularly in the area of the data-movement services. A data-movement service is necessary every time data crosses system boundaries. Your conceptual picture will differ depending on the details of your particular end-to-end environment.)

It's *extremely* important to plan, design, and otherwise think about data warehouse middleware in terms of the *individual services* just listed (and described in the following sections) rather than in generic terms, such as "extraction tools." The reason is that many different vendors provide some, many, or all of these services as part of a single product or a suite of products. The challenge (problem) is usually that a tool with strong mapping and transformation services, for example, may be weak in data-loading services, or another tool that provides a rich set of extraction services may be less effective in the mapping and transformation space, in addition to data quality assurance.

Before selecting a tool for your data warehousing project (if that's the route you take rather than custom coding, which is discussed in the following section), make sure that you have a good idea about the particular challenges in your environment. If you have relatively straightforward data-extraction needs, for example, but challenging data-quality problems, concentrate on finding the highest-quality-assurance tool available, even if it has only so-so extraction capabilities. (This advice applies even if the tool has no extraction capabilities, in which case you have to combine it with another tool.)

Should you use tools or custom code?

In the early days of data warehousing, most organizations handled middleware services through custom coding rather than with the few tools available at the time, as shown in this example:

1. An organization writes a program in a programming language such as COBOL, or perhaps in an environment such as SAS, to handle the data extracts and then do the quality assurance checking and the transformation.

2. A file-transfer service, such as standard FTP (File Transfer Protocol), is used to copy the transformed and "cleansed" data to the machine on which the data warehouse will reside.

3. Plain old SQL is used to load a relational database with the new (or updated) contents of the data warehouse.

Nothing is wrong with this programmatic approach, even today. Always determine for your specific environment whether custom coding or tools are the right way to go. Don't automatically assume that you should implement your data warehouse using middleware tools.

 Here's a guideline for your tools-or-code decision. If your organization already extracts data from operational systems and copies it into a "sort of" data warehouse (it's really a file extract, as discussed in Chapter 21) for reporting or querying, you probably have a suite of programs already written in COBOL, SAS, or some other programming language to perform these middleware functions. In this case, strongly consider using your existing programs, perhaps upgrading them as necessary instead of having your team members start all over in the learning curve (in addition to the evaluation process) of data warehousing middleware tools. If your organiza- tion doesn't use file extracts for analysis, however, and you're embarking on a data warehousing project, tools (rather than code) are probably the best way to go.

What Each Middleware Service Does for You

This section describes each of the data warehousing middleware services and what they mean to your data warehousing environment.

Data selection and extractions

The primary purpose of the data-selection and -extraction service is to select (find) from a data source the data that will move into the data warehouse and then extract (pull out) that data into a form that can be readied for quality assurance services.

You can use one of two different types of selection and extraction services for your data warehousing environment:

- ✔ **"Get 'em all and sort 'em out later":** Find and extract all the data elements in a source that will be loaded into your data warehouse regardless of whether a specific element has been previously extracted.

- ✔ **Change oriented:** Find and extract *only* the data elements that have been either newly added to the data source since the last extraction or updated since the last extraction.

The first type of service requires less complex logic in order to perform the extraction. You will deal with larger volumes of data (sometimes *much* larger volumes), however, than with the second type, the change-oriented service.

The change-oriented method of selection and extraction is fairly straightforward when your source is a relational database with a time stamp you can use to detect when a row of data was added or last updated. You can compare a row of data against the date and time of the last extraction process to determine whether data needs to be selected and extracted. When the data is stored in a file (a VSAM file, for example) that does not have a time stamp, however, this process can be significantly more difficult.

Another challenge you have to consider for either a file or a database is for source data that has been *deleted*. If the business rules for your data warehousing environment call for the deletion of corresponding data from the warehouse, you must have a way to detect deletions that were made since the last extraction process to ensure that appropriate deletions are made.

The result of the selection and extraction is, well, an extract of data that's ready to undergo additional processing: checking out the data quality.

Data quality assurance (QA), Part 1

Two different quality assurance (QA) services should be in the flow of middleware services. You have to perform the first QA tasks against the extract from the data source *before* any more middleware services are performed. You should try to catch (and correct) errors and problems as early in the process as possible. Moving data down the pipeline toward the data warehouse is pointless if problems are so significant that they either require significantly more effort to correct later in the process or simply can't be corrected and if the source-to-warehouse process must therefore be halted.

So what types of problems should you look for? Here are a few:

- **Values in data elements that exceed a reasonable range:** A customer has submitted 150 million purchase orders in the past month, for example, or an employee who (according to the employee database and the stored hiring date) has worked with the company for 4,297 years.

- **Values in data elements that don't fit the official and complete list of permissible values:** A value may have an A code, for example, when the only permissible values for a field are supposed to be M and F. (If that field were labeled GENDER, A may stand for androgynous!)

- **Cross-table inconsistencies:** For entries in the CUSTOMER_ORDER table, no corresponding entries (as identified by CUSTOMER_ID) exist in the CUSTOMER_MASTER_TABLE.

- **Cross-field inconsistencies:** Records with an incorrect state or zip code for the city indicated.

- **Missing values:** Records with missing values in certain fields where they should have contents.

- **Data gaps:** For example, a source table should contain one row of data with total units sold and sales dollars for each month over the past two years. For a large number of customers, however, no rows exist for at least one of those months.

- **Incomplete data:** If information about every product the company sells is supposed to be available, for example, are all products included in the extract?

- **Violations of business rules:** If a business rule states that only one wholesaler can sell products to any one of the company's customers, you should check to see whether any customer records indicate sales made through more than one wholesaler, which could indicate incorrect data in the source.

- **Data corruption since the last extract:** If extraction occurs monthly, for example, you should keep track of data values or sums that should be constant, such as SALES PER CUSTOMER PER MONTH. If, in a subsequent month, the value of SALES PER CUSTOMER PER MONTH is now different for a given customer for a previous month than it had once been, it's possible that the underlying data has been corrupted.

- **Spelling inconsistencies:** A customer's name is spelled several different ways, for example.

What do you do when you find problems? You can try one of the following techniques:

- ✔ **Apply an automatic-correction rule.** When you find an inconsistent spelling, for example, do a lookup in a master table of previous spelling corrections and automatically make the change in the data.

- ✔ **Set aside the record for a team member to analyze and correct later.** In this case, the human part of the QA may be done in conjunction with automatic correction. For example, automatic corrections are made, if possible, and a report about other problems are put into a separate file and sent to the QA person. When all manual corrections have been made, they're merged back into the data that has gone through the automatic QA process.

- ✔ **Cool your jets.** If you discover enough problems and they're serious enough or require an indeterminate amount of research, consider halting the entire process until later.

The QA process is much more efficient, and much less problematic, when you perform a thorough *source systems analysis,* as described in Chapter 15. If you have a fairly good idea about what types of data problems you may expect to find in each data source, your QA process can be preprogrammed to detect and (hopefully) correct them before continuing.

Most organizations now treat the data warehouse QA process as a one-directional flow. Problems are corrected before the data is moved further into the flow of middleware processes *but is never corrected in the data sources.* In a growing trend, though, a *feedback loop* from the QA process returns to the data source to correct the source data.

Data movement, Part 1

In most situations, the two services I've already described (selection and extraction and quality assurance) take place on the same platform (system) on which the data source resides. If your data warehouse will be hosted on a different platform than that data source, though, you have to use a *data-movement* service to effect the system-to-system transfer of the data.

This service is likely to be a relatively simple one (handled by a simple file-transfer program, for example). The primary purpose of the movement service, if it's necessary at this point, is to move the QA'd data into the environment in which additional transformation will take place.

Data mapping and transformation

Figure 7-1 shows an environment in which data is being extracted from three different data sources for inclusion in a data warehouse and each of the three is on a different platform. At some point in the middleware process, these QA'd extracts must be brought together for a *combined* mapping and transformation process.

The mapping and transformation service handles classical data warehousing problems. Suppose that one data source stores customers with a five-character customer ID and another uses a six-digit numeric customer identifier. To enable comparisons and other data warehouse processing, a common method of customer identification must exist: One of the identification schemes must be converted to the other, or perhaps a third, neutral identification system, depending on that environment's characteristics.

In addition to handling cross-system incompatibilities, additional transformations may include

- ✔ **Data summary:** A summary can be performed earlier in the process, before cross-system movement, depending on the peculiarities of your specific data warehousing environment.

- ✔ **Selective inclusion of data:** You may include records from only one data source, for example, if a comparable record is coming from another extract. You don't know, until all the data source's contributions are converged, how selective inclusion rules are applied.

- ✔ **Data convergence:** Certain elements from one data source are combined with elements from another source to create one unified record for each customer, product, contract, or whatever type of data with which you're dealing.

The main point to remember about the mapping and transformation service is that you should have, at its conclusion, a *unified* set of data that's ready to be loaded into the data warehouse — as soon as a few more steps are completed.

In increasingly complex data warehousing environments, you may want to consider multiple transformation processes. As shown in Figure 7-2, for example, data extracts converge at several different levels of transformation before moving further down the middleware pipeline.

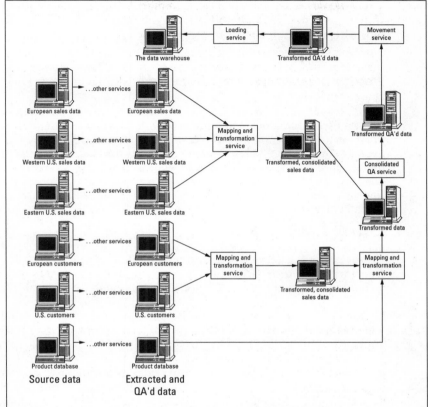

Figure 7-2:
Complex
data
warehousing
environments
may have
several
different
mapping
and trans-
formation
points.

Data quality assurance (QA), Part II

Following completion of the transformation processes, data must be QA'd —
again. Why? Simply because you never know what type of errors or discrepancies may have been introduced into the data as a result of the
transformation process. After changes have occurred, any previous QA
processes are no longer valid.

You want to run the consolidated, transformed data through the same type
of QA steps discussed earlier in this chapter, in the section "Data quality
assurance (QA), Part I." Although you probably won't find as many rudimentary errors (such as spelling or values that are out of range) if you did a
thorough job on your first-level, component QA, you still should make sure.
Furthermore, you should ensure that the code or scripts used for data
transformation didn't accidentally cause new errors to creep in.

The goal of this second-level QA is to make sure that your consolidated and transformed data is ready to load into the data warehouse, as soon as one more step occurs, if necessary.

Data movement, Part II

If your transformation and QA processing is occurring on a platform that's different from what will run your production data warehouse (on a development server, for example, rather than on the operational server), you must execute one more data-movement service to get the data to the place where it will eventually reside. Again, this process is usually a relatively simple file transfer.

Data loading

The data-loading service is the process of loading the extracted, QA'd, transformed, and "re-QA'd" data into your warehouse. You may load data via a customized program, SQL (an INSERT statement, for example), or a utility.

If you need to load a large volume of data, try to use a fast-loading utility, which usually involves much less time than a programmatic or SQL-based approach.

If you use SQL to load your data into a relational database, try to make the loading as efficient as possible by turning off logging if your DBMS product permits it. If the loading job is abnormally terminated, all you have to do is use the DROP statement to get rid of your partially loaded table, fix the problem that caused the termination, and restart the job. This process usually is much faster than if you have turned on the facilities needed for OLTP-style data and transaction integrity (with accompanying overhead).

Replication Services for Data Warehousing

Replication is a special case of middleware services that combines selection and extraction, movement, and loading from one database to one or more others, *usually* managed by a single DBMS product. (The source database and all the targets are all Oracle, all Sybase, or all Microsoft SQL Server, for example.)

Replication across multiple DBMS products — from a DB2 source to an Oracle replicate, for example — is a growing trend. As far as I can tell, however, few environments have been built with cross-DBMS replication.

Although replication service capabilities vary among DBMS products, traditionally they have been *snapshot-oriented:* A snapshot of either an entire database or the changes since the last replication occurred are extracted, at a predetermined time, from the source and copied over a networked environment to the intended targets. The data is then transmitted and loaded as is (no transformation occurs).

Although the rumor mill says that DBMS products are incorporating data-transformation services (summarization) into their replication models, I think that it's still early in the game for these value-added approaches. You should check out any claim of this type if it may apply to your environment.

Does replication replace the long list of data warehousing middleware services discussed in this chapter? No! The primary place for replication in a data warehousing environment is *after* the data has been loaded into a data warehouse and is then being extracted and sent to data marts, as shown in Figure 7-3.

Figure 7-3:
RDBMS-
based
replication
services
extract
snapshots
of certain
data and
transmit
it to depart-
mental data
marts.

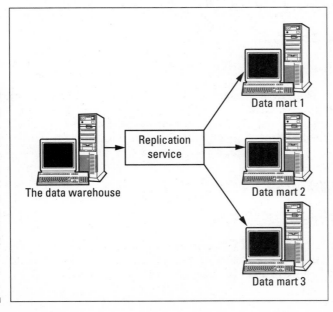

Vendors with Middleware Products for Data Warehousing

This section lists the names of vendors with data warehousing middleware products that may be of interest to you.

Chapter 29 lists some Web sites that provide links to these and many other product vendors, in addition to product listings by category. Check 'em out!

Carleton Corporation

www.carleton.com/

Carleton Corporation produces PASSPORT, which automates the process of extracting, transforming, cleansing, formatting, and mapping data, from source production database management systems (DB2, IMS, Oracle, Sybase, or VSAM, for example) to targeted relational database management systems.

Evolutionary Technologies International (ETI)

www.evtech.com/

ETI-Extract, from Evolutionary Technologies International, is a middleware tool the company markets not only for data warehousing environments but also as useful for data migration/system migration efforts. ETI calls ETI-Extract a "best of breed" product that works with other tools.

Informatica

www.informatica.com/

Informatica, the maker of PowerMart, bills itself as "the enterprise data mart company." Its Web site describes PowerMart as an "advanced set of tightly integrated, highly visual client/server software tools."

An editorial: Data warehousing middleware — or not?

Not everyone would agree that the services and tools discussed in this chapter should be classified as data warehousing middleware. Some people consider data warehousing middleware to be cross-database access tools and other types of gateways. These folks consider tools that perform the types of services discussed in this chapter to be part of the extraction, data cleansing, and loading product group.

I believe that it's simply a matter of semantics. In my view, the services described in this chapter have as much of a middleware flavor to them as any distributed transaction processing manager or distributed security service or any of the other categories of traditional TP-oriented middleware.

Furthermore, you may have seen the current trend toward making warehouse-enabling applications capable of pushing data out toward the warehouse rather than toward an external service (such as the one performed by traditional extraction tools). This trend also ensures that the data has gone through its QA phase and transformation on the way to the data warehouse.

Call it what you want — I call it middleware, but use the term you prefer. You still have to perform these functions — *that's* the important thing to remember after reading this chapter.

Platinum Technology

www.platinum.com/

Platinum Technology offers a suite of products that perform the various data warehousing middleware services described in this chapter. Here's a list of some of its products, with features listed on the company's Web site:

- ✔ **PLATINUM InfoPump:** Performs bidirectional (back and forth) replication between heterogeneous (different product) databases.
- ✔ **PLATINUM InfoRefiner:** Performs extraction, refinement, and movement of large volumes of legacy data to client/server platforms.
- ✔ **PLATINUM InfoTransport:** A high-speed data-movement tool.

Praxis International

www.praxisint.com/

OmniReplicator, from Praxis International, provides a variety of different cross-product replication capabilities.

Prism Solutions

www.prismsolutions.com/

Prism Solutions offers the Prism Warehouse Executive, which, according to its Web site, provides these features:

- ✔ A graphical depiction of data sources and targets
- ✔ A graphical depiction of the flows within a data warehousing environment (including data marts)
- ✔ The generation of programs, according to templates, for the various phases of data warehouse construction (extraction and transformation, for example)
- ✔ The generation of load files and scripts
- ✔ A metadata management facility

Reliant Data Systems

www.dcle.com/

Reliant Data Systems produces the Data Conversion Language Engine (DCLE). This codeless migration engine, according to information at the DCLE Web site, simplifies data movement for both data warehousing and database migration tasks.

Sagent Technology

www.SagentTech.com/

Sagent Technology has a suite of products oriented for data marts, including Sagent Design Studio. The company describes the product as a visual environment that enables developers to embed Visual Basic or C++ code into extraction and transformation routines for building data marts.

VMARK

www.vmark.com/

VMARK describes its DataStage product as an integrated product suite for multisource extraction, transformation, integration, and maintenance of data.

Part III
Business Intelligence and Data Warehousing

In this part . . .

No, the phrase *business intelligence* is not an oxymoron. You have no reason to build a data warehouse, in fact, if your objective is not to provide business intelligence to members of your organization.

What is business intelligence? The chapters in this part of the book explain different aspects of business intelligence — from the simplest to the most complex — in down-to-earth, hypefree language complete with examples and a description of products that may interest you.

Chapter 8

An Intelligent Look at Business Intelligence

In This Chapter

▶ What business intelligence is

▶ What business intelligence means to data warehousing

▶ Which categories of business intelligence are important to you

In Chapter 5, I discuss the controversy over whether relational database management systems (RDBMSs) are suitable for data warehousing. One cause of the controversy was the mistaken belief, in the early days of data warehousing, that a data warehouse would be used *solely* for online analytical processing (OLAP) functionality.

As I said in Chapter 5, that's *wrong!*

You could even make the generalization that a data warehouse is created for the purposes of business intelligence. One variety of business intelligence is indeed OLAP functionality, and others exist.

If you build a data warehouse without clearly understanding what types of business intelligence are important to your organization, you're almost certain to build and put into use something that doesn't even come close to providing the business value you're seeking, regardless of how error-free your data is, how sophisticated your user tools are, and how wonderful your environment's performance is.

This chapter helps you make sense of the business intelligence quandary. (*Note:* Much of the information in this chapter is explored in-depth in the other chapters in this part of the book. This chapter, however, provides a place where you can skim through the descriptions of each of these categories to see how they relate to each other.)

The Four Main Categories

At the outset of your data warehousing project, don't focus on the type of tools you need — yet. Instead, concentrate on figuring out the types of questions users will ask against the warehouse's contents, the types of reports that will be run and for what purposes, and the general models of processing that will occur.

To help you get past hype, buzzwords, and technojargon, use the model shown in Table 8-1, which describes the four main categories of business intelligence functionality.

Table 8-1	Business Intelligence Categories	
Type	*Information You Want*	*See This Chapter*
Basic querying and reporting	"Tell me what happened."	9
OLAP	"Tell me what happened and why."	10
Data mining	"Tell me what may happen" or "Tell me something interesting."	11
EIS	"Tell me lots of things, but don't make me work too hard."	12

Each of these four categories describes a way of accessing data, doing something with the information that's retrieved, and providing information to whomever requested it. Each category, however, has different attributes.

Querying and reporting

Basic querying and reporting is most representative of traditional uses of data for analytical purposes. The data is retrieved in accordance with either regular standard reports or in response to a particular question (an ad hoc query, for example); then it's formatted and presented to the user either on-screen or on a printout. The interaction model is usually a set of regular, *predictable* steps:

1. **Make a data request.**

2. **Retrieve the data.**

3. **Manipulate the data slightly.**

   Summarize or reorganize, for example, if necessary.

4. **Format the data.**

5. **Present the data.**

OLAP

OLAP, in contrast, introduces analytical processes and a degree of variability into the user interaction model. Conceptually, the first steps are pretty much the same as the five in the preceding section for querying and reporting, but then the user takes over:

6. Manipulate the data.

Look at it in a different way or request the "data beneath the data," such as the details underneath a summary.

7. View the new results.

From that point, the variability of the process may iteratively cycle through Steps 6 and 7 (continually manipulating and reviewing the new results, for example) or even add new data for more analysis.

Data mining

Data mining, the newest entry in the business intelligence family, is an area also laden with hype (what a surprise). Data mining is often presented as a magical technique that's used to uncover the secrets of the universe from your organization's data.

In reality, data mining is an umbrella term for a series of advanced statistical techniques and models born in the 1980s as part of artificial intelligence research (neural networks, for example). Without focusing here on individual technologies (you can read about them in Chapter 11), you should understand data mining as a technique that has one or both of these aspects:

- **Predictive:** Data mining tools and capabilities search through large volumes of data, look for patterns and other aspects of the data in accordance with the techniques being used, and try to tell you what *may* happen based on the information the data analysis found. Notice the emphasis on the word *may:* Data mining is a technique of probability, not a fortune-telling service.

- **Discovery-oriented:** Both the basic querying-and-reporting and OLAP categories of business intelligence tools provide business intelligence based on questions users explicitly ask (sort of the question of the moment) or "institutionalized" questions that members of the organization ask in the form of regular reports (or both). The key word is *question;* no questions asked, no answers forthcoming.

Data mining's discovery-oriented nature is intended to provide answers even if no questions are asked. (I always refer to this model as "tell me something interesting, even if I don't know what questions to ask.") The data mining system typically provides these answers by building complex models that are used to analyze data, look for something that may be appropriate, and then let you know what it found.

Executive Information Systems (EIS)

The early and mid-1980s experienced a frenzy in *executive information systems (EIS)* technology, a sort of predecessor to the 1990s data warehousing boom. Early EIS technology received a mixed welcome and sort of faded away near the end of the decade. Some people therefore consider EIS to be a predecessor to, but not a relative of, data warehousing.

When you consider the aspect of entire systems, this view seems accurate because many EISs were built on top of relatively simple data extracts (described in Chapter 21) with a narrow range of content.

In this new era of data warehousing, though, EIS is alive and well. EIS environments best serve the *broad* category of users who want very much to receive key business information and indicators but who don't want (for whatever reason) to use OLAP tools or querying and reporting tools. They certainly don't want to sift through reams of printouts from dozens or hundreds of reports. The philosophy of the EIS user is, "Tell me what I need to know — just a little information or a great deal of it — but *please* don't make me work too hard to get to it!"

EISs are typically fed by results from either querying and reporting tools or from OLAP tools. A tool in one of those categories does the work, and the result is made available through an EIS.

EISs aren't only for executives! Executives don't use only EISs to the exclusion of other categories of tools. Focus on the *concept* of EISs, not on the word *executive* in the acronym.

EIS technology involves two major types of environments (both discussed in Chapter 12): briefing books and command centers. A *briefing book* is an electronic (though it can be printed) sequence of key information and indicators that someone regularly uses for decision-making or performance monitoring. Users typically don't "wander" through information; rather, they take a relatively particular path.

The *command center* may be a console of on-screen push-buttons (perhaps lots of them), each of which shows the user a different report, document, image, or indicator.

Command center EIS interfaces are tailor-made for multimedia "knowledge management," as explained in Chapter 24, to include nontraditional data as part of a business intelligence environment.

Other Types of Business Intelligence

Alas, the neat, organized model with four different types of business intelligence categories is somewhat more complex. For example, an OLAP or EIS tool may have geographical information system (GIS) capabilities — or maybe not. As shown in Figure 8-1, several other horizontal categories of business intelligence can apply to some or all of the categories discussed in the preceding section.

Figure 8-1:
Horizontal business intelligence categories may span some or all of the vertical types.

Statistical processing			
Querying and reporting	OLAP	Data mining	EIS
Geographical information systems			

Statistical processing

Most tools in the querying/reporting or OLAP categories do rudimentary statistical processing, such as averages, summaries, maximum values, minimum values, and standard deviations.

Think back, though, to that statistics class you endured in college. (If statistics class was easy for you, more power to you.) Remember z-scores? Chi-square tests? Poisson distributions? Some folks in the real world really use those concepts (and many other related remnants that most of us left way behind) as part of their jobs.

For these people, it's always valuable to have statistical functionality integrated into a querying and reporting tool or OLAP tool instead of having to save results from one tool into an intermediate storage facility (such as a spreadsheet file) and importing that data into a statistical tool for processing. Tool integration is a good thing!

Additionally, a large part of some data mining processing is based on "heavy stats" (advanced statistics, such as probabilities). Some environments include simulation and gaming capabilities to identify and test various outcomes and to try to handle sophisticated what-if processing based on real data rather than on assumptions and hypotheses.

Geographical information systems

Another category of business intelligence functionality that spans multiple categories is geographical information systems (GISs). The simplest way to understand GIS technology is to consider the concept of maps. You could, for example, do querying or OLAP processing in a tabular manner and show product sales by country. Those sales are divided into product sales by territory and then broken down into product sales by increasingly smaller groupings (down to, for example, product sales by department in each store).

Another way of viewing this information is by using maps. Suppose that countries colored in red indicate that sales revenue is lower in the most recent quarter than it was in the preceding quarter. If you click your mouse on any of those countries, another map is displayed that's divided into sales territories and again color-coded. Clicking on a red-colored territory displays another map (a U.S. map by state, for example) with additional levels of detail.

The point of GIS technology is that data is not just managed in a hierarchy such as the following:

Departments⇨stores⇨states⇨territories⇨countries

The data is also managed *spatially:* in a manner that's sensitive to on-screen layout. For example, when you click on a map of Pennsylvania, the GIS would "know" that you want to see sales in Pittsburgh, without having to type or otherwise select that city from a drop-down list or other on-screen control.

Business Intelligence Architecture and Data Warehousing

The early days of business intelligence processing (any variety except data mining) had a strong, two-tier, first-generation client/server flavor. (Some business intelligence environments hosted on a mainframe and doing querying and reporting were built with a centralized architecture.)

Conceptually, early business intelligence architectures made sense, considering the state of the art for distributed computing technology (what really worked rather than today's just-out-of-reach generation).

Many of these early environments had a number of deficiencies, however. Because tools often "captured" a client desktop (prevented other work from being performed), long-running reports and complex queries often bottlenecked regular work processes.

Also, most tools were designed and built as *fat clients:* Most of their functionality was stored in and processed on the desktop. In addition to the bottleneck problem, because software changes and upgrades were often complex and problematic, especially in large user bases, all users' PCs had to be updated.

The beginning of a new era of business intelligence architecture has arrived, whether your tool of choice is a basic querying and reporting product, an OLAP product, an EIS system, or a data mining capability. Although product architecture varies between products, of course, you should keep an eye on some major trends when you evaluate products that may provide business intelligence functionality for your data warehouse:

- ✔ **Server-based functionality:** Rather than have most or all of the data manipulation performed on users' desktops, server-based software (known as a *report server*) handles most of these tasks after receiving a request from a user's desktop tool. After the task is completed, the result is made available to the user, either directly (a report is passed back to the client, for example) or by posting the result on the company intranet.

- ✔ **Web-enabled functionality:** Almost every leading tool manufacturer has promised or delivered Web-enabled functionality in its products. Although product capabilities vary, most post widely used reports on a company intranet rather than send e-mail copies to everyone on a distribution list.

- ✔ **Support for mobile users:** Many users who are relatively mobile (users who spend most of their time out of the office and use laptops to access office-based computing resources) have to perform business intelligence functions when they're disconnected from the company network. In one model, mobile users can dial in or otherwise connect to a report server or an OLAP server, receive a download of the most recent data, and then, after detaching and working elsewhere, work with and manipulate that data in a stand-alone, disconnected manner.

- ✔ **Agent technology:** In a growing trend, intelligent agents are used as part of a business intelligence environment. An intelligent agent may detect a major change in a key indicator, for example, or detect the presence of new data and then alert the user that he or she should check out the new information.

✔ **Push technology:** The concept of an operational data store (described in Chapter 23) is likely to be based on the real-time, or almost real-time, updating of information for business intelligence instead of having to wait for traditional batch processes. In these situations, an application must be warehouse-enabled and be capable of pushing data into the ODS instead of having the data pulled out, as with traditional data-extraction services (described in Chapter 7). In these situations, the business intelligence tools must detect that new data has been pushed into its environment and, if necessary, update measures and indicators that are already on a user's screen. (In most of today's business intelligence tools, on-screen results are frozen until the user requests new data by issuing a new query or otherwise explicitly changing what is displayed on the screen.)

Chapter 9

Simple Database Querying and Reporting

Querying and reporting is the low end of the spectrum of *business intelligence* functionality that applies to your data warehouse. (Chapter 8 discusses business intelligence in-depth.) Querying and reporting handles "Tell me what happened" processing that, for the most part, is relatively static and predictable. The data is retrieved in accordance with either regular standard reports or in response to a particular question (an ad hoc query, for example). Then it's formatted and presented to the user either on-screen or on a printout.

The interaction model for querying and reporting business intelligence typically follows a pattern of regular, *predictable* steps (these steps are also in Chapter 8, so you can skip ahead if you've already read it):

1. **Make a data request.**

2. **Retrieve the data.**

3. **Manipulate the data slightly.**

   Summarize or reorganize, for example, if necessary.

4. **Format the data.**

5. **Present the data.**

These steps don't vary much between tools, scenarios, or users. If a user decides that the presented result looks odd or otherwise needs to be augmented, the process usually just begins again with a new request.

What Functionality Does a Querying and Reporting Tool Provide?

To help you understand the functionality a querying and reporting tool offers, this list describes some of the tasks it can help you perform:

- **Run regular reports:** Your organization may regularly produce standard reports that come from an operational system or from data extracted from one or more of those systems.

- **Create organized listings:** You may produce a list of all the salespeople in your company or those who meet a specific criteria (they cover more than two territories, for example) and their sales in the most recent month. *Organized* means that your report or query can be listed alphabetically by salesperson's last name; alphabetically by customer name and the salesperson who covers that customer; by rank, from highest sales revenue generated to the least; or any other way you want to look at the data. Figure 9-1 shows an example using fictional company names.

- **Perform cross-tabular reporting and querying:** Cross-tabular reports, sometimes called cross-tabs, are slightly more complex than a basic organized listing of data. In addition to the sequential, ordered vertical listing (the company's salespeople), you see across the top (the other axis) of the report a decomposition of various categories and values associated with each category. In the example shown in Figure 9-2, sales revenues are broken down by product.

The barriers between OLAP tools and products that have historically (in earlier versions) been oriented toward querying and reporting are getting somewhat "grayer." It's not uncommon, for example, for a query tool to also permit some level of *drill-down,* an OLAP function that enables you to see underlying, more detailed data, as explained in Chapter 10.

Sales revenue for August 1997
From highest to lowest total sales revenue

Salesperson	Customer	Sales revenue	
Sam Mayday	National Brew Pubs, Inc.	$9,999	
	Total		$9,999
Barney Collins	Unique Halloween Costumes, Inc.	$3,216	
	Canes R Us	$2,189	
	Total		$5,405
Nick L'Deon	Recycled Old TV Shows, Inc.	$3,355	
	Total		$3,355
Harry Chevrolet	Desert Explorer Hats, Inc.	$1,000	
	Space Fighters, Ltd.	$1,000	
	Cold War Relics, Inc.	$200	
	Total		$2,200

Figure 9-1: You can use a querying and reporting tool to produce a comprehensive, organized listing of monthly sales revenue by company salesperson.

Video rental volume by store: March 1985
In order of total store revenue

Store	Total Rental Revenue		Action		Icky Romance		Comedy		Family
Kolb and Speedway	$	25,425	$	4,948	$	8,484	$	9,872	$ 2,121
Park Mall	$	14,905	$	2,928	$	9,873	$	983	$ 1,121
Northwest	$	10,139	$	8,866	$	151	$	602	$ 520
Bear Canyon	$	9,423	$	4,297	$	3,938	$	1,100	$ 88
Midtown 1	$	6,447	$	2,112	$	1,112	$	2,112	$ 1,111
Midtown 2	$	4,444	$	1,111	$	1,111	$	1,111	$ 1,111

Movie category

Figure 9-2: This cross-tab breaks sales revenue down by product.

The role of SQL

SQL is the official database language of the National Football League; any use of an SQL tool without the express written consent of the National Football League is strictly prohibited.

(Sorry about that — a little too much Denver Broncos fever there.)

SQL is the official database query language used to access and update the data contained within a relational database management system, or RDBMS.

Doesn't OLAP do querying and reporting also?

Without having you jump ahead to Chapter 10, let me answer a question you may be wondering about if you have OLAP experience: Wouldn't an OLAP tool have the capabilities listed in the preceding section, plus many more?

Absolutely! Querying and reporting is, at least conceptually, a subset of OLAP functionality. OLAP architectures and capabilities are more complex than those oriented toward reporting and querying, though.

If all you need is basic querying and reporting capabilities — and you're absolutely sure of it! — you may not want to deal with the overhead of setting up and maintaining an OLAP environment if you don't anticipate gaining much business benefit from those capabilities (if you just don't plan to use them, for example).

The roots of SQL go back to IBM and its research labs during the early days of relational database technology. IBM and Oracle were among the first to adopt SQL as the language used to access their relational products (other RDBMSs used different languages that were invented by their respective vendors). In the mid-1980s, SQL was submitted for approval to both the American National Standards Institute (ANSI) and the International Organization for Standards (ISO), and, during the next few years, other database access languages faded away. Later versions of the SQL standard were published every few years (the most recent is SQL-92); the SQL3 standard is being finalized for publication, most likely in late 1998.

The significance of SQL for querying and reporting (and for data warehousing) is that the language has represented a *mostly* standard way to access multiple RDBMS products.

Each RDBMS product has a slightly different SQL dialect. Although the basic syntax is the same, especially for the most commonly used commands, all SQL dialects are slightly different. In the early 1990s, despite these syntactical differences, several different efforts provided a common gateway to SQL RDBMS products. The most successful was Microsoft Open Database Connectivity (ODBC). The phrase *ODBC-compliant* grew in importance in RDBMS applications in the early and mid-1990s.

The use of SQL as the basis for most querying and reporting tools was both good and bad for data warehousing. On the positive side, many more product-to-product matchups were possible in data warehousing environments than in previous years, when data access tools were primarily vendor-specific because they were provided by (sold by) each RDBMS vendor.

On the negative side, though, SQL is a relatively complex language after you get past the basics.

Back to the positive side: Most querying and reporting tools provided visually oriented environments that enabled developers and users to design screens for report layouts, the data columns for the report, or what rows of data should be selected (only salespeople who have met their quota, for example).

Back to the negative side: Using all this "painted" information, most tools would create (as they said back in 1991) "the mother of all SQL statements" if a large number of tables or other complexities was involved. As discussed in Chapter 5, until recently, most RDBMS products would confront an overly complex query that had a large number of tables involved by doing the technological equivalent of throwing its hands up in the air and saying, "I dunno — you tell me."

Relief is at hand! Query and reporting tools (and ROLAP products) are increasingly taking an approach to "smart query generation." Instead of generating a single, overly complex SQL statement that would get you an A in database class but draw a disgusted shake of the head from someone who has done this stuff in the real world, a sequence of SQL statements (usually taking advantage of temporary tables for intermediate results) is generated. This sequence, in effect, decomposes the query into a more efficient series of steps.

The idea of managed queries and reports

Turning the average group of users loose with a querying and reporting tool and directing them to "go forth and ask all kinds of questions against the data warehouse" is a dangerous idea. Even with visual tools to aid in generating queries and reports and even with wizards (online context-sensitive user assistance) to help even more, at least some of these people will undoubtedly issue all kinds of overly complex queries that do little more than bring your data warehouse to its knees.

Although it's certainly a good idea to enable power users (technically sophisticated users) to do whatever they need to do, you should handle average users differently.

In a *managed querying and reporting environment,* users are given templates of queries that are the means by which they ask questions and perform business intelligence functions in the data warehousing environment. Each template is set up so that it's not too rigid and not too flexible — it's just right.

Suppose that a user must run a report periodically (weekly, monthly, or quarterly) and needs different data, depending on which period is indicated. For example, the user may need to run a weekly report for all product sales to wholesalers, a monthly report for all product sales directly to retailers, and a quarterly report for wholesaler, retailer, and cross-company product sales. Also, one variation of the report must show sales for the entire United States, and another report for each sales territory must be distributed to the appropriate sales manager.

To complicate matters, sales managers sometimes request a weekly preview run of what would ordinarily be a quarterly or monthly report. The reports can't be totally "canned" (set up once and never modified), and each run requires a little (although not much) human input.

The managed environment may have a preset format and links to the tables that are needed. Before running the report, however, the user is prompted for which type of customer should be included; whether the report is for the entire United States or for a specific territory (or perhaps more than one); and any other parameters (for a previous month's sales in case someone requests a rerun of a previous report, for example).

Other than these types of guided inputs, the queries and reports are managed and controlled to reduce the chance of runaway queries that use an enormous amount of system resources and may never run to completion.

Is This All You Need?

Suppose that querying and reporting sounds like a good idea, but you really want to check out "that OLAP stuff" too.

You can give some users basic tools and still let others use OLAP tools (and, for that matter, let your statistician use a data mining product). One of the benefits of designing and developing your data warehouse in this flexible, component-oriented manner is that you can equip users with the tools that are most applicable to their respective missions and the business value they're expected to provide from using the data warehouse.

Designing a Relational Database for Querying and Reporting Support

Your data warehousing environment or a specific data mart that will be fed by your main data warehouse may have the mission of generating a finite and predictable set of reports. This section gives you one approach to designing a relational database to support that mission. This approach is built around the principle of *database denormalization,* or deliberately violating good relational database design principles in the interest of performance efficiency. (Chapter 5 discusses normalization, if you're interested in the background to this approach.)

Denormalization is best suited for "quick hit" solutions, in which you must get a small-scale relational data warehouse or a data mart up and running quickly and you have a *specific* charter to produce a certain set of reports that, for example, may become unavailable as a result of a legacy systems migration effort. Although denormalization isn't quite a dead end, a great deal of duplicate data is involved, and the database structures you create don't have much flexibility. Additionally, your querying capabilities (in addition to your standard reports) are likely to be limited, closely tied to the reporting structures formalized in the table design. Still, this approach is worth checking out.

A simple example of this approach is shown in Figure 9-3. It shows what the source database tables look like in an application that tracks sales performance, with those tables structured primarily according to standard relational database design principles (they're normalized). To support the report format shown at the bottom of the figure, the source structures are mapped into a denormalized table from which the report can be generated without having to join any tables when you run the report. (To put it more simply, your report will run very quickly.)

Note: A real-world example would involve many more tables (from 10 to 50 or more) and many more reports that need to be reported. Figure 9-3 should get the idea across, however.

Source
database

CUSTOMERS

CUST_ID	CUST_LAST_NAME	CUST_FIRST_NAME	CUST_TYPE	GROUP_ID
12345	Johnson	Bill	W	1
22233	Smith	Jane	W	2
88888	Marcuson	Susan	R	2

CUST_TYPES

CUST_TYPE	TYPE_DESCRIPTION
W	Wholesaler
R	Retailer
O	Other

PRODUCT_MAIN

PRODUCT_ID	PRODUCT_DESCRIPTION	CATEGORY_CODE
1000	Glasses	1
2000	Coffee cups	1
3000	Ski poles	2

GROUP_TYPES

GROUP_ID	GROUP_DESCRIPTION
1	Exporter only
2	Importer only
3	Importer/exporter

PRODUCT_CATEGORIES

1 Drinking containers, households
2 Athletic gear

SALES

DATE	CUST_ID	PRODUCT_ID	QUANTITY	DOLLARS
3/19/76	12345	1000	3	$ 4.50
3/20/76	22233	2000	15	$ 22.50
3/10/85	88888	1000	55	$ 82.50
7/6/85	12345	3000	1	$ 25.00
7/27/85	22233	1000	1	$ 1.50
9/5/85	22233	2000	30	$ 35.00

Figure 9-3:
Normalized
database
tables in a
source
application.

──────── Required sales report format ────────

PRODUCT_CATEGORY	SALES DATE	GROUP_TYPES	TOTAL_QTY	TOTAL_$	WH_QTY	RET_QTY	OTHER_QTY	WH_$	RET_$	OTHER_$
Drinking containers, households		Exporters only	XX	$ XX	XX	XX	XX	$XX	$XX	$XX
	XX/XX/XX	Importers only	XX	$ XX	XX	XX	XX	$XX	$XX	$XX
	XX/XX/XX	Importer/exporter	XX	$ XX	XX	XX	XX	$XX	$XX	$XX
Athletic gear	XX/XX/XX	Exporters only	XX	$ XX	XX	XX	XX	$XX	$XX	$XX
	XX/XX/XX	Importers only	XX	$ XX	XX	XX	XX	$XX	$XX	$XX
	XX/XX/XX	Importers/exporters	XX	$ XX	XX	XX	XX	$XX	$XX	$XX

Alternatively, you may want to follow the principles and techniques of
dimensional design, as discussed in Chapter 6. Because RDBMSs now have
much less trouble dealing with dimensionally oriented structures than in the
past, you're likely to get adequate performance for your reporting needs and
still have the flexibility to support a large variety of ad hoc, multidimensional queries.

For rapid deployment that's reporting-oriented, though, at least consider
denormalization-based design for relational data.

Vendors with Querying and Reporting Products for Data Warehousing

This section lists the names of some vendors who provide querying and
reporting tools you may want to consider using with your data warehouse.

Chapter 29 has a list of Internet Web sites that provide up-to-date product
information and evaluations, including links to vendors' Web sites for other
products in this category. Check it out!

Andyne

www.andyne.com/

Andyne produces GQL, a querying and reporting tool that has in its latest version (4.1.1) fully integrated spatial analysis functionality using technology from MapInfo Corporation. This feature enables geographical information system (GIS) processing, as discussed in Chapter 8.

Business Objects

www.businessobjects.com/

Business Objects sells a product also called Business Objects, in addition to the new WebIntelligence, a Web-based decision-support system (DSS) for ad hoc query, reporting, and analysis.

Cognos Corporation

www.cognos.com/

Impromptu, from Cognos Corporation, has a Report Wizard feature for building ad hoc reports, a unified querying and reporting interface, the capability to publish HTML reports for viewing in a web browser, and integration with PowerPlay, the company's OLAP product. (Chapter 10 discusses OLAP in-depth.)

Information Builders

www.ibi.com/

Information Builders, Inc., (IBI) produces the Focus family of reporting and querying products, which has its roots in the mainframe Focus system. Information at the company's Web site says that WebFOCUS, the latest generation of Focus (FOCUS Six for Windows is also available), enables you to create an embedded link between your existing HTML pages and dynamic data resident in any corporate database. The basic FOCUS product family contains capabilities for cross-tab and other reporting capabilities, including support for FOCEXECs (FOCUS executable programs).

Microsoft Corporation

www.microsoft.com/MSAccess/default.htm

Don't forget about Microsoft Access for querying and reporting tools. Many users have (shall I say it?) access to Access through their standard client desktops.

Seagate Software

www.img.seagatesoftware.com/

Seagate Software has two products that have traditionally been popular for querying and reporting.

Crystal Reports has a variety of features, such as cross tabs, summarization, drill-down, and report distribution. Crystal Info has a three-tier client/server reporting system that features shared folders containing existing queries and both ad hoc and user-created reports.

Chapter 10

Online Analytical Processing (OLAP)

Aman walks down the street in Manhattan carrying a data warehouse under his arm. From the other direction, a woman approaches, carrying an OLAP. (Bear with me — this stuff will make sense in a second.)

The man sees a billboard advertising a watch he has had his eye on, and now it's on sale. To catch the ending date for the sale, he keeps his eyes on the billboard as he walks.

The woman notices a crowd of people gathered outside a theater and looks in that direction to see what the commotion is. She too continues walking.

Suddenly, the man and woman collide. Stunned for a moment, the man looks down and then says to the woman, "Hey, you got OLAP in my data warehouse!" The woman recovers from her surprise, looks down, and says to the man, "Hey, you got a data warehouse on my OLAP!"

Together, they both say, "Mmmmm. . . ."

If you're at least as old as I am, this scenario should bring back memories of a series of commercials for a certain chocolate-covered peanut-butter-cup candy. If it doesn't sound familiar, check out the retromercials (old, original television commercials) on *TV Land* on Nickelodeon. You may see this one.

Step over from *TV Land* to Data Warehousing Land. Without OLAP, data warehousing would hardly be the mania it is today. At the same time, the roots of OLAP — or more precisely, *multidimensional analysis* — go back to the 1960s.

OLAP and data warehousing made each other what they are today: an intensely popular mode of data analysis that almost every organization has either implemented or is considering.

An interesting history of OLAP, written by Nigel Pendse, is available on the Internet, at `www.olapreport.com/origins.htm`. It traces multidimensional analysis back to the APL programming language, developed at IBM in the late 1960s based on work done a few years earlier. Products were introduced throughout successive decades, including a convergence with spreadsheet technology in the 1980s. Not until the early 1990s, though, when data warehousing became popular, did the two disciplines click and history was made.

Despite the natural synergy between data warehousing and OLAP, I caution elsewhere in this book that you can, and likely will, do more with a data warehouse than with OLAP. For that matter, OLAP isn't performed exclusively against a data warehousing environment. (If you want, you can use an OLAP tool against multidimensionally oriented tables in a low-volume production database.)

What Is OLAP?

OLAP is "Tell me what happened and why" processing that you do after you build your data warehouse. Unlike querying and reporting tools, OLAP functionality enables you to dig deeper, poke around a little, and (hopefully) come up with the "why" aspect of what's happening in your business.

The distinguishing characteristic about OLAP is that it enables you to perform *multidimensional analysis*. As discussed in Chapter 6, users have a natural tendency to view business results in different ways, organized by various dimensions. By using the dimension of time, for example, you can perform trend analysis. By using other dimensions particular to a given fact (products, business units, and geography, for example), you can get down to the nitty-gritty of finding problem areas, pinpointing your company's strengths, and generally getting a clear picture of what's going on and why it's happening.

The OLAP Acronym Parade

In the data warehousing world, OLAP hit the big time by operating against multidimensional databases specially structured to support this type of processing. These environments have come to be known as *multidimensional OLAP (MOLAP)* systems.

A corresponding approach (the archenemy of MOLAP) is *relational OLAP,* or *ROLAP.* ROLAP uses plain old relational databases rather than specialized multidimensional structures. As discussed in Chapter 6, however, ROLAP requires that the DBMS products perform cross-table joining of data somewhat more efficiently than they traditionally have done.

Ah, but I'm not done yet. *Hybrid OLAP,* or *HOLAP,* is an attempt by vendors to call a truce in the ROLAP-versus-MOLAP war and bridge the gap. Different vendors are taking different approaches. Some are linking a MOLAP front end to a ROLAP back end and routing user requests to the appropriate engine where the answer can be served most efficiently. Others are caching multidimensional aggregated results for subsequent use rather than re-creating those aggregates.

Want more? How about *desktop OLAP,* or *DOLAP,* environments, in which a client system rather than an OLAP server is the primary storage repository for a specialized multidimensional structure. DOLAP is particularly useful for laptop users who want to perform OLAP in a detached manner (while they're not hooked up to the company network) while on the road or at a client site.

First, an Editorial

Before discussing OLAP features, I should provide some valuable context to the OLAP hype you may face, if you haven't already.

Don't get sucked into the hype. Just browse the Internet, and check out vendors' white papers about OLAP. They make a serious amount of definitive, "This will not work" statements about whatever approach is *not* the one they sell.

Here's my opinion: No OLAP silver bullet exists, at least not today. Here are some guidelines and trade-offs:

✔ Strongly consider a MOLAP solution (and check out ROLAP alternatives) if response time is a key factor, if your business intelligence mission can be handled primarily by summarized data rather than by detail-level data, and if your data volumes won't grow to more than 50 gigabytes.

✔ Some financial-analysis and budgeting packages are tied to a particular multidimensional database product. In these cases, you may want to set up a financial-analysis data mart using MOLAP technology, regardless of the other data marts and data warehouse databases in your environment.

✔ If detail-level data is important to your business intelligence processing and if you're likely to have a very large database (VLDB) environment, you should consider ROLAP solutions. You may want to consider a HOLAP environment, however, as described earlier in this chapter.

✔ Regardless of the approach you take, check out products carefully. Look for hidden performance "gotchas," recalculation times for multidimensional structures, inefficient relational processing in ROLAP environments, scalability problems (after you reach a certain number of users or a certain database size, problems occur), and other events that can cause your data warehousing environment to be less than satisfactory.

OLAP Features: An Overview

This section presents a brief list of *some* OLAP features to give you an idea of what to expect from products.

For more details about OLAP, check out vendors' Web sites (see the list at the end of this chapter), product brochures, and demos; OLAP textbooks and tutorials; magazine articles; and other sources. Because it's impossible to discuss this subject in detail in just a few pages, I hit just the strategic highlights to show you what this area means to you and your data warehouse.

Drill-down

Drill-down analysis is probably the OLAP feature average users use most frequently. The concept is fairly simple: As required, you can see *selective* increasing levels of detail.

Figure 10-1 shows a report you may run to see Zip's Records and Video third quarter sales, initially broken down by region on one axis and by product on the other.

Suppose that you want to see the next level of detail for sales in the northeast region. You typically double-click on that row to display what's shown in Figure 10-2: an additional level of detail for sales by product in New Jersey and Pennsylvania.

Figure 10-1:
Initial level
of detail on
a quarterly
sales
report.

Zip's Records and Video
Sales for Q3 1985

	LPs	Cassettes	8-Tracks	CDs	Video Sales	Video Rentals	Total
Total Sales	$ 398,146	$ 195,832	$ 232,279	$ 284,794	$ 72,164	$ 130,986	$ 1,314,201
Northeast region	$ 78,683	$ 22,172	$ 59,945	$ 42,158	$ 12,439	$ 27,473	$ 242,870
Southeast region	$ 88,661	$ 51,121	$ 19,877	$ 77,655	$ 8,875	$ 21,334	$ 267,523
Midwest region	$ 66,496	$ 38,341	$ 15,902	$ 58,241	$ 15,531	$ 16,001	$ 210,511
Northwest region	$ 77,578	$ 44,731	$ 17,889	$ 67,948	$ 12,203	$ 18,667	$ 239,017
Southwest region	$ 86,728	$ 39,468	$ 118,666	$ 38,792	$ 23,115	$ 47,512	$ 354,280

Figure 10-2:
Drilling
down to the
next level of
detail for
one region
doesn't
affect other
summary
levels.

Zip's Records and Video
Sales for Q3 1985

	LPs	Cassettes	8-Tracks	CDs	Video Sales	Video Rentals	Total
Total Sales	$ 398,146	$ 195,832	$ 232,279	$ 284,794	$ 72,164	$ 130,986	$ 1,314,201
Northeast region	$ 78,683	$ 22,172	$ 59,945	$ 42,158	$ 12,439	$ 27,473	$ 242,870
Pennsylvania	$ 56,000	$ 8,130	$ 26,344	$ 22,366	$ 7,171	$ 14,986	$ 134,997
New Jersey	$ 22,683	$ 14,042	$ 33,601	$ 19,792	$ 5,268	$ 12,487	$ 107,873
Southeast region	$ 88,661	$ 51,121	$ 19,877	$ 77,655	$ 8,875	$ 21,334	$ 267,523
Midwest region	$ 66,496	$ 38,341	$ 15,902	$ 58,241	$ 15,531	$ 16,001	$ 210,511
Northwest region	$ 77,578	$ 44,731	$ 17,889	$ 67,948	$ 12,203	$ 18,667	$ 239,017
Southwest region	$ 86,728	$ 39,468	$ 118,666	$ 38,792	$ 23,115	$ 47,512	$ 354,280

Suppose that you're curious about the additional level of detail for sales in cities in Pennsylvania. A double-click there, and — presto! — you have the results shown in Figure 10-3: sales for each city.

Now you want to see the sales amount for each store. After a few more double-clicks on each city, you see the lowest level of detail, as shown in Figure 10-4.

Figure 10-3:
Drilling
down even
further, you
can see
sales by
city in
Pennsylvania.

Zip's Records and Video
Sales for Q3 1985

	LPs	Cassettes	8-Tracks	CDs	Video Sales	Video Rentals	Total
Total Sales	$ 398,146	$ 195,832	$ 232,279	$ 284,794	$ 72,164	$ 130,986	$ 1,314,201
Northeast region	$ 78,683	$ 22,172	$ 59,945	$ 42,158	$ 12,439	$ 27,473	$ 242,870
Pennsylvania	$ 56,000	$ 8,130	$ 26,344	$ 22,366	$ 7,171	$ 14,986	$ 134,997
Pittsburgh	$ 28,888	$ 3,232	$ 8,590	$ 15,722	$ 840	$ 12,088	$ 69,360
Wilkes-Barre	$ 2,112	$ 544	$ 88	$ 5,000	$ 4,433	$ 777	$ 12,954
Philadelphia	$ 25,000	$ 4,354	$ 17,666	$ 1,644	$ 1,898	$ 2,121	$ 52,683
New Jersey	$ 22,683	$ 14,042	$ 33,601	$ 19,792	$ 5,268	$ 12,487	$ 107,873
Southeast region	$ 88,661	$ 51,121	$ 19,877	$ 77,655	$ 8,875	$ 21,334	$ 267,523
Midwest region	$ 66,496	$ 38,341	$ 15,902	$ 58,241	$ 15,531	$ 16,001	$ 210,511
Northwest region	$ 77,578	$ 44,731	$ 17,889	$ 67,948	$ 12,203	$ 18,667	$ 239,017
Southwest region	$ 86,728	$ 39,468	$ 118,666	$ 38,792	$ 23,115	$ 47,512	$ 354,280

Zip's Records and Video
Sales for Q3 1985

	LPs	Cassettes	8-Tracks	CDs	Video Sales	Video Rentals	Total
Total Sales	**$ 398,146**	**$ 195,832**	**$ 232,279**	**$ 284,794**	**$ 72,164**	**$ 130,986**	**$ 1,314,201**
Northeast region	**$ 78,683**	**$ 22,172**	**$ 59,945**	**$ 42,158**	**$ 12,439**	**$ 27,473**	**$ 242,870**
Pennsylvania	$ 56,000	$ 8,130	$ 26,344	$ 22,366	$ 7,171	$ 14,986	$ 134,997
Pittsburgh	$ 28,888	$ 3,232	$ 8,590	$ 15,722	$ 840	$ 12,088	$ 69,360
Oakland	$ 15,533	$ 2,121	$ 4,297	$ 8,111	$ 393	$ 3,222	$ 33,677
Downtown	$ 13,355	$ 1,111	$ 4,293	$ 7,611	$ 447	$ 8,866	$ 35,683
Wilkes-Barre	$ 2,112	$ 544	$ 88	$ 5,000	$ 4,433	$ 777	$ 12,954
Downtown	$ 2,112	$ 544	$ 88	$ 5,000	$ 4,433	$ 777	$ 12,954
Philadelphia	$ 25,000	$ 4,354	$ 17,666	$ 1,644	$ 1,898	$ 2,121	$ 52,683
New Jersey	$ 22,683	$ 14,042	$ 33,601	$ 19,792	$ 5,268	$ 12,487	$ 107,873
Southeast region	**$ 88,661**	**$ 51,121**	**$ 19,877**	**$ 77,655**	**$ 8,875**	**$ 21,334**	**$ 267,523**
Midwest region	**$ 66,496**	**$ 38,341**	**$ 15,902**	**$ 58,241**	**$ 15,531**	**$ 16,001**	**$ 210,511**
Northwest region	**$ 77,578**	**$ 44,731**	**$ 17,889**	**$ 67,948**	**$ 12,203**	**$ 18,667**	**$ 239,017**
Southwest region	**$ 86,728**	**$ 39,468**	**$ 118,666**	**$ 38,792**	**$ 23,115**	**$ 47,512**	**$ 354,280**

Figure 10-4:
Drilling down to the lowest level of detail: quarterly sales by product and by store.

What's so great about this drilling stuff?

"Big deal," you may be thinking. "I can run reports with varying levels of detail in the query tool I've been using for the past five years. What's so wonderful about this drill-down and drill-across business?"

The major advantage of OLAP drilling capability as compared to traditional methods of getting this information is that basic querying and reporting tools usually have had to run separate database access queries for each level of detail (often using the SQL GROUP BY clause). Each run would be a separate SQL statement issued to the database, a separate pass through the database, a separate return of all the requested data, and a separate formatting of the results.

Multidimensional analysis and its drilling capability, on the other hand, are instantaneous because the information you need is staged for you. By clicking the mouse or selecting a command, you see less detail, more detail, or whatever you want. The tool and the database don't have to collaborate for successive data access requests — it's all there for you.

Hint: If you haven't used a drill-down feature and want to get a feel for it, try using the HIDE and UNHIDE features for rows and columns in your spreadsheet program. Set up a set of detailed rows of data, total them into another row, and then do the same thing again. When you HIDE the detail rows, you're performing a drill-up function; when you UNHIDE them, you're drilling down.

As mentioned in Chapter 9, some reporting tools now have OLAP drill-down capabilities, which blurs the distinction between members of these two classes of business intelligence tools.

Drill-down analysis can be selective. Suppose that your particular area of interest is the northeast region but you're filling in for the analyst who usually handles Arizona because that person is on vacation. You may use drill-down on only the portions of the total result set, as shown in Figure 10-5.

Zip's Records and Video
Sales for Q3 1985

	LPs	Cassettes	8-Tracks	CDs	Video Sales	Video Rentals	Total
Total Sales	**$398,146**	**$ 195,832**	**$232,279**	**$ 284,794**	**$ 72,164**	**$ 130,986**	**$ 1,314,201**
Northeast region	**$ 78,683**	**$ 22,172**	**$ 59,945**	**$ 42,158**	**$ 12,439**	**$ 27,473**	**$ 242,870**
Pennsylvania	$ 56,000	$ 8,130	$ 26,344	$ 22,366	$ 7,171	$ 14,986	$ 134,997
Pittsburgh	$ 28,888	$ 3,232	$ 8,590	$ 15,722	$ 840	$ 12,088	$ 69,360
Oakland	$ 15,533	$ 2,121	$ 4,297	$ 8,111	$ 393	$ 3,222	$ 33,677
Downtown	$ 13,355	$ 1,111	$ 4,293	$ 7,611	$ 447	$ 8,866	$ 35,683
Wilkes-Barre	$ 2,112	$ 544	$ 88	$ 5,000	$ 4,433	$ 777	$ 12,954
Downtown	$ 2,112	$ 544	$ 88	$ 5,000	$ 4,433	$ 777	$ 12,954
Philadelphia	$ 25,000	$ 4,354	$ 17,666	$ 1,644	$ 1,898	$ 2,121	$ 52,683
Suburban	$ 10,000	$ 1,122	$ 8,812	$ 1,211	$ 999	$ 1,121	$ 23,265
Center City	$ 15,000	$ 3,232	$ 8,854	$ 433	$ 899	$ 1,000	$ 29,418
New Jersey	$ 22,683	$ 14,042	$ 33,601	$ 19,792	$ 5,268	$ 12,487	$ 107,873
Monmouth County	$ 18,637	$ 2,036	$ 30,258	$ 2,604	$ 2,615	$ 8,965	$ 65,115
Freehold	$ 9,761	$ 1,717	$ 28,282	$ 1,717	$ 1,616	$ 1,211	$ 44,304
Colt's Neck	$ 8,876	$ 319	$ 1,976	$ 887	$ 999	$ 7,754	$ 20,811
Ocean County	$ 1,000	$ 2,340	$ 1,580	$ 656	$ 887	$ 664	$ 7,127
Jackson	$ 1,000	$ 2,340	$ 1,580	$ 656	$ 887	$ 664	$ 7,127
Middlesex County	$ 3,046	$ 9,666	$ 1,763	$ 16,532	$ 1,766	$ 2,858	$ 35,631
New Brunswick	$ 2,309	$ 8,766	$ 776	$ 6,654	$ 990	$ 2,213	$ 21,708
Somerset	$ 737	$ 900	$ 987	$ 9,878	$ 776	$ 645	$ 13,923
Southeast region	**$ 88,661**	**$ 51,121**	**$ 19,877**	**$ 77,655**	**$ 8,875**	**$ 21,334**	**$ 267,523**
Midwest region	**$ 66,496**	**$ 38,341**	**$ 15,902**	**$ 58,241**	**$ 15,531**	**$ 16,001**	**$ 210,511**
Northwest region	**$ 77,578**	**$ 44,731**	**$ 17,889**	**$ 67,948**	**$ 12,203**	**$ 18,667**	**$ 239,017**
Southwest region	**$ 86,728**	**$ 39,468**	**$118,666**	**$ 38,792**	**$ 23,115**	**$ 47,512**	**$ 354,280**
Arizona	$ 83,189	$ 35,327	$ 110,575	$ 37,574	$ 19,918	$ 45,981	$ 332,563
Phoenix Metro	$ 14,999	$ 27,392	$ 4,578	$ 20,980	$ 4,140	$ 13,621	$ 85,709
Camelback	$ 2,655	$ 10,081	$ 892	$ 7,652	$ 1,139	$ 2,545	$ 24,964
Tempe	$ 5,766	$ 5,200	$ 1,434	$ 4,270	$ 1,069	$ 5,149	$ 22,888
Scottsdale	$ 3,438	$ 6,237	$ 950	$ 4,866	$ 901	$ 3,141	$ 19,531
Northwest	$ 3,140	$ 5,874	$ 1,302	$ 4,193	$ 1,031	$ 2,786	$ 18,326
Tucson	$ 68,190	$ 7,935	$ 105,997	$ 16,593	$ 15,779	$ 32,360	$ 246,854
Kolb	$ 21,302	$ 2,327	$ 34,585	$ 2,976	$ 2,989	$ 10,247	$ 74,426
Mall	$ 34,169	$ 4,449	$ 69,154	$ 5,163	$ 5,065	$ 12,604	$ 130,603
Bear Canyon	$ 9,551	$ 343	$ 2,126	$ 954	$ 1,075	$ 8,343	$ 22,393
Northwest	$ 3,168	$ 816	$ 132	$ 7,500	$ 6,650	$ 1,166	$ 19,431
Nevada	$ 3,539	$ 4,141	$ 8,091	$ 1,218	$ 3,197	$ 1,531	$ 21,717

Figure 10-5:
Selective drill-down: You can pick and choose the level of detail you want to see in mix-and-match mode.

Drill-up

Drill-up analysis is, obviously, the exact opposite of drill-down analysis. Using a detailed report such as the one shown in Figure 10-5, you could drill up to group the results from all the stores in the northeast region to the city level, and then all the cities to the state level, and eventually all the states to the regional level.

Drill-across

Drill-across analysis is used to take some value on a horizontal axis (in the example in Figures 10-1 through 10-5, the type of product) and receive additional level of detail. Suppose that you want to see why 8-track sales are so high in your New Jersey stores (not that you're complaining). Figure 10-6 shows how to get this increased level of detail by doing a drill-across function.

Figure 10-6:
Drill-across analysis, combined with drill-down, can give you a fix on problem areas.

Increasing level of detail
for 8-track sales by category
(Viva la Springsteen!)

Zip's Records and Video
Sales for Q3 1985

	LPs	Cassettes	8-Tracks	Country	Springsteen	Other Rock	Comedy	CDs	Video Sales	Video Rentals	Total
Total Sales	$ 398,146	$ 195,832	$ 232,279	$ 10,000	$ 200,000	$ 10,000	$ 12,279	$ 284,794	$ 72,164	$ 130,986	$ 1,374,146
Northeast region	$ 78,683	$ 22,172	$ 59,945	$ 1,577	$ 48,776	$ 2,850	$ 6,742	$ 42,158	$ 12,439	$ 27,473	$ 302,815
New Jersey	$ 22,683	$ 14,042	$ 33,601	$ 1,343	$ 28,776	$ 1,850	$ 1,632	$ 19,792	$ 5,268	$ 12,487	$ 141,474
Monmouth County	$ 18,637	$ 2,036	$ 30,258	$ 1,282	$ 26,976	$ 1,000	$ 1,000	$ 2,604	$ 2,615	$ 8,965	$ 95,373
Freehold	$ 9,761	$ 1,717	$ 28,282	$ 1,282	$ 25,000	$ 1,000	$ 1,000	$ 1,717	$ 1,616	$ 1,211	$ 72,586
Colt's Neck	$ 8,876	$ 319	$ 1,976	$ -	$ 1,976	$ -	$ -	$ 887	$ 999	$ 7,754	$ 22,787
Ocean County	$ 1,000	$ 2,340	$ 1,580	$ 25	$ 1,000	$ 25	$ 530	$ 656	$ 887	$ 664	$ 8,707
Jackson	$ 1,000	$ 2,340	$ 1,580	$ 25	$ 1,000	$ 25	$ 530	$ 656	$ 887	$ 664	$ 8,707
Middlesex County	$ 3,046	$ 9,666	$ 1,763	$ 36	$ 800	$ 825	$ 102	$ 16,532	$ 1,766	$ 2,858	$ 37,394
New Brunswick	$ 2,309	$ 8,766	$ 776	$ 26	$ 700	$ 25	$ 25	$ 6,654	$ 990	$ 2,213	$ 22,484
Somerset	$ 737	$ 900	$ 987	$ 10	$ 100	$ 800	$ 77	$ 9,878	$ 776	$ 645	$ 14,910

Drill-through

In *drill-through analysis* (sometimes referred to as *reach-through* analysis), you get as much detail as possible from your data and still want more. The data warehousing environment then is set up (ideally, in a behind-the-scenes manner) so that users can access additional levels of detail from a supplemental database. In a typical scenario, you get from a data mart the types of reports shown in the figures in this chapter and then request to see daily sales by store, perhaps further divided by hour. Your environment drills through, for example, to a main relationally based data warehouse with a large store of detailed data, pulls out the information that applies to your request, and sends it back to you.

Because it's still early in the game for drill-through, check out this type of capability carefully, especially if you're looking at multivendor, multiproduct solutions. Because this feature is a frequently requested one, expect to see increased capabilities in this area soon.

Drill-bit

Just kidding!

Pivoting

Another OLAP capability is *pivoting*. You can rearrange the look of an on-screen report (drag spreadsheet columns over to become rows, for example) with a few drag-and-drop mouse operations.

Trending

One of the strengths of OLAP dimensionality is that you can perform trending analysis relatively easily when time is one of the dimensions in your data warehouse (as it usually is). You can see, for example, how sales data or market share or units sold or any other measure changes over time without having to go through a number of gyrations in your database model to support this capability.

Vendors with OLAP Products for Data Warehousing

This section lists some vendors who provide OLAP products and where you can find them on the World Wide Web. You should check out these vendors' products (and those from other companies).

Arbor Software

`www.arborsoft.com/`

Arbor Software produces (in addition to associated products) Arbor Essbase, a MOLAP/MDDB environment. Arbor says that a strategic relationship between it and IBM will integrate the Arbor Essbase OLAP engine directly with the IBM DB2 and other RDBMS products.

Brio Technology

`www.brio.com/`

BrioQuery, a MOLAP tool from Brio Technology, is now accompanied by Brio.Insight and Brio.Quickview for browser-based access to the data warehouse's contents.

Gentia

www.gentia.com/

Gentia (formerly known as Planning Sciences) produces a MOLAP tool by the same name. The product's Smart Agents act as personal assistants within the Gentia environment; for example, agents can be instructed to alert users automatically to information they need to know.

Information Advantage

www.infoadvan.com/

Information Advantage produces the ROLAP products DecisionSuite and WebOLAP.

Information Advantage and Brio Technology recently announced a strategic partnership to integrate the Brio Brio.Insight Web-browser-based OLAP product and the Information Advantage server-based OLAP solution, DecisionSuite.

Informix

www.informix.com/

Informix produces INFORMIX-MetaCube, a ROLAP product that supports SQL algorithms, mathematical summarization, cross-tabulation, pivoting functions, and comparisons and rankings.

MicroStrategy

www.strategy.com/

MicroStrategy produces a suite of ROLAP products that are part of its DSS family: DSS Agent, DSS Web, DSS Objects, DSS Server, DSS Architect, DSS Administrator, and DSS Executive. The DSS Server provides the core ROLAP engine and isolates decision-support applications from changes in the data warehouse schema.

Oracle Corporation

www.oracle.com/

Oracle Corporation purchased the Express product family and has integrated Oracle Express Objects, Oracle Express Analyzer, and the Oracle Express Server into its data-management architecture along with its flagship Oracle RDBMS product.

Seagate Software

www.img.seagatesoftware.com/

Seagate Software (also mentioned in Chapter 9) provides Seagate Holos, a MOLAP tool, formerly produced by Holistic Systems.

Chapter 11

Data Mining: Hi-Ho, Hi-Ho, It's Off to Mine We Go

In This Chapter

▶ What you use data mining for

▶ Data mining techniques

▶ Data mining products

*T*he distinguishing characteristic about data mining, as compared with reporting and querying or even OLAP, is that you can get information without having to ask specific questions.

Data Mining without the Hype

Data mining serves two primary roles in your business intelligence mission. The *predictive* mission says, "Tell me what may happen," and the *discovery-oriented* mission says, "Tell me something interesting."

The "Tell me what may happen" role

The first role of data mining is predictive, in which you say, in effect, "Tell me what *may* happen." Using "hidden knowledge" locked away in your data warehouse, probabilities and the likelihood of future trends and occurrences are ferreted out and presented to you.

The "Tell me something interesting" role

In addition to possible future events and occurrences, data mining also tries to pull out interesting information you probably should know about, such as a particularly unusual relationship between sales of two different products and how that relationship varies according to placement in your retail stores. Although many of these interesting tidbits are likely to exist, what questions should you ask if you were using a querying or OLAP tool, and how would you interpret the results? Data mining assists you in this arduous task by doing much of the grunt work for you.

Data Mining in Specific Business Missions

Data mining is particularly suited for these specific types of business missions:

- ✔ Detecting fraud
- ✔ Determining marketing program effectiveness
- ✔ Selecting who, from a large customer base or the general population, should be targeted as part of a marketing program
- ✔ Managing customer life cycle, including the customer retention mission
- ✔ Performing advanced business process modeling and what-if scenarios

Think about what's behind each of the business missions in the preceding list:

- ✔ A large amount of data
- ✔ An even larger number of combinations of various pieces of data
- ✔ Intensive results set analysis, usually involving complex algorithms and advanced statistical techniques

Now think about what you would have to do using a reporting or OLAP tool to accomplish these missions. To *thoroughly* perform any of the preceding missions would be virtually impossible to if you had to ask a question and get a result, ask another question and get another result, and then keep repeating those steps.

Haven't I Heard This Before?

If you've been in the information technology (IT) field for at least a decade, some of the preceding terms may sound vaguely familiar. Unlocking hidden knowledge? Predictive functionality? Wait a minute — now I remember! That's artificial intelligence!

From the earliest days of commercial computing, computer scientists have long been interested in developing "thinking machines" that can process large amounts of data and "make decisions" based on that analysis. Interest in artificial intelligence (AI) hit its zenith in the mid-1980s. At that time, database vendors worked on producing *knowledge base management systems,* or *KBMSs,* which were databases that not only stored data but also had artificial intelligence capabilities built into the DBMS engine. Other vendors came out with *expert system shells,* or AI-based application development frameworks that used artificial techniques to advise users about decisions. Also, neural networks (discussed in the follow section) were positioned as the next big AI development. Interest in AI waned near the end of the decade, when expectations exceeded available capabilities and other "frenzies," such as client/server migration and, of course, data warehousing, took center stage.

Now, AI is back.

Data Mining and Artificial Intelligence

The highest-profile AI technique used in data mining is neural networks. *Neural networks,* or *neural nets,* are systems designed to mimic the highly parallel processing techniques of the brain's neural system. Neural nets were originally envisioned as a processing model that would mimic the way the human brain solves problems, using neurons and highly parallel processing to do pattern solving.

By applying neural network algorithms to the areas of business intelligence that data mining handles (again, predictive and "Tell me something interesting" missions), a natural match seems to have been made.

Although it's still early in the data mining/neural network game, it's definitely worth checking into related products (and the specific techniques each one uses) somewhat carefully before making a full-scale commitment to bringing this type of processing into your business intelligence framework.

Data Mining and Statistics

The more mature area of data mining is the application of advanced statistical techniques against the large volumes of data in your data warehouse. Different tools use different types of statistical techniques.

Here are two of the statistical methods that are important to data mining:

- ✔ **Classification:** Looking at large amounts of data and then informing you that, for example, "Customers who are retained through at least two generations of product purchases tend to have these characteristics: They have an income of at least $30,000, and they own their own homes."

- ✔ **Association:** Noting that, for example, if a customer purchases a particular software package, there's a 65 percent chance that within two weeks at least two product-specific add-on packs will also be purchased.

Many more methods exist. Dust off that old statistics book and start reading.

Some Vendors with Data Mining Products

This section lists vendors who sell data mining products. You should take the time to check them out, and other data mining vendors' products, to see how their products — and techniques — apply to your predictive and knowledge discovery situation.

CrossZ Software

www.crossz.com/

After interviewing the user about a business objective, the Voyager Business Goal Wizard determines which variables in the sample data set are most relevant to that goal. Voyager then develops a QueryObject-based data mart. (QueryObject is another of the company's products.)

DataMind Corporation

www.datamindcorp.com/

The DataMind Agent Network Technology (ANT) is based on the interaction of intelligent agents representing data relationships. ANT, which is the core of the company's DataCruncher product, is used for classification, clustering, and association problems. DecisionAR is an association rule system for determining whether events will occur together in one instant or whether they will follow each other in a logical progression.

The company's Web site also has some interesting white papers about data mining.

HNC Software

```
www.hnc.com/
```

DataBase Mining Marksman, from HNC Software, is a predictive modeling system tailored to the database analysis needs of direct-marketing professionals. The Marksman software uses advanced computational intelligence techniques to automate the mining, modeling, and profiling of customer and prospect data.

HNC also sells the Database Mining Workstation, which uses neural network technology to detect patterns in databases and form predictions for use in government, consumer and commercial lending, sales forecasting, direct mail, banking, and manufacturing.

IBM

```
www.software.ibm.com/data/intelli-mine/
```

IBM offers Intelligent Miner, which supports deviation detection, classification and predicative modeling, association discovery, sequential pattern discovery, and database segmentation.

NeoVista Solutions

```
www.neovista.com/
```

NeoVista Solutions produces the Decision Series product family:

- ✔ DecisionAccess performs automatic translation of data between relational databases and pattern discovery tools.

- ✔ DecisionNet is an advanced neural network tool that learns to recognize patterns from training examples.

- ✔ DecisionCL uses clustering techniques to find groups of items that are similar.

- ✔ DecisionAR is an association rule system for determining whether events will occur together in one instant or follow each other in a logical progression.

Thinking Machines Corporation

www.think.com/

Darwin, from Thinking Machines Corporation, reveals hidden patterns, trends, and correlations and then makes predictions

The company also has a Knowledge Discovery Laboratory (KDL) located in its Bedford, Massachusetts, headquarters, that focuses on data mining and knowledge discovery. You can enlist the KDL as a consulting center or as a service bureau to perform your data mining functions for you.

Chapter 12

Executive Information Systems (EIS)

*T*hink about how a child learns to read. You begin by reading a picture-oriented book to the child, one with a short sentence at the bottom of each page ("See the bunny eat lettuce!"). Pretty soon, the child learns how to read the book without your help. The child turns the pages, occasionally squealing in delight because of that favorite picture coming up on the next page.

Now, think about how behavioral researchers work with dolphins or chimpanzees to better understand how they think. When the chimp pushes a button, a banana drops down; when the dolphin presses a lever with a flipper, it's rewarded with a dolphin treat (whatever that is).

These are the principles behind executive information systems: a briefing book and a command center, respectively.

Wait a minute! Stop that booing and hissing, and put down those rotten vegetables! I'm not trying to insult anyone!

I'm very serious. An executive information system (EIS) is intended to be a ridiculously easy way to provide online business intelligence to people who are "too busy" to learn how to use reporting or OLAP tools.

EIS Principles

The fundamental principle behind an EIS is, "Tell me lots of things, but don't make me work too hard to get the answer." Despite the best efforts of vendors; despite all the human factors and usability research that has gone into OLAP tools and reporting and querying products; and no matter how much training you provide to your data warehouse users, at least one person doesn't grasp the concept of painting a report screen, doing a drill-down analysis, or taking full advantage of the power available from today's tools.

This person and others may be, as mentioned, "too busy" to learn. Believe it or not, the mentality that computers are for "clerical types" still pervades many of corporate America's executive suites. Most of these folks grudgingly accept delivery of that brand-new, supercharged PC (although they still refuse to type their own letters) and want to do "just a couple of things" with it to show that they're really using it.

Should those people be shut out of the world of business intelligence in your data warehousing environment? No!

The answer is, in most cases, to use an EIS environment. The EIS, like other areas of business intelligence, predates the data warehousing era and was a hot item for a while during the mid- and late-1980s. Alas, like early multidimensional analysis (pre-OLAP OLAP), the full power of an EIS wasn't realized at the time, and the EIS faded to the background as OLAP took hold along with data warehousing.

Some people consider OLAP to be the successor to EIS, in much the same way as EIS was the successor to early decision support system (DSS) environments. OLAP and EIS are complementary to one another, at least as defined in the business intelligence framework described in Chapter 8 and mentioned throughout this part of the book, and they coexist in most organizations.

An EIS isn't just for executives. Almost any user in an organization with the requirement of "Give me lots of information, but don't make me work too hard" can be an EIS user. This approach is often preferable to organization-wide business intelligence over giving everyone the "official" OLAP tool and having three-quarters of the group never use it.

Don't assume that anyone classified as an executive (above a certain level) in your organization should automatically be given an EIS to the exclusion of other tools. Many a computer-savvy executive can wind up as the primary user of OLAP or a reporting tool.

The Relationship between EIS and the Other Parts of Business Intelligence

While I'm on the subject of EIS and OLAP, I should mention an important point about EIS environments. An EIS is often linked to results from other business intelligence tools, representing a presentation mechanism rather than an analytical mechanism. For example, the "pages" of a briefing book (discussed later in this chapter, in the section "The Briefing Book") may be created from the results of various standardized reports (run from the reporting tool) in addition to a rudimentary multidimensional analysis from the organization's OLAP tool that is "ready to go" for inclusion in the briefing book.

An important aspect of an EIS environment is often the inclusion of geographical information system (GIS) capabilities, as described in Chapter 8. An EIS–GIS (say that five times fast!) would present, for example, a series of standardized views of important information to a user using maps or other geographical tools as the primary interface. The EIS user then could take a cursory look through each screen of information; if everything looks okay, the user can continue to the next page, or, if something looks askew, perform GIS operations, such as double-clicking on a map to reach the underlying data.

EIS and Key Indicators

In keeping with the philosophy of "Don't make me work too hard for my information," many EIS environments are built around the concept of *key indicators*. An executive may have, for example, a handful of (seven or eight) items that are monitored on a weekly basis and represent the pulse of the organization. If all these items are okay (whatever that means for each measure), all is well, and it's off to a quick nine holes of golf during a long lunch break.

On the other hand, an indicator that's out of whack likely means that you should do a little digging — or maybe a great deal of digging — in that particular area.

A quick snapshot of key indicators (ideally, all on one screen) can therefore be a valuable part of a well-organized EIS environment.

Customize EIS implementations! One executive's key indicators aren't likely to be the same as another's. An EIS is an *environment,* not an unvarying, rigid set of screens installed on several users' respective computers.

During the scope phase of your project, spend enough time working with likely EIS users to determine each person's key indicators. Explore other possibilities, and show examples; in the end, however, let users decide which ones they want to see and how they should look.

The Briefing Book

If you've ever used a presentation program, such as Microsoft PowerPoint, that contains a slide show feature, you have a basic understanding of the briefing book concept. A *briefing book* is usually constructed to flow from one screen to another, covering key information, indicators, and other pertinent data in a relatively predictable manner.

You can design a briefing book to have an up-front screen or indicator that provides an overall assessment: "All is well" or "Update your résumé," for example. Then each successive screen displays the important items to that EIS user.

 One interesting aspect of a well-architected briefing book is that you must strike a balance between not enough detail and too much detail in the information presented to a user. For example, an on-screen button usually should be labeled More Information (or a link, if the EIS is web-enabled) to provide additional detail. A large part of the simplicity of the briefing book, however, is that the flow from screen to screen is predictable and not too complex, as described earlier in this chapter. Therefore, users' "more information" navigation paths should allow access to only one more screen, perhaps two. If additional information must be provided, the EIS user may need assistance getting it. Don't lose the flow of the briefing book by trying to make the environment overly elegant and flexible.

The Command Center

The command center is another type of EIS that is in one way less predictable than a briefing book environment but in another way just as predictable.

Huh?

The "less predictable" aspect is that, unlike the sequentially oriented nature of a briefing book, a command center user may choose to check out a particular set of information — or maybe not. An on-screen scan of visual indicators with an all-is-well indication means that no more information access occurs.

The "just as predictable" part, though, is that each command center user should have an environment tailored to a set of reports or sets of data that are important to that particular user. A sales executive, for example, may have a series of buttons (or some other type of control) on a command center: one for each region the person is responsible for, with a visual indicator to provide a quick look at the state of that region. The visual indicator may be a stoplight, for example: green for "Everything's okay," yellow for "Better check this out before things get worse," and red for "Uh-oh."

A command center EIS interface is tailor-made for multimedia business intelligence environments (as described in Chapter 24). Certain buttons on a command center can lead, for example, to posted results from standard OLAP-generated reports that are posted on the company's intranet. Other buttons can lead to the company's latest ads, product diagrams, training videos, or other elements. An EIS can be just like a spiffy Web site home page with both structured and unstructured data underneath.

Command centers can also be used operationally rather than analytically. Sometimes the distinctions between the two are subtle. In an operational command center, an executive usually monitors the environment regularly (daily or perhaps more frequently) as an active part of operational decision-making; analytical command centers are usually accessed less frequently (weekly or monthly, for example), with the purpose of determining "How did we do?" rather than "What's going on now, and what do I have to do?"

Who Produces EIS Products

Because most reporting and OLAP tools now have an EIS component to them, I recommend checking out EIS environments as you research business intelligence tools in these other areas.

Alternatively, you can use Internet technology to develop your own EIS environment as part of a web-enabled business intelligence framework for your users. You can develop an EIS home page, for example, that uses hyperlinks to guide users through briefing books or to enable them to navigate among command-center-driven capabilities.

Part IV
Data Warehousing Projects: How to Do Them Right

The 5th Wave   By Rich Tennant

WE CALL HIM "DATA WAREHOUSE" BECAUSE HE TAKES UP SO MUCH ROOM.

In this part . . .

A data warehousing project is just like any other application development project. Or, to be more blunt, you can mess up a perfectly good data warehouse effort in lots of ways: poor project management, putting the wrong people on the development team — you get the idea.

If you want to learn how to do a data warehouse project the *right* way, this part of the book is for you!

Chapter 13

Data Warehousing and Other IT Projects: The Same but Different

- -

In This Chapter

▶ Why it's important to understand the similarities *and* differences between data warehousing projects and other application development efforts

▶ Why the phenomenon of secondhand data complicates data warehousing projects

▶ Why top-level buy-in is important to your project's success

▶ An approach you should use for large projects to keep things on track

- -

*P*sst! Yes, *you.* Do you want to know a secret? No, this isn't the Beatles song; this secret is about data warehousing projects and how you can almost *guarantee* success.

I thought that would get your attention! Listen closely because I sum up this secret in three sentences:

✔ Data warehousing projects are remarkably (about 95 percent) similar to any other application development project.

✔ The 5 percent that's different is solely because of the reliance on data from other applications' databases and files (the phenomenon of secondhand data, as mentioned in Chapter 1).

✔ By applying your organization's application development "best practices" to the 95 percent portion (as though this project is just like any other) and by following a few guidelines to handle the other 5 percent, you will almost certainly develop your data warehouse successfully.

What — you want more details? Then continue reading!

Why a Data Warehousing Project Is (Almost) Like Any Other Development Project

I want to start this section by describing something about the way some organizations conduct data warehousing projects that never fails to amaze me.

Way back in the mid- and late-1970s, when disco reigned supreme, IT professionals realized, in developing computer applications and systems, that certain things made sense and other things didn't. One of the things that made sense was that before choosing hardware, off-the-shelf products (such as DBMSs), and even programming languages, you *first* had to determine the business requirements you were trying to satisfy and then take a number of steps to specify and design the programs you would try to develop. *Then,* after gaining a good understanding of these details, you could better choose your hardware and development software than if you did that as your first step before conducting your analysis and design.

Jump ahead to the early 1990s and the beginning of the tremendous interest in data warehousing. I can't tell you how many times I've sat in a room with clients, discussing their upcoming data warehousing projects, when someone (not me!) says, "I think that we want to use Brand X OLAP tool and the Brand Z extraction-and-transformation product." They make this choice *before* they've even begun to analyze their business requirements, let alone specify their architecture or do any design work.

Hello! What happened to the lessons we learned in the 1970s? Although I realize that they were confusing times, some of the application development revelations about choosing hardware and software that are appropriate for the business problem at hand still make a great deal of sense for *any* type of project — even a data warehousing project.

Maybe it's because of the data warehousing vendors and their product hype: The phrase "It slices! It dices!" is appropriate for OLAP software. (OLAP is discussed in Chapter 10.) Rather than try to find someone to blame, however, how about if everyone agrees to make a fresh start? Let's have no premature selection of hardware, database software, OLAP tools, middleware products, or *any* other products without first concentrating on business requirements and then doing appropriate analysis and design work.

How to Apply Your Company's Best Development Practices to Your Project

I hope that your company has jumped on the application development methodology bandwagon and has published a set of guidelines you're supposed to use in developing applications. If not, read this section anyway because it describes how your company is *supposed* to develop applications.

The current conventional wisdom says that no matter how large or complex the business problem that's the reason you're developing an application, you should, if at all possible, divide that problem into chunks, each of which can be delivered in a manageable, relatively short time (typically three to nine months).

A number of methodologies exist based on this philosophy of manageable chunks. My company, Cambridge Technology Partners, uses an approach that's oriented toward *extremely fast* delivery of results, with each project (each project chunk) divided into several different phases:

1. **Scope:** All relevant people reach consensus about what is to be built, why it should be built, and other factors.

2. **Rapid solutions workshop (RSW):** Visible results are delivered in a few weeks. (You can sit down at a keyboard and *do* something.)

3. **Design phase:** All the technical details are decided to make sure that development (the next phase) both goes smoothly and delivers an application that meets the business requirements.

4. **Development:** Databases are created, user screens developed, and code written, for example.

5. **Deployment:** The customer delivers the application to the users, and they begin using it.

Here's the important part. For my company's data warehousing projects, we follow the *same* methodology as we do for traditional applications. Although the data warehousing version of the methodology is tailored for that 5 to 10 percent difference I mentioned earlier to handle the transfer of data from the source systems into the data warehouse, our employees begin, for example, by working with clients on the project scope to build the business case for the data warehouse. They collect requirements and help them determine the business value to expect from the data warehouse. We *don't* sit down with a client in the first meeting and, after hearing that they're interested in developing a data warehouse, tell them "Okay, you should use Brand X OLAP tool and the Brand Z extraction-and-transformation product. Now what do you want this data warehouse to do?"

Remember the key: If your company's application development methodology works (if you usually deliver projects on time and on budget), use it as the foundation for your data warehousing project, and make adjustments such as the ones described in the following section to handle the unique properties of data warehousing.

How to Handle the Uniqueness of Secondhand Data

One element your company's standard application development methodology probably does *not* cover is how to handle all the issues of secondhand data that are an integral part of your data warehouse. Most applications create data in their databases as a result of transactions (a customer making a savings account deposit, for example, or someone placing an order for season tickets to Pittsburgh Steelers games). As long as the application's internal processes that create, store, modify, and retrieve the data are correct, you most likely don't have to worry about data problems within your application.

The following steps for your warehouse's data environment are different from the steps in a traditional application development project. The project phase is listed in bold (I use the phases of the Cambridge Technology Partners methodology described in the preceding section), followed by a brief explanation of how the task is different from a traditional application:

Scope

1. **Identify all candidate data sources.** This step is usually not part of a traditional application (or is only a minor part).

2. **Prioritize data sources.** Most applications don't use external data. Because those that do use it *need* the data for processing, prioritization isn't done: The application won't work without the data.

RSW

3. **Obtain several data extract samples.** This step is more important than in a traditional application, even if external data is used.

4. **Quickly create a database design.** The design must be oriented toward the type of business intelligence the warehouse supports (reporting and querying and OLAP, for example) rather than general purpose.

5. **Do preliminary determinations of data summary levels.** This step is usually not applicable in a traditional application; only rarely is any kind of intra-database summarization done.

6. **Populate database design with extracted data.** This step is usually not done in a traditional application.

7. **Get feedback from users about whether they like the views of the data you created.** This step is usually not important in a traditional application.

Design

8. **Create a complete database design.** The design of the data warehouse must be oriented toward business intelligence rather than toward transactions.

9. **Do complete inventory of source data elements.** This step is much more extensive than even a traditional application with external data needs.

10. **Spend time meeting with owners of source data.** This step is much more extensive than even a traditional application with external data needs.

11. **Dig into source data.** Analyzing data integrity and other issues is an important part of the process (see Chapter 14).

12. **Create transformation algorithms.** This step is much more extensive than even a traditional application with external data needs.

13. **Dig into old versions of the data that may be needed in the data warehouse (look for different versions of the data and different codes, for example).** This step is rarely done in a traditional application because old data is not applicable.

14. **Select tools, or design code, to handle middleware tasks.** This step is usually not applicable for a traditional application.

15. **Make sure that middleware functions exist for initial warehouse loading *and* updates.** This step is usually not done in a traditional application.

16. **Define quality assurance (QA) procedures for all source data.** This step is much more extensive than even a traditional application with external data needs.

17. **Conduct preliminary tests for all the source-to-warehouse data extraction, transformation, movement, and loading.** This step is much more extensive than even a traditional application with external data needs.

Development

18. **Spend extensive time coding, or using tools, to extract, transform, move, and load data.** This step is much more extensive than even a traditional application with external data needs.

19. **Conduct end-to-end performance tests.** This step is similar to performance testing in a traditional application but more complex because of the unpredictability of how users will access data.

20. **Conduct performance tests for user access to data.** This step involves different measurement techniques than a transaction-processing application.

Deployment

21. **Perform initial population of the warehouse's database.** This step is much more extensive than the initial population of a traditional application's database.

22. **Monitor the data warehouse reloading process.** This step is much more extensive than the equivalent in a traditional application.

23. **Put plans in place to keep track of source data changes.** Again, this step is much more extensive than that of a traditional application.

Why Your Data Warehousing Project Must Have Top-Level Buy-In

Although your data warehousing project may be the most important part of *your* job, you must keep in mind that your perspective is *not* likely to be the same as that of others within your company. For example:

✔ Most of the people who operate the applications from which you acquire data will see your project as one large nuisance that does little other than cause them to work a number of overtime hours.

✔ Some users who already perform rudimentary analytical tasks using extracts from an application's database (quasi-warehouses, as discussed in Chapter 21) won't want to change the way they operate, even though the data warehouse will provide them with a much richer set of data.

✔ When you try to divide a large data warehouse project into the chunks mentioned earlier in this chapter, each business organization will see its piece as the most important, and you'll have on your hands a battle over whose is most important.

Many other issues may arise that are a result of organizational politics and have nothing to do with data warehousing *technology*.

This situation calls for a hero — a courageous person willing to take a stand and look at the "big picture." This person is someone willing to make *and enforce* statements such as, "You *will* support this data warehousing project. Put some people on it; if you don't have any, go hire some consultants." Or the person may say, "Hold on, your group will certainly be supported by this data warehouse, but you'll be in the second phase of development. In the meantime, I need you to participate in evaluating OLAP tools and put a couple of people on source data analysis." (We data warehousing consultants love people who say things like that.)

In case you haven't guessed, this job calls for an executive, someone as high up as possible in the organizational chart, such as the company's chief executive officer (CEO) or at least the chief operating officer (COO) or whatever title the director of operations has. Better yet, you should try to get a joint directive from the COO and the chief information officer (CIO) for everyone to be on the same page of the playbook, indicating that both the business and technology organizations are behind the data warehousing project.

So what's the big deal? This prospect seems straightforward, right? Unfortunately, the complications usually occur in large (Fortune 500-size) companies with a number of different business divisions, each having its own organizational structure, from a president on down. Each division also often has its own CIO and COO and its own data center. To put it bluntly, determining who in the overall picture reports to whom is difficult. All it takes is a data warehousing project that crosses these divisional boundaries, and the turf wars soon spring to life. Unless you're one of these high-powered individuals, the best you can hope for is that whoever sponsors your data warehouse project has enough clout and interpersonal skills to get everyone to support it. If not, be prepared.

How Do I Conduct a Large, Enterprise-Scale Data Warehousing Initiative?

Very carefully! Seriously, you can choose one of three main approaches to large data warehousing projects that cross a large number of organizational boundaries and are complex (the upper bounds of the data warehouse deluxe group, as described in Chapter 3):

- ✔ Top-down
- ✔ Bottom-up
- ✔ Mixed-mode (combining the best aspects of the other two methods)

Top-down

To develop a large data warehouse in a top-down manner, follow these steps:

1. **Proceed with scope and design phase activities (discussed earlier in this chapter) from the perspective of the entire data warehousing environment, no matter how large.**

2. **Create an all-inclusive data model of your data warehouse (called an *enterprise data warehouse model*).**

   For your blueprint, use all the data elements that will be stored anywhere in the data warehouse and the sources for each one.

3. **Decompose the enterprise data warehouse model into as many component models (smaller models) as appropriate for your environment.**

   Group data elements and subject areas according to the primary function of each submodel area, with *little or no data overlap* between models. (Your goal is to have one official storage place for each data element.)

4. **Begin developing each part of your data warehouse, with each part containing one of the component models.**

 This approach is similar to the way most people have been taught to handle any type of large problems, not just those in the information technology business: Get an idea of the "big picture," decompose the problem into manageable chunks, and then work on each one. The problem is that although this approach makes sense *conceptually,* carrying it out successfully in the real world is difficult. The major stumbling block is the creation of the enterprise data warehouse model. It's difficult to create because of the large number of source applications for an enterprise-scale data warehousing project. Even if you're successful, keeping that large of a model up-to-date, especially with all the data sources you have to consider, is even more difficult than to create it in the first place. More often than not, the enterprise view of data turns out to be of little value.

Bottom-up

You can also develop a large data warehouse environment from the bottom up. After you identify a number of different subject areas, or groups of subject areas, that are within the scope of your project, you treat each one as a separate project with little overlap among them. When everything is completed, you have your data warehouse — sort of.

The major risk of this approach is that even if each of the smaller projects is successful, eventually the components of the data warehouse won't fit together neatly, and the environment eventually falls into disuse.

Mixed-mode

In mixed mode (the preferred approach), you combine the best parts of the top-down and bottom-up methods. Follow these steps, as shown in Figure 13-1:

1. **Start with a project scope phase.**

   As discussed earlier in this chapter, explore the business mission, vision, and other defining constraints for the overall data warehouse environment you want to build.

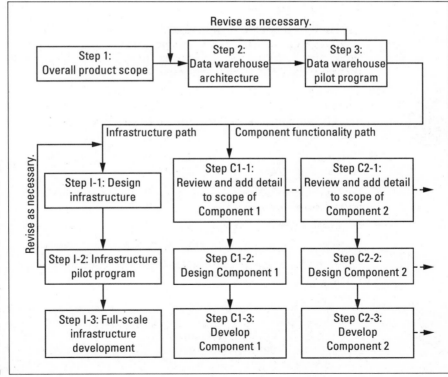

Figure 13-1: If you follow this approach for large data warehouse projects, your chances of success increase dramatically.

2. **Initiate a separate data warehouse architecture phase.**

   Concentrate on the overall architecture for the enterprise. For example, catalog all the data sources and the platforms on which they run; identify the entire user community and who will perform which functions; and identify which external data sources are likely to be necessary. The goal of this phase is to create a complete *conceptual* picture of your corporate data environment (from the data sources to the data warehouse and all points in between) and identify the pieces that overlap and the pieces that are stand-alone.

3. **Create a data warehouse architecture pilot program.**

   All the overlapping pieces of your environment (the pieces that must communicate with one another) undergo an evaluation, both in concept (such as checking out vendor literature) and in implementation (such as seeing whether vendor products do what they're supposed to do and whether they're suitable for your environment).

4. **Revise the data warehousing architecture, based on the results of your pilot program.**

5. **Create two separate design and development paths: one for *infrastructure capabilities* (the shared pieces used across much or all of your data warehouse) and another path for the functionality of each component of the data warehouse.**

   Assign "systems people" (IT staff members) to the design and development tasks for the infrastructure capabilities. Assign a mix of business and IT people to the tasks associated with developing the component data warehousing features.

6. **Decompose the component data warehousing functionality into a series of projects.**

   Each series lasts from three to nine months and has few dependencies on any other project piece.

7. **Continue with the other project phases described earlier in this chapter: RSW, design, development, and deployment.**

   Each project piece *and* your infrastructure will incorporate all these phases.

Create a data warehousing project office, with representatives from each thread of development activity, including the infrastructure development. Even though each thread of development activity should proceed as independently as possible, to make your overall effort proceed as smoothly as possible, ensure that information such as OLAP product evaluation, issues, and risks can be shared.

Chapter 14

Building a Winning Data Warehousing Project Team

In This Chapter

▶ Understanding the roles that are necessary on your data warehousing project team

▶ Finding good technologists and managers for your data warehousing project

*Y*our attention, please. Here's the starting lineup for your data warehousing project.

Batting first, and playing project architect, with four years of data warehousing experience, Linda. (Applause from the crowd.)

Batting second, your project manager, with seven years of project management experience and three of those years spent in the data warehousing area, Mike. (More applause.)

Batting third, last year's most valuable player for her key role on a 90-day data mart development project that was delivered two weeks ahead of schedule, and serving as the senior developer, Carrie. (Still more applause.)

Okay, being part of a data warehousing team isn't exactly like being a member of a major-league baseball team. In reality, it's *nothing* like being a member of a major-league baseball team, except for one thing: teamwork.

Your best chances of data warehousing project success lie in building a winning team. As in baseball, your team must have a balance of skills across a variety of roles. If your baseball team has ten excellent pitchers bound for the Hall of Fame but all the infielders play baseball like I did in Little League, you probably won't win many games.

Don't Make This Mistake!

A development team that does a top-notch, bang-up job of developing traditional applications (an inventory-management system, for example, or a system designed to handle large volumes of product orders by telephone) may also do a great job if it's assigned to a data warehousing project.

Then again, it may not. Don't make these assumptions:

- A person who can code in Visual Basic or C, for example, can handle those data warehousing OLAP tools.

- A project manager, comfortable with and successful in transactional, production-oriented application development, can handle the twists and turns of informational, analytical data warehousing projects.

- A database administrator who can tune a database for transaction-processing performance has the knowledge and skills to do the same for data warehousing performance, which has different access patterns.

In short, don't assume *anything* about building your data warehousing project team, such as the role of each team member and the qualifications of the people who will fill those roles.

The Roles You Have to Fill on Your Project

The following statement may seem obvious: The size of your data warehousing project dictates the number of team members you need.

Wow! You're reading this chapter for *that* piece of wisdom? Wait! Don't skip ahead, thinking that the rest of this chapter is a waste of your time.

The reason I made that statement is that although the number of people on your project may vary, the *roles* they fill almost always remain constant from one data warehousing project to another. Depending on the size and complexity of your project, it may have

- One person filling each role

- One person filling more than one role

- More than one person filling a single role

Later in this chapter, I discuss how to determine the matchup of people and roles. For now, it's important to focus on the *roles* you must assign, before you begin to choose people to fill them.

The following roles almost always have to be filled in a data warehousing project:

- Project manager
- Technical leader
- Chief data warehousing architect
- Business requirements analyst
- Data modeler and conceptual/logical database designer
- Database administrator and physical database designer
- Data movement and middleware specialist
- Front-end tools specialist and developer
- Quality assurance specialist
- Source data analyst
- User community interaction manager
- User community executive sponsor
- Technical executive sponsor

If you don't assign one or more of these roles, either explicitly or because of an oversight, your data warehousing project is at risk. In all except the rarest circumstances, each of these roles is critical to the success of your project.

Project manager

Here's Rule Number One about your data warehousing project manager: The manager *must* be a full-time, dedicated resource. Dedicated means, in this case, 100 percent assigned to the data warehousing project, not dedicated as in "very interested in and passionate about" (although fulfilling the latter definition doesn't hurt).

I mention this rule because I've seen more data warehousing projects get totally messed up because someone wanted to scrimp on the resources or budget assigned to the project, and the temptation is often to say, "Well, maybe we need a project manager assigned to this job on only a half-time basis." Before you know it, someone has been assigned as your project's manager on an additional-duty basis, schedule conflicts pull this person all over the place, and the project goes to pieces.

This situation seems to happen more often on data warehousing projects (particularly smaller-scale projects that can be classified as data marts) because of the tendency to think, "It's not a *real* application being developed; it's only one that's copying data from a bunch of different places to another. How difficult can that be?" This type of tremendously shortsighted thinking often occurs when one of these situations occurs:

- An organization, already short on resources, has so many projects taking place that an internal full-time project manager "just doesn't make sense."

- Because of budget pressures, the people responsible for a data warehousing project being contracted out to one or more consulting firms have this attitude: "We can save thousands of dollars over the life of the project by having only a half-time project manager and being billed accordingly."

Forget the shortsighted thinking. Assign, pay for, or find a full-time project manager for your data warehousing project.

Does the same person have to manage all phases of the data warehousing project?

No! Although some project managers are skilled in managing all phases of a project (scope, rapid development workshop, design, development, and deployment, as described in Chapter 13), others may be more adept at one or two of the phases than at others. An individual may be a top-notch project manager for the construction activities of development (screen development in OLAP tools and database creation, population, and testing, for example) and struggle during the early phases of a project, such as scoping the project and working closely to determine its requirements. Other people may have a knack for early-phase activities and have problems with all the nitty-gritty details of development and deployment.

An organization with a number of data warehousing initiatives may reasonably have a pool of project managers, some of whom concentrate on the earlier phases (scope and design) of a data warehousing project and others who concentrate on development and deployment. Projects can be handed off from early-phase project managers to managers skilled in the latter phases, in much the same way as a starting pitcher in baseball may regularly leave the game after the seventh or eighth inning (no matter how well he had been pitching) and yield the pitching mound to the ace reliever to close out the game. (Sorry, I couldn't resist another baseball analogy.)

Even if this type of setup makes sense for your organization, however, the key is to make sure that the project manager (whoever is filling that role) is still at any phase a resource 100 percent dedicated to the project.

Your data warehousing project manager should be able to do the following:

- ✔ Create, manage, and adjust to project plans.

- ✔ Communicate effectively, both verbally and in writing, to people in both the technical and user communities.

- ✔ Weather project storms without "falling to pieces."

- ✔ Stick to your project plan and, at the same time, be flexible. That's not a contradiction: When a project is going well, the project manager must ensure that it continues to go well; when a problem surfaces, however, the project manager must be able to steer team members around the obstacle without losing sight of the objective.

- ✔ Be both responsive to team members' needs and dedicated to the successful completion of all project tasks.

- ✔ Be organized.

- ✔ Be diplomatic without being wishy-washy.

- ✔ Know enough about data warehousing to be able to be effective in the role.

- ✔ Make timely decisions.

Technical leader

From the first stages of design activity through the successful deployment of the data warehousing environment, the technical leader is the person that other team members look to for, well, technical leadership. All the details, all the issues, all the product problems, and all the interface issues eventually fall under the realm of the person in this role. The role of project manager may be to make assignments and ensure that they're successfully completed. As these assignments are completed, the technical leader's responsibility is to make sure that they all fit together and lead toward a successful data warehousing implementation.

Chief architect

The role of chief architect is *not* the same as the role of technical leader. (As discussed later in this chapter, though, one individual sometimes fills both roles.) Although the technical leader is responsible for making sure that all aspects of the data warehousing technology (front-end tools, networking, databases, and middleware tools, for example) are successfully implemented and deployed, these activities occur according to the initial architecture created primarily by the project's chief architect.

The architect performs architectural functions, based on the convergence of business needs, the state of the art of data warehousing and computing technology, and an organization's internal standards and guidelines. When that work is completed, though, the implementation becomes the responsibility of the technical leader and team members involved in the development process.

When only one person serves as both chief data warehouse architect (in the early phases of the project) and, later, as the technical leader, he or she must "change hats" at the appropriate time. Specifically, the role of data warehousing architect has an element of creativity to it: The architect has to take a fresh look at how technology and products can be used to meet business objectives or to solve business problems. An architect should look at a number of different approaches and architectures and then choose (or recommend) one that's most sensible for that specific environment. As the architect changes roles and becomes the technical leader, though, he or she must restrain creativity. Looking at different ways a selected OLAP tool may perform some task and then implementing a better method is a reasonably creative job for a technical leader. It's risky, however, for that person to begin adjusting the data warehousing architecture several weeks into development because of new product announcements or similar occurrences.

Business requirements analyst

During the data warehousing project's scope phase, the business requirements analyst's role is to collect, consolidate, organize, and prioritize business needs and problems the user community presents. The eventual objective is to create a set of requirements which ensure that the data warehouse accomplishes its original intent when it's deployed.

The role of business requirements analyst is therefore an important one. Unless business needs and problems, and all their characteristics, are correctly noted and subsequently validated, you run a substantial risk of creating a data warehouse that's successful in a technological sense (users can make requests and receive data back) but a *failure* in a business sense. No business value is obtained from making requests and getting responses, no matter how quickly or how elegantly the results are formatted.

The business requirements analyst must

- ✔ Be a good listener.
- ✔ Ask insightful questions.

✔ Be able to create a consolidated set of requirements from bits and pieces of information that surface throughout the early days of a data warehousing project.

✔ Understand the basics of data warehousing (that most or all of the data exists somewhere and that it's important to find out what pieces are *really* necessary and how to prioritize those needs).

✔ Be a diplomat, especially in dealing with user groups created from different organizations that are likely to have conflicting objectives and priorities.

Does a business requirements analyst have to be an industry specialist?

A school of thought in not only the data warehousing realm but also general applications development says that unless the people serving in the business requirements analyst role are industry specialists (sometimes referred to as *vertical-market* specialists), it will be difficult (if not impossible) to accurately specify business requirements to be handed off to people in the design phase.

My opinion is not only that this school of thought is wrong but also that the *exact opposite* is true.

During the first days (the scope phase) of a data warehousing project, the business requirements analyst must ask *many* questions of users. One of the dangers of vertical-market specialists serving as data warehousing requirements analysts is that they tend to do two things:

1. Enter into a project with solutions already in mind, based on previous successes.

2. Close their minds to new, innovative possibilities for how data can be transformed into business intelligence (the "Aha!" factor), because they already have the answers (and the data required to support those answers) in mind.

In the worst extremes, an industry specialist can seem arrogant when interacting with a group of users, particularly when an outside vertical-market consultant fills the business requirements analyst role (as described in Chapter 22).

Whoever leads the scope phase must ask lots of questions; users, in turn, must provide lots of explanations. It's a *good* thing when a business requirements analyst continually asks users questions such as, "Can you explain why you use (some group of data elements) in this way?" and "What would the business impact be if it weren't available until the second phase of the project rather than at the initial delivery?" A data warehousing project is much more likely to deliver a high degree of business value when users are provoked into thinking about and justifying their data needs and the expected usefulness of the data warehouse than when some expert leads them into a solution that may or may not be suitable for their business requirements.

Data modeler and conceptual/logical database designer

After business needs have been collected and validated, the resulting bucketful of data elements *must* be organized in a manner that can be implemented in whatever database management system the warehousing environment features. The person who does this organizing is the data modeler (sometimes known as the conceptual/logical database designer).

The person in this role concentrates on the *conceptual* side of the data requirements, a business- and application-specific focus rather than physical and implementation-specific issues, such as tuning the database for performance and the various nuances of a particular database management system. (These tasks are performed by the person filling the role of the physical database designer and database administrator, as described in the following section. Although one person can fill both these roles, they are distinct roles.)

The data modeler creates data structures that are in tune with the way users will access data and the types of reports and queries they will run, as determined during the scope phase and the early design stages. Facts and dimensions are identified if the implementation database has a dimensional nature (refer to Chapter 5); if it features relationally oriented structures with some degree of denormalization (again, refer to Chapter 5), the data model is structured in that way.

In a data warehousing environment, unlike a traditional application environment, the conceptual data modeling process is complicated by source-to-target data mappings. The conceptual data modeling function concentrates on the target side (the data warehouse) rather than on the source side and various transformations. The data warehousing middleware specialist (discussed later in this chapter) is responsible for mapping and transforming source data into the target environment the data modeler specifies. Again, both these roles can be filled by one person, or by a team of individuals, each with his or her own assignments and responsibilities, on a larger project. Regardless of how the team and their assignments are established, the data modeler must concentrate on data delivery needs and avoid getting bogged down in the difficulties and problems of data transformation and quality assurance. People in this situation also have to make sure that they're wearing the right "hat" at the right time.

Database administrator and physical database designer

A conceptual data model is a wonderful thing because it makes an environment understandable by grouping data elements into structures such as entities or facts. The relationships among different data objects present a fairly clear picture of which data relates to certain other data.

Until a conceptual data model is implemented, however (which is the physical database designer's job), it's useful only in a descriptive manner.

The physical database design role is extremely important. The person in this role takes a set of concepts created by the conceptual data modeler and adjusts them for the constraints of the real world. Whoever fills this role typically also serves as an ongoing database administrator during development, by performing these tasks:

- ✔ Creates the initial database schema (the physical structure).

- ✔ Modifies the database schema as required throughout development.

- ✔ Runs load scripts to handle initial population of the database with either test data or real data, and runs scripts to reload the database with new data (the data warehouse restocking processes).

- ✔ Tunes the database for performance by analyzing where response-time problems occur and how the database structure can be tweaked to make it run faster.

- ✔ Performs backup and restore operations as necessary.

Front-end tools specialist and developer

The conceptual data modeler and database administrator deal with the database environment. Just as important are the developers who evaluate, select, and build programs in the front-end tools that users have on their desktops: Tools used for simple reporting and querying, online analytical processing, data mining, or executive information systems. (Part II of this book describes these various types of business intelligence tools.)

The role of front-end tools specialist is much the same as any developer's role — create code based on specifications and designs that were created based on user requirements. Many of a traditional (C or Visual Basic) programmer's characteristics and skills apply to a data warehousing tools specialist. In addition to being creative, a tools specialist must be able to

- ✔ Debug code.

- ✔ Determine which of several different implementation strategies makes the most sense in a specific environment — and why.

- ✔ Follow design and specification guidelines to ensure that whatever is implemented is correct. (This requirement is probably the most important.)

Middleware specialist

The unique nature of data warehousing (specifically, the reliance on extracting, transforming, and moving data across environments) requires that the middleware functions of extraction, selection, transformation, and other tasks (as described in Chapter 7) be performed to change source data into warehouse-ready data.

The middleware specialist is chartered with making sure that data is moved efficiently *and accurately* into the data warehousing environment, whether tools or custom code are used for these tasks.

Quality assurance (QA) specialist

When I was starting out in the world of computers, people fashionably referred to the "garbage in, garbage out" metaphor in discussing the process of edit-checking input data before writing it to a file or database. That metaphor is just as valid today, especially in data warehousing environments.

The source data isn't the only thing that that has to undergo rigorous quality checking. Someone (the QA specialist) must determine whether variables and parameters in the tools are used correctly; whether all the transformation algorithms and code are done correctly; how exception handling will work when data errors occur; and all the other QA tasks necessary for any application development.

You may be tempted to let quality assurance be done after the fact — after a system has been developed and is ready for deployment. *Don't make this mistake.* Quality assurance must be performed from day one in any data warehousing project. Don't think about saving money in your budget by ensuring quality only near the end of a project, and don't think about how much faster you can meet scheduled deadlines if QA doesn't "interrupt" design and development. Pay attention to quality from the first day of a project, and assign someone full-time to this role (on a large project, assign more than one person).

Source data analyst

Source data analysis plays a key role in a data warehousing project because all the subsequent extraction and transformation processes depend on what's *really* in the data sources. Chapter 15 describes source data analysis — how to do it *and* why. After reading that chapter, you can't possibly question why the source data analyst role is necessary on a data warehousing project. The success or failure of the project often depends on whether a source data analyst has done a thorough job.

User community interaction manager

Chapter 16 discusses the importance of actively involving users in all aspects of a data warehousing project. This concept is so important that a definitive, formal role is necessary in order to let someone manage interaction with the user community: their requests, issues, and concerns — everything.

Technical executive sponsor

Even though the project manager serves as day-to-day Project King or Queen, it's important for someone (usually a "high-placed muckity-muck") in the information technology (IT) organization to be recognized as the project's executive sponsor. As issues and conflicts surface during the project (and they will), resolution and getting back on track often depends on the executive sponsor's taking a stand, such as saying in a more formal way, "This is my project. Stop acting like children, solve your problems, and get this thing going again."

The technical executive sponsor does more than just step in when a situation starts getting bad. This person is also usually responsible for the project's budget, sticking up for the data warehousing project during budgeting time (especially during potential cutbacks), and "selling" the importance of the data warehouse to even higher levels of management.

The technical executive sponsor, though not officially a day-to-day team member, should be more than just a figurehead or a name that shows up on a project's organizational chart. The more involved this person is (by attending regular status meetings and briefings, for example), the more likely the hands-on team members are to take the role seriously and make use of it as necessary.

User community executive sponsor

The counterpart to the technical executive sponsor from the user community side is, of course, the user community executive sponsor. Everything about the technical executive sponsor (as mentioned in the preceding section) applies also to this person: Don't be a figurehead, be involved on a regular basis, sell the project's importance — the whole bit.

And Now, the People

So much for the roles on the data warehousing project. How should those roles be filled?

✔ In a large data warehousing project, a bunch of hands-on people should fill all the different database, middleware, and front-end development roles.

✔ In a smaller data warehousing project, you may be safe to have some individuals fill more than one role (one person can be both the business requirements analyst and the data modeler, for example, or both the data modeler and the physical database administrator).

How's that for stating the obvious? You were expecting something of substance in this section, weren't you?

Try this suggestion: Don't make assumptions about or explicit assignments for the composition of your team until you know what you're dealing with. Because you know that John is not only a top-notch data modeler but also a pretty darned good database administrator, you probably can have him handle both tasks *if* the workload and the project schedule allow for it. Or you may realize that Sherry is a first-rate data warehousing project manager and that her diplomatic manner makes her the perfect person to be the primary interface with the user community. Because the upcoming project she'll be assigned to is small and fairly straightforward, the project management role will be mostly managed by exception after things get going. Why not have her fill both those roles?

You may want me to make more definitive statements in this section, such as "You need one source data analyst if you have three or fewer data sources, two analysts for four to six sources, and three analysts if you have seven to nine sources." Because every data warehousing project (or every project in general) is unique, however, generalizations about exact staffing levels and who should fill which role don't provide anything of value and can cause harm to your project if you don't make these determinations.

After you've been creating data warehouses for a while, you begin to get a sense that "this one feels like a five-person project," for example. You may think, "This one's so big that we need a project manager *and* a project control person to do nothing other than manage the project plan, to free the project manager to handle all the issues that are likely to surface." You begin to know the people (the "best athletes") who can handle a variety of tasks, such as analyzing source data, modeling the data warehouse's database, and serving as the project's database administrator. You also get to know the specialists who may be good in one particular role but who really don't have the background and experience to perform other roles. This insight helps you figure out your team's composition a little faster than if you have no knowledge of people and their capabilities and no sense of a project's complexity.

Do not, however, let this data warehousing "sense" strictly govern the way you assign people to project roles. Plan your data warehousing project and its roles, and decide carefully who will fill those roles.

Chapter 15

Analyzing Data Sources

• •

In This Chapter

▶ Digging into source data

▶ Putting together an action plan for analyzing source data

▶ Ensuring that you assign the right people to the job

▶ Employing different techniques to analyze source data

▶ Analyzing what's *not* there

▶ Introducing mapping and transformation logic

• •

*A*lthough the process of extracting, transforming, and moving data from its sources to the data warehouse is complicated, some people would have you believe that it's still a relatively straightforward mapping exercise that's done at the structural (database definition) level.

I would (and do) argue that the structural transformation is the *least* complicated part of the process of determining what should be in the data warehouse and populating it. The most complicated piece of the puzzle is digging through the source data (the files, databases, and archived tapes) and finding whatever quirks, oddities, omissions, and outright errors are waiting to bite you directly in the — you get the idea.

Source data analysis plays a key role in a data warehousing project because all the subsequent extraction and transformation processes depend on what's *really* in the data sources.

A couple of years ago, I was working on a data warehouse lite project (see Chapter 3) that was being done in conjunction with an application migration project. One team (another consulting company) was working on the application migration, and my team was developing a reporting and querying environment to replace the one that would be retired along with the legacy system.

The other team was responsible for converting the source data files into the new application's database environment (DB2/400 running on an IBM AS/400). As phases of the database migration were completed, the converted data was made available to my team so that we could check out our scripts and screens against real data. Until that point, we had been working to build our reporting environment from a long list of database table definitions and their accompanying data element descriptions and database-enforced business rules (lists of permissible values and rules for cross-table data relationships, for example).

After we began receiving the post-conversion data, though, I decided to dig into the data to see what was there. Using plain old SQL SELECT statements through a terminal-emulation interface on my PC, I poked around, looking for nothing in particular — just interesting little tidbits of information.

While browsing through a list of the company's customers, I saw the name of an Arizona supermarket chain where I had held a summer job in college (as a janitor, if you must know). Because I couldn't remember, 16 years later, the specific store number and address, I issued an SQL SELECT statement to return all the store numbers so that I could see whether an address would jog my memory.

(Because the client's customers were organized and grouped according to how their contracts were issued, a master customer record was linked to all the members — in many cases, individual store locations belonging to that customer. The use of SQL to get my "show me all their stores" query answered was, therefore, relatively easy.)

Much to my surprise, I found the address of the store where I had worked and others where I had occasionally shopped. (I even found the location of a store in another part of Phoenix where my college girlfriend had worked.) I also found records, however, for individual stores from several different national drugstore chains, linked back to the master record for this regional grocery chain. Puzzled at first and then suspicious, I dug a little more into the database and found a number of similar discrepancies (or so I assumed) in which the associations between customer master records and individual stores seemed to make no sense.

The strange records had shown up because problems with the data-conversion routines had messed up the associations between a large number of customer data records. After fixing the problem, the application-migration team had to redo most of its data conversion.

You should remember two things from this story:

> ✔ Unless someone (perhaps more than one person) is filling the role of source data analyst, by digging into files and databases to see what's there and trying all sorts of different *hands-on* inquiries to find problems, your data warehouse may be populated with all kinds of erroneous information, which puts the success of your entire project at risk.

✔ Because I had once worked as a janitor — computer jobs were hard to come by in the late 1970s, before personal computers became popular — I was able to use in my data warehousing career something I had learned on my janitorial job, even if it was only the store's address and location. (It probably wouldn't have worked the other way around: putting data warehouse knowledge and experience to use in a career as a janitor.)

Begin with Source Data Structures, but Don't Stop There

Before you begin digging into the data, it's best to spend some time looking at the structural definitions of your warehouse's various data sources:

✔ Database table and column definitions, constraints, and other *Data Definition Language* (DDL) statements

✔ The structures of source data files (VSAM or ISAM files on an IBM mainframe or RMS files on a VAX/VMS system, for example), as described in source program listings

✔ COBOL "copy book" definitions (if they're used)

✔ Definitions that may be stored in a centralized data dictionary or repository

Begin with program listings and other paper material, and then get online and look at the files and databases as soon as possible. You must ensure that your analysis is based on the most recent information available.

Your goal is simple: Begin building up your knowledge about the data that's likely to find its way into your data warehousing environment.

You may have to study more than just the current versions of database and file structures. If your data warehouse contains historical information — which is likely, especially if you perform any type of trend analysis — you're likely to use archived data from the past one, two, three or more years that has been "dumped" from the active production systems onto tape, optical disk, or some other storage medium (even regular disk files just "sitting around"). Over time, data structures are almost certain to have been modified because of application changes. For each iteration of archived data, you must determine the structure that was in use at that time in order to understand what data elements and their respective characteristics (data types and size, for example) you have to bring into the data warehouse.

Identify What Data You Need to Analyze

Suppose that you face the following situation:

- ✔ The data warehouse obtains data from five different source systems.

- ✔ Two of the source systems have more than 200 database tables apiece, with more than 3,000 data elements apiece (the two systems have more than 6,000 data elements between them).

- ✔ Two other source systems have approximately 100 database tables apiece and collectively another 3,000 data elements (a total of 9,000, if you're counting).

- ✔ A fifth data source has 50 database tables and 1,000 data elements, for a grand total of 10,000 data elements across the five data sources.

To do the source system analysis in this scenario, therefore, you must study the structural definitions for approximately 650 database tables and 10,000 data elements, right?

Wrong! (Fortunately.)

Under the guiding principles of the good data warehousing seal of approval, you want to bring into your warehouse only the data that's part of your business intelligence picture. Therefore, you have to study only the data that's aligned with the set of business needs for which you're building the data warehouse!

As mentioned elsewhere in this book, you don't do data warehousing for the sake of doing data warehousing. After you have a specific business mission in mind, align everything you do in designing and building the data warehouse to meet that mission. This point may seem repetitive, but I can't stress it enough.

Considering the preceding advice, how do you put an action plan in place to help sift through the numerous volumes of data elements in a reasonable, timely manner? Here's how (Chapter 13 has more details about the recommended data warehousing project phases):

1. During the scope stage, when you're trying to figure out what you need to do with a general business objective that "feels like" a data warehouse, you identify a number of facts as they relate to possible data warehousing functionality.

   To support the function of "analyze each store's by department sales against how the same store did in the preceding month," for example, you note that your data warehouse must have sales data. Digging a little more into the project's specific needs during the scope, you (or users taking part in the scope work) may determine that the sales data must have dollar and unit amounts by product and by department and be cross-referenced with the staff member responsible for the sale.

2. Based on the consolidated set of facts (and the data it represents), you begin to identify the data sources necessary to provide the elements to build those facts within the data warehouse.

    For example, two different applications may have sales information recorded as part of the production environment: one that handles the eastern half of the United States and another that handles the western half. These systems are different from one another: The western stores are part of the overall environment from a corporate merger, and the systems conversion (to get everyone on the same sales-tracking application) hasn't occurred yet. (When you're identifying likely data sources, you're still in the scope phase.)

3. At the beginning of the data warehouse design phase and while your data modeler begins designing the warehouse's database environment (as described in Chapter 14), the source systems analyst begins figuring out what data will be needed from the various sources and what must happen to the data to bring it into the data warehouse.

    The source systems analyst begins studying each data source and its tables or files to match them against the facts and data sources identified during the scope phase. If no need has been identified for data in a source, you don't have to analyze it any further (for now, anyway). It's that simple.

In addition to continually checking the guidelines developed in the scope phase, you can use a couple of tricks to make the source systems analysis go even faster by eliminating data you almost certainly won't need for your data warehouse. Here are the guidelines you should follow:

✔ Any source database table that's used for systems management purposes, such as storing the physical addresses of nodes on a network, usually can be eliminated from additional analysis because that data is of no value for the business intelligence mission of the data warehouse in most (if not all) situations.

✔ Any source database table that contains only a single column with a nondescript name and CHARACTER(80) data type (or some other large number of characters) and with a description indicating that it's an "interface table" for electronic data interchange (EDI) or some other type of inter-environment data exchange is usually not useful to your data warehouse and you don't have to look at it anymore.

✔ Any source database table that's commented with "reserved for future use," despite having what seems to be a complete list of database columns, is likely to be empty. No data, no more analysis.

In these cases, you must ensure that the table is empty and that it isn't just an old comment you're looking at. The best way to do that quickly is to issue the SQL statement SELECT COUNT(*) FROM table-name. If a value of zero is returned, the table is empty, and you should just move on.

Line Up the Help You'll Need

Never, never, never call up a person responsible for maintaining an application and its database (or files) and say something like this: "Hey, Ellen, can you do me a favor? I need to analyze that inventory application you maintain to see what the data looks like. If you have some time later in the week, could you let me know whether the data has any problems I should know about? Thanks. I'll talk with you Friday."

The person (or people, for larger projects with multiple data sources) assigned to perform source systems analysis for your data warehousing project usually should not be the same staff members responsible for maintaining the applications and their data.

Why? You simply want a fresh set of eyes and a curious mind looking at every data source — someone who wants to hunt out little oddities and tidbits of information. If you assign the source systems analyst role to someone who struggles to keep the application running day after day, it doesn't matter how conscientious the person is: You're unlikely to get the same level of data analysis as you would with someone from the "outside."

That outside person can be an external consultant or even an internal person working on the data warehousing project whose "home" is another organization. If you rationalize that the source systems analysis will go faster if someone familiar with the application and its data does it, you're probably right. I can almost guarantee, however, that the quality of the analysis work won't be as good as when someone else has to dig around a little to get the answers and find all kinds of interesting items in the process.

Techniques for Analyzing Data Sources and Their Content

As mentioned earlier in this chapter, you have to consider both the structures of the data sources and each source's contents (the data). Here are some techniques you can use to accomplish these tasks:

✔ If your source data is stored in a relational database management system (Oracle, Informix, Sybase, DB/2, DB2/400, or Rdb/VMS, for example), consider SQL to be your best friend. The more skilled you are with variations of the SQL SELECT statement, particularly nested subqueries for cross-table data relationships, the more productive and efficient your source data analysis. You probably won't use many UPDATE or DELETE statements as part of your source data analysis, unless you're using temporary tables for interim results storage and subsequent comparison.

✔ Use the SQL SELECT COUNT(*) FROM table-name statement frequently to obtain quick counts of the rows in a table to quickly determine whether one table has missing data based on relationships with the content of another.

✔ Use the DISTINCT phrase in SQL to quickly identify duplicate key values.

✔ Use SAS functions for running statistical frequencies of source data to find values that shouldn't be there.

✔ Look at all coded data fields (A = ACTIVE or I = INACTIVE, for example) that are candidates for inclusion in your data warehouse to see whether any data rows or records have invalid values, as shown in this example:

SELECT * FROM CUSTOMERS WHERE STATUS <> A AND STATUS <> I

Be careful to use AND, not OR; otherwise, every row is returned to you.

✔ Look at all fields that seem to have date information in them to see whether you have a Year 2000 problem (for example, the year is stored as a two-character 85 or 91 rather than as 1985 or 1991, respectively). Identify all the fields for additional analysis concerning Year 2000 sensitivity.

✔ Check out the summary tables that are in some application databases. A point-of-sale application, for example, may contain, in addition to the details of every time-stamped sales transaction, a by-day and by-product summary (how many of each product were sold that day) and a monthly summary also organized by product. When you're doing your source systems analysis, you probably don't yet know the level of detail in the data warehouse. It may be (as in this example) at the daily or monthly level or even at the level of every recorded sales transaction.

For now, the level of detail doesn't matter. What does matter is what you do with these application-generated summary tables. Check them out! See whether the sales dollars and units recorded for a specific product on a specific day match the sum of all the detailed transactions for that day. See whether the daily dollars and units roll up correctly into the monthly table. This way, when the level of data warehouse detail is chosen, you know that you can extract the appropriate information from your data source (at the right level of detail) and that it's correct.

Analyze What's Not There: Data Gap Analysis

As challenging as it is to analyze what's in a source system's data, it's even more of a challenge to determine what should be there — and isn't. This *data gap analysis* is an important piece of your source systems analysis. Here's what you should look for:

- ✔ **"Holes" in otherwise complete data, such as no sales data for February 1991:** These holes may exist because, for example, a systems migration occurred that month and data was lost during the cut-over or because a monthly archive tape is missing from the library or a similar reason.

- ✔ **An inadequate level of detail to support the business needs of the data warehouse being built:** Here's a real-life example: A client purchased external data about its competitors' product sales activity. (Chapter 17 describes external data in a warehousing environment.) In concert with a systems migration, the client was changing its data-purchasing policies and would still be acquiring competitive sales data from the same source except that its data would be summarized at a higher level of detail. The problem: To do the business analysis functions that were a key part of the reason it was building the data warehouse, the client needed the lower level of detail it had previously been receiving. The result is a (subtle) data gap. Competitive sales data was still there; it just wasn't adequately detailed for the client's needs.

- ✔ **Changes over time in the structure and contents of a data source:** For example, programming changes may have been made a year earlier that resulted in some "not so important" data values no longer being stored in the database tables after they were used during the processing of an incoming transaction (a purchase order, for example). For trend analysis, however, those data values *are* important — or they would be, if they were available.

When you're using SAS, SQL, or some other language to analyze data contents, make sure that you issue a number of queries to find and list spaces, zeroes, or null values in place of data. Suppose that a mail-order processing application has a MAIL_ORDERS table and a NUM_PRODUCTS_NOT_IN_STOCK column originally used to record how many products on the order weren't available and had to be back-ordered. Because no one used this column, the code was changed during a maintenance update so that it no longer calculates and writes a value into this column when a new database row is written. From an *analytical* perspective (how you use your data warehouse), however, this information is *extremely* valuable. You have identified a data gap. At a certain point, you can no longer get information on an order-by-order basis about the number of products that were ordered but are no longer available.

Handling data gaps can be either easy or difficult. In some cases, history can be re-created by doing the following:

- ✔ Run old programs to re-create missing files (if the starting data values were known or had been saved in some type of transaction log).

- ✔ Repurchase missing externally provided data from the original source.

- ✔ Dig through old transaction logs, and, by writing specialized programs, create the missing data elements.

In other situations, data gaps cannot be filled, and decisions must be made about how the data warehousing environment should handle these issues. (If only partial data exists, for example, forget it because it's of little value without the missing pieces.)

Determine Mapping and Transformation Logic

You perform source systems analysis as part of a data warehousing project for one important reason: When you write code or use a tool to extract and transform source data, you must ensure that the data warehouse can handle any type of conditions or oddities in the source data you find. Newcomers to data warehousing often think of the transformation process as being fairly straightforward: "If Source A has a five-character alphabetic customer identifier and Source B uses a four-digit numeric customer identifier, just select one. For the other source, have a conversion table on hand to unify the customer data from the two sources."

How about customers who are inactive? If the data warehousing functionality is intended for only active customers, why should data about inactive customers (perhaps a large volume of data) be brought into the data warehouse if it won't be used?

Or how about the SUPPLIER_TYPE column in the SUPPLIERS table in Source C, the one that's supposed to have a value of either W for Wholesaler or F for Factory but actually has a large number of rows in which SUPPLIER_TYPE is equal to B? (Originally, the source analyst thought that the B stood for Bob, a guy on the street corner who used to occasionally provide parts that were in high demand, but no one ever asked any questions about "the Bob connection.") Should those rows be brought into the data warehouse? If so, should the code stay as the unknown B or be changed to U for Unknown?

Without doing the source data analysis and knowing the real contents of the data, the mapping and transformation portion of your data warehousing project is, at best, a hit-or-miss proposition. Is development slowed, therefore, to handle these problems that weren't identified earlier? Will someone (not you, of course) say, "Oh, the heck with it. Just load the data anyway, and we'll deal with it in the warehousing environment"?

Doing a thorough source systems analysis goes a long way toward preventing unpleasant surprises during a data warehousing project. As a certain shoe company's motto says, just do it.

Chapter 16

User Testing, Feedback, and Acceptance

▶ Why users are important team members from Day One

▶ Why real business problems should determine how to meet business needs

▶ Why you should get feedback from *all* users

▶ Why you should stick to the definition of user acceptance

*A*nd now, presenting *The Data Warehousing User's Anthem,* as sung by a misinformed, snooty data warehousing specialist (with apologies to James Taylor):

Don't know much about the OLAP tool
I think data mining is for fools
Don't know what a database is for
Just give me a bunch of data to the core.

Now, I don't claim to be a technologist
But I'll pretend to be
Cause then I can sit in meetings all day long
Rather than become just another worker bee.

This song summarizes the most contemptible attitude I've seen (occasionally) on the part of those who deem themselves data warehousing professionals.

To be perfectly clear, this is not *my* view of users in a data warehousing project (or any project, for that matter). Increasingly, however, I've noticed a changing perception among some data warehousing specialists. They seem to be saying, "We know what's best for their data warehouse — not just the tools but also how they should use the data and what levels of detail they should have — all of that. Step aside, step aside: professionals at work."

I'll say it only once: Without user involvement during all stages of a data warehousing project (from the first moments of the project's scope, not just during after-the-fact testing of what has been developed "for them"), the project cannot be successful.

Recognizing that Early User Involvement Is Critical to Data Warehousing Success

You should not build a data warehouse unless the project is directly related to a specific set of business needs. Furthermore, the purpose of the data warehouse is to make selected data available to business users (maybe just a handful and maybe a number of them) to help them perform informational and analytical functions, such as "Tell me what happened and why" or "Tell me what might happen."

I hope that you consider it difficult (or impossible) to argue with this premise of data warehousing tied to business value. Considering the business value premise, who else other than the organization members who do the business work should establish and prioritize the data warehouse's functionality?

It's valuable to ask questions of users, such as "Why do you do a particular task this way?" or "What would the effect be if you couldn't perform this task the same way you do it now?" You must handle what's likely to be an overflow of requests for features in some sort of order. Users will need some help with prioritization and figuring out which features should be delivered first and which ones can wait.

A skilled data warehousing technologist must work with users while they evaluate tools in order to point out various products' advantages and disadvantages (using real-world examples) and to help users choose products to fit their needs.

When a data warehousing initiative crosses organizational boundaries and corporate politics inevitably become part of the picture, someone with no vested interest in those politics *must* be able to steer or cajole people from various organizations toward a potential win–win solution.

Every data warehousing professional, every executive sponsor (on either the IT or business side), and everyone else involved in a data warehousing initiative must keep the following statement in mind: Unless a data warehouse is used regularly (over a period of at least six months) and real business decisions and actions are based on information from the data warehouse, the project is a failure. This statement is true even if a database has been built, tools deployed, outside consultants re-engaged for a follow-on phase or for another project, and a congratulatory party — with cake and ice cream — held in the company cafeteria.

So where is my soapbox heading? Unless you want your data warehousing project to be one that "grasps defeat from the jaws of victory" (I've always loved that little saying), make sure that what you're building will be used when it's implemented and deployed.

If you complete the scope phase of your data warehousing project and you don't have user consensus about the warehouse's functionality and purpose, you're in trouble. Consensus implies common consent or general agreement (direct from my thesaurus); unless you can describe the collective frame of mind of the user community in these terms, you should seriously think about delaying the start of the design phase.

Using Real Business Situations

One frustration that both users and data warehousing professionals experience during the early stages of a project is that discussions are often too conceptual and too imprecise for many people to relate to. From the outset of the project, all discussions about warehouse functionality, the data necessary to support that functionality, and the effect of not having these capabilities available must be tied to real business situations.

Regarding real-world business situations, make sure that you discuss and analyze both business *problems* (situations that could benefit from more accurate, timely information) and business *opportunities* (situations that aren't now part of the business environment that, with appropriate information available, could soon become important).

As in golf, be sure to follow through. Don't just touch on real business situations and then say, "Okay, let's put that one on the functionality list. What's next?" Dig into each item. Explore the end-to-end impact, all the way through the system (the customer life cycle) to learn what will happen if a data warehouse is successfully implemented with the features and capabilities you're discussing. Then discuss what will happen if the project fails.

At some point, you have to brief the executive sponsors or possibly even people higher up in the organization — and data warehousing projects should *not* be a "technology sell" (getting people interested in the project based on how cool the idea of data warehousing is). Frankly, no one on the business side of your organization who's being asked for project funding or continued support should care about items such as ROLAP versus MOLAP or Product A versus Product B. These folks want to know what this $700,000 or $1.5 million or whatever amount the funding request is will buy them in business value — either a hard return on investment (ROI) or at least "softer" returns, such as improved customer service or better supply chain management. Using real-life examples from the proposed data warehousing functionality, you should be able to walk decision-makers through the end-to-end processes of how that data will help people in your organization do whatever must be done.

Ensuring That Users Provide Necessary Feedback

Behold, the reluctant user — drafted into the data warehousing scope phase, ticked off because "real work" is waiting to be done, and resistant to any project that takes away those comfy little extract files that have been used for the past five years and work just fine, thank you.

You must do whatever it takes to break through this reluctance, determine why a user is skeptical about or resistant to the project, and ensure that each individual contributes to the data warehousing project. If you don't, that person may become a one-person threat to your project's success.

I'm a firm believer in facilitated work sessions as the primary vehicle for involving users as efficiently as possible when you're trying to determine and prioritize data warehousing functionality. With reluctant users, however, it's often valuable to have one-on-one discussions (perhaps in an informal setting, such as over lunch) to try to draw out the true reasons for their reticence or resistance.

Whoever's running the data warehousing work sessions during the scope phase has the responsibility to keep a checklist of each user's level of interaction and involvement. As in most group settings, a small number of (perhaps only one or two) strong personalities will emerge who dominate conversation, perhaps intimidating others into silence. The facilitator (the person standing up in front of the room and leading the discussion about functionality and data needs) must call on others as necessary to achieve a more balanced view. That person can use techniques such as voting and going around the room and requesting that everyone state an opinion or make a contribution.

For larger user groups, don't overlook the value of breakout sessions: dividing the overall group into a number of smaller groups and sending them to separate rooms for discussion. Cluster stronger personalities together where they can counteract each other so that you can draw out the opinions and specific business needs of people in other groups.

After the Scope: Involving Users during Design and Development

Most of the discussion in this chapter about the importance of user involvement has focused on the scope phase — the point at which critical discoveries and decisions are made about the business mission of the data warehouse, its specific functionality, and the data necessary to support that functionality.

User involvement does not end as the scope phase moves into the design and development phases, to be picked up later in the life cycle with user acceptance testing, as described in the following section. Rather, users should be involved throughout all phases, performing roles such as the ones in this list:

- Try out and provide feedback about different user interaction options, screen layouts, and other features of front-end tools.

- Help with the source data analysis process (as described in Chapter 15) to decipher often cryptic codes and to assist in analyzing potential source data problems and data gaps.

- Work with the quality assurance (QA) team members as early as possible to ensure that requirements are being implemented correctly.

- Participate in regular status meetings to discuss issues such as training, deployment, desktop integration issues, and the next phase of development.

Understanding What Determines User Acceptance

One way of looking at *user acceptance* is to say that users have collectively accepted the warehouse when they stop making last-minute requests for changes in functionality or database contents and begin *using* it.

I don't like this approach. It's too haphazard and depends too much on imprecise criteria. The exact criteria to determine user acceptance should be set early in the project — ideally, during the scope phase. Although the exact nature of the acceptance criteria varies from one project to another, all parties should agree to these types of statements:

✔ **What constitutes preliminary user acceptance:** Usually, development has been completed, the development team has run the final QA processes, and a user QA team has verified that the system is performing correctly.

✔ **What constitutes final user acceptance:** Training has been completed, tools are deployed to all appropriate desktops, and all users have performed a series of "check it out" steps to ensure that they can correctly access data with acceptable performance.

As mentioned earlier in this chapter, user acceptance does not occur when everyone gathers in the company cafeteria for the congratulatory party. The key is that the data warehouse is *truly* being used.

Part V
Data Warehousing: The Big Picture

The 5th Wave   By Rich Tennant

I DON'T KNOW - MY SPREADSHEET TELLS ME WE SHOULD BASE OUR OVERHEAD BUDGET ON SALES FIGURES RATHER THAN FIXED, MY PLOT CHART INDICATES WE SHOULD ESCALATE OUR MARKETING THRUST, AND MY PSYCHOANALYSIS PROGRAM TELLS ME I DEPEND TOO MUCH ON OUTSIDE INPUT AND SHOULD TRUST MY INSTINCTS MORE.

In this part . . .

No data warehouse is an island.

This part of the book describes a data warehouse in the context of many other parts of your professional life: how the folks in the executive boardroom look at data warehousing, how to acquire external data about your customers or your competitors and what to do with it after you get it, and how to avoid letting changes in other applications affect your data warehouse in, shall we say, unpleasant and unfortunate ways.

Chapter 17

Dealing with External Data

• •

In This Chapter

▶ Understanding why your data warehouse usually needs data from outside your company

▶ Determining what external data you need

▶ Analyzing and loading external data successfully

▶ Dealing with the challenges of external data

▶ Acquiring external data (including the Internet) and updating sources as necessary

• •

*Y*our data warehouse is most likely incomplete until it includes data that comes from sources outside your company. It's one thing to build a picture of sales activity across all your divisions for the past three years; wouldn't it also make sense to include competitors' sales results so that your data warehouse users can see how your company is doing in comparison?

If you were to call a competitor's chief information officer to ask whether someone could send you a regular tape with data pulled from the company's sales applications or reports from the consolidated sales analysis data warehouse that it has already built, the response probably would be, of course, "Are you crazy?" Fortunately, you can obtain much of this type of information from publicly available sources.

Identifying Data You Need from Other People

Simply ask yourself this question: Looking at the complete list from within our company of all data sources that will provide data to the warehouse, what else do we need that's not already on the list and is not available somewhere else within the company to help make business decisions?

Here's a list you can use as a starting point:

- ✔ Your competitors' unit and revenue sales results in the regions in which you both compete (or will compete)

- ✔ Historical demographic data, such as population trends, per-household and per capita income, and local and regional unemployment data

- ✔ Economic forecasts

- ✔ Information about your customers' activities and behavior with companies other than your own

Recognizing Why External Data Is Important

This type of information is important for one simple reason: To ensure that your business decisions are the right ones, you have to be able to see the "big picture," which usually means that not all the answers are stored in your company's various computer applications and databases. Here are some examples:

- ✔ Your data warehouse may be able to tell you that a customer's bill-paying record throughout all her accounts with you has been satisfactory, with only an occasional brief blip. Before you offer a dramatically increased credit limit, however, wouldn't it be good to know that this same customer has been continually 60 days late with payments almost everywhere else and has a poor credit bureau rating?

- ✔ According to the consolidated results in your data warehouse, pulled in from 20 different sales applications across the world, the trend is "up, up, up!" no matter how the data is sliced and diced. Your archenemy competitor, however, is doing much better than you and, worse, is getting 75 percent of all new business in key geographic regions, leaving you only the crumbs.

- ✔ Your unit sales across your entire product line have been increasing steadily in all stores nationwide except for *every* store in Colorado. Is the problem an economic slowdown there? New competitors moving into the area? A steady, dramatic population decrease during the past 12 months?

Viewing External Data from a User's Perspective

This section provides a clear understanding of a data warehouse user's perspective of external data and its importance. Consider these two tables:

Region (and Assessment)	1996 Q1 Results	1997 Q1 Results	Change
Northeast (Good)	$2,000,000	$2,500,000	+25 percent
Southeast (Good)	$1,500,000	$2,000,000	+33 percent
Midwest (Good)	$2,000,000	$2,200,000	+10 percent
Southwest (Good)	$1,000,000	$1,200,000	+20 percent
Pacific (Good)	$3,000,000	$3,300,000	+10 percent

Region (and Assessment)	Us (Good Guys, Inc.)			Them (Bad Guys, Ltd.)		
	1996 Q1 Results	1997 Q1 Results	Our Change	1996 Q1 Results	1997 Q1 Results	Their Change
Northeast (Problem)	$2,000,000	$2,500,000	+25 percent	$1,500,000	$2,000,000	+33 percent
Southeast (Good)	$1,500,000	$2,000,000	+33 percent	$0	$0	N/A
Midwest (Good)	$2,000,000	$2,200,000	+10 percent	$0	$0	N/A
Southwest (Big problem)	$1,000,000	$1,200,000	+20 percent	$1,000,000	$2,000,000	100 percent
Pacific (Uh-oh!)	$3,000,000	$3,300,000	+10 percent	$0	$2,000,000	—

The first table doesn't lie: It shows Good Guys, Inc., analysts and executives that its sales in every region have increased in the first quarter of 1997 as compared with the first quarter of 1996. The assessment in each region can easily be considered good, based solely on year-to-year sales increases.

The big picture, though, as shown in the second table, should tell even the most out-of-touch executive that if something isn't done soon, all those stock options will be about as valuable as a flowery Hawaiian shirt, baggy shorts, and sandals at the North Pole.

Determining What External Data You Really Need

Don't overdo it. The same rule that applies to internal data in your warehouse is just as applicable to externally sourced data: Make sure that your analysis and decision-making has *true* business value before you go through the trouble of analyzing, transforming, storing, and making available all this data. If your competitors' sales data provides a clearer picture of how you're doing, go get it. If the knowledge that certain city populations are dramatically increasing or decreasing will have no bearing on your company's decision-making, why bother acquiring and storing that data?

Suppose that the database service bureau from which you have decided to purchase sales data has an extensive catalog of companies, time periods, and types of data elements, with a variety of package prices available. When you're considering raw data, the temptation nearly everyone faces in constructing a data warehouse is "more is obviously better." Just as with internally provided data, however, you have to apply your business needs analysis before you begin to consider what data to acquire.

How? First, it's likely that some, perhaps many, of the data warehouse users will apply the simple "Tell me what happened" style of querying and reporting, not OLAP or data mining. (Part III describes the different types of business intelligence.) Because simple querying and reporting almost always has an internal focus, consulting those types of users about external data needs isn't necessary.

By process of elimination, therefore, the remainder of the user community must be part of the external data business-needs analysis. The trick is to make this determination as soon as possible to focus your analysis and design efforts toward users who will be externally focused. Follow these steps:

1. **Start with your total user universe (everyone in the company who has been identified as a potential data warehouse user, as described in Chapter 14), and revalidate the list.** Is everyone on the list still a candidate to use the data warehouse? (Or, if the data warehouse has already been deployed, is everyone on the list using it?) Is anyone not on the list who should be on it? If you're satisfied that the answer to the first question is yes and the answer to the second question is no, move ahead. If not, make sure that you adjust the list until it's correct.

2. **For each person on the list, answer this single question:** To perform most effectively the business functions this person has been assigned, is there any data that's not available from the company's internal computer systems?

3. **Using the results from your interviewing, create a consolidated list of external data needs, the sources from which the data can be obtained, prices and fees, restrictions, and contact information.** Then, it's off to the budget-approval game to make the request and do whatever else is necessary in your company.

Often, in dealing with large user populations (100 or more people), data warehousing developers have a tendency to take a shortcut and apply the preceding question to groups of users, not to individual people, in the interest of meeting deliverable schedules. If a bank's credit-analysis organization, for example, has five people (Martha, Robin, Karen, Robert, and Sidney), all with the same title of credit risk analyst, all of whom report to Suellen as peers on the organizational chart, and who all have been identified as data warehouse users, the same data needs apply across the entire group, right?

Don't make this mistake. In more cases than not, a group of this size has at least two distinct business roles, each of which requires different external data (not to mention internal data). Robin and Robert may focus, for example, on credit card risk and require credit bureau scores and market data only for bank cards; others in the group may concentrate on installment loan risk and need external credit-bureau and other market data for different types of installment loans, such as auto, small business, and signature. If you were to work with Robin and find out that she needs credit-card-oriented external data but wouldn't do anything with externally provided installment-loan data even if it were available, it would be absolutely incorrect to assume that no one else in Robin's organization would need installment-loan data and that you have no need to pursue that information any further.

Talk to everyone, even if it takes a little extra time.

Ensuring the Quality of Incoming External Data

After you have determined what external data you need, you then place an order (similar to ordering clothes or a fruit basket from a mail-order catalog). After you begin receiving data on tape or by file transfer or by some other means, it's smooth sailing — or is it?

Not so fast. What about the quality of the incoming data? You absolutely must apply the same set of quality assurance (QA) procedures to externally provided data as you do to data coming from your own internal systems. Just because the information is being purchased on the open market does *not* guarantee that the acquired data is flawless.

Here's a list of QA procedures you should apply to every incoming batch of data:

1. **Find out whether the incoming data has check values appended to the files.** Some examples of check values are the number of records in each file, the total value of each numeric column (total sales dollars for all records and total units sold for all records, for example), and subsets of the total column values (by-state total amounts of sales and units, for example). If check values are provided, they must be stored and used as part of the end-to-end loading procedures. No official updates to the warehouse's contents should be made until the check totals agree with your own calculations made when the data is prepared for loading.

2. **If no check values are provided, request them.** Although the request may take a few cycles (a few months, for example) to fill, any data provider interested in providing a high level of customer service would surely take this type of request seriously and strive to make the requested control information available.

3. **During your loading procedures, filter each row and make sure that the following conditions are true:**

   • Keys (unique identifiers for each record) are correct across all the information. For example, if each record in the SalesMasterRecord group of data must have exactly 12 related records in SalesDetailRecord (one for each month), make sure that all the detail records are present by comparing record key values.

   • Ranges of values are correct. Product sales per month, for example, must be within reasonable bounds for that type of product (airplanes are different from bolts, for example).

   • Missing fields of information (a likely, almost inevitable, occurrence with externally provided data) do not distort the meaning of the incoming data. For example, although the absence of supplemental pieces of data (defined according to the business rules for your specific industry or organization) may not be too serious of a problem, if half the incoming records have an empty space where UnitsSold or TotalSalesPrice or some other critical type of information should be, the value of the data is questionable at best.

   • Especially in the early stages of acquiring external data (the first three or four months, for example), use your analytical tools, as described in Chapter 10, to perform data quality analysis before your users use the same tools to perform business analysis.

   Search for oddities, anomalies, puzzling results, inconsistencies, apparent paradoxes, and anything else that "just looks weird."

Then drill down to the roots of the data to check things out. Remember that you're probably dealing with many millions of rows of incoming data: In addition to not being able to personally check out every single row, setting up your filtering and QA checking criteria for every possible condition is difficult. Anyone who has ever done anything with externally provided source data has come across all kinds of strange situations in the incoming information. By putting yourself in the place of users and using the same tools they use, you probably will discover a thing or two that, after they're corrected, will make your data warehouse a much better store of valuable business information.

Filtering and Reorganizing Data after It Arrives

The same rules regarding levels of detail and the organization of data-warehouse-resident information (refer to Chapter 1) apply to externally provided data. If your provider sends you a tape with detailed transaction-level information on it, you have no reason not to summarize and regroup that data into a more manageable format that takes up less disk space.

If you choose to summarize incoming information before it's loaded into your warehouse, do you lose the detailed data? Not necessarily. Even though your main data warehouse may have sales for all your competitors summarized by state and by week, you can keep the raw data that comprises those summarizations in a "data warehouse auxiliary" — some storage mechanism that's not routinely used but can be accessed on a just-in-case basis. This information can be stored on some type of media, including

- ✔ Your corporate mainframe in a flat file

- ✔ CD-ROMs or optical disks and distributed to each of your branch offices, to be used if necessary

- ✔ Modern, high-speed magnetic tape kept in the corporate tape silo in near-online mode

To help train and educate all your data warehouse users about these supplemental places to seek business intelligence data, they should receive a guidebook with a section titled "All the other places other than the main data warehouse where you can possibly find additional detailed information in case you need it."

Restocking Your External Data

You have to determine, based on your data warehouse business requirements and source analysis (refer to Chapter 15), which of the following four
models apply to *each* externally provided source when a new batch of data
is received and you update (restock) your data warehouse:

Model	*What Happens*	*Why*
Complete replacement	Incoming data overwrites older, now obsolete data in the warehouse.	Because the information provider is continually updating all data, even historical information may be different from the last time data was received.

Example: Although the information provider collects sales data from many
different chemical companies, the chemical companies provide not only new
sales (those in the past month, for example) but also "old sales" that had
not previously been provided. Historical sales are then constantly changing;
to make sure that your data warehouse has the most accurate information,
you have to do a complete replacement.

Model	*What Happens*	*Why*
Append	Incoming data is appended to existing data in the warehouse.	History never changes; only new information is provided.

Example: Each quarterly incoming tape from the credit bureau contains
activity and credit score changes since the last tape was made, in addition
to the most recent balances. To perform trend analysis over multiple time
periods, your data warehouse should always retain the old credit information and add the new information as it's acquired.

Model	*What Happens*	*Why*
Rolling append	Although incoming data is appended to existing data in the warehouse, the oldest data is deleted to make room for new data.	Some analysis is done on a 24-month rolling basis, for example; any data older than 24 months is useless and no longer has to be kept in the data warehouse, although it can, and should, be retained in the archives.

Example: You receive a quarterly tape that contains econometric and
demographic data, and your statistical models are all built for, at most, 16
quarters of data. The oldest quarter's data in the data warehouse can
therefore be deleted and replaced by the incoming data.

Model	What Happens	Why
In-place update	Each record of incoming data is applied to some record (or records) in the data warehouse, doing the same as an SQL UPDATE statement.	Although this scenario is least likely for externally provided data (it's more common with internal sources), in some circumstances the volume of change to the group of data is such a small percentage of the overall size that it's more efficient to send along only change information.

Example: You receive not only full information provided quarterly by a credit bureau but also weekly file-transfer critical-information reports about any of your customers whose credit rating has changed dramatically. You don't get a complete list each week — only a list of customers who meet some "I want to know about this!" criteria (typically about 2 percent of your total customer list). You can apply this update information directly to those records in your data warehouse.

Acquiring External Data

So now I've convinced you that you usually need externally provided data to get maximum value from your data warehouse. What can you do about it?

Finding this type of information

If you're looking for industry-specific data, your industry probably has some type of clearinghouse from which you can purchase data consolidated from many different sources — a megawarehouse to provide data to your own data warehouse, if you will.

Where do these industry clearinghouse companies get the data they sell? Directly from you — and your competitors. If you ask around in your information systems organization, you probably can find a person or small department responsible for sending a regular "feed" of results data to one or more of these clearinghouses. A monthly or quarterly transmission is typically done via tape or, increasingly, direct file transfer that contains information such as sales by product or by geographic region. Standards often dictate the format and content of these transmissions; if you're curious about the details, find out who in your company is responsible for sending data to the clearinghouse company and ask.

Some industry-specific clearinghouses

Any company that deals with retail credit (that of individual persons and some small businesses) can purchase data from Fair, Isaac that it pulls together and consolidates from the three major credit bureaus: Equifax, TRW, and TransUnion. Fair, Isaac provides a menu of attribute groups to choose the amount of information most suitable to your data warehouse's needs.

Pharmaceutical companies can buy competitive sales data from several different sources, including IMS America or Walsh.

Fair, Isaac: www.fairisaac.com/

IMS America: 162.44.245.4/
communications/
ims_america.html

AC Nielsen: www.acnielsen.com/

Just why in the world would someone in your company make this information available so that your competitors can get their hands on it? The answer is simple: so that you can have access to your competitors' detailed results. One of the first rules of most private providers of industry sales data is that if you don't participate and send your information, you're not allowed to buy information from them.

In some cases, the process of acquiring external data is not as simple as the old song: "If you want it, here it is; come and get it." (Nostalgia check: What song is the line from, and which group sang it?) Some companies that collect industry-specific sales results from you and your competitors attach restrictions to what information may be available to you. You may be able to obtain only certain types of credit information and ratings for your customers and anyone who wants to be your customer. Before performing any detailed analysis and design on the external data that will be in your data warehouse and how the information will be used, make sure that you learn all the rules and restrictions that apply.

Gathering general information

You can get lots of other information that cuts across most, if not all, industries. Econometric data (lots of statistical stuff) and demographic and population data are some examples. You can obtain this type of information from a variety of private and public governmental sources.

Cruising the Internet

The Internet is changing the relationship between data warehousing and external data. With increasing frequency, you can find the data you need somewhere on the Internet. Clearinghouse companies and bureaus that have traditionally handled only tape-based exchanges of data with their customers are joining the 1990s and creating Web sites that publish their information.

If you already subscribe to an external data service for your data warehouse but are still using tape or special-purpose file transfers, ask your customer contact at the clearinghouse company about its Internet plans.

Maintaining Control over External Data

Imagine ordering by mail a couple of expensive, white, cotton, button-down dress shirts from one of those catalog places in New England. After you receive the package, you eagerly open it and say, "Hey — this isn't what I ordered!" as you stare at two chocolate brown, polyester, no-top-button shirts that would have gone great with your lime green leisure suit and platform shoes in the mid-1970s. The same sort of thing (but less startling) happens occasionally when you acquire externally supplied data for use in your data warehouse.

(If you're a female reader, I apologize for the lack of gender neutrality in this example. You have to admit that women's fashions didn't take nearly the nosedive in taste that men's fashions did during the disco years. I just couldn't think of an equivalently shocking example.)

Last month, perhaps PRODUCT-FAMILY was a three-character field that, within each record structure, came right after MARKET-CODE. On this month's tape, four characters and a new field called MARKET-SUBTYPE-CODE are listed before PRODUCT-FAMILY. What the heck is going on here?

Staying on Top of Changes

Sometimes the changes aren't as obvious as new data fields — or missing data fields — or easy-to-spot modifications to the data types. Have regions been shuffled and rearranged? Have certain products been dropped from the provider's database for some reason? Has one of your competitors stopped providing information to a certain clearinghouse because the competitor is now using another one? You have a right to know whether situations will change from one month (or quarter or whatever your acquisition timetable is) to the next because you're paying for this data.

One thing you should *demand* from your customer liaison at any company providing you with external data for your warehouse is that you be told of upcoming changes before they show up on your doorstep. You don't want surprises when they affect your data warehouse. Play the customer-service card as much as necessary. You're paying for information you can easily integrate with your internal data, not a surprise package you have to continually adjust every time a new version appears.

Knowing What to Do with Historical External Data

If your company has been acquiring external data for a while for specialized analysis outside a data warehouse (building files or statistical data sets, for example), when you begin building a data warehouse, one of your data sources probably will be a couple years' worth of tapes that are sitting in the tape library and collecting dust.

Be prepared to analyze each tape for its structure and content before loading the data into the warehouse. You can't stop your data analysis after you study only the *current* format and content guidelines because at least a few things probably have changed over the period those tapes represent.

Determining When New External Data Sources Are Available

Suppose that you finally get everything situated in the external source corner of your data warehouse. What about six months from now? Or next year? One phenomenon of the Internet era has been the proliferation of homegrown service providers, with small companies encroaching on larger ones by being able to quickly and cost-effectively deliver information to you. How do you know when new, potentially valuable sources of data appear?

Pay close attention to your industry's trade periodicals. New providers, mergers of existing information bureaus, and similar events almost always are announced and the impact of those occurrences analyzed.

Switching from One External Data Provider to Another

Knowing what you need to do to switch to another data provider depends on these considerations:

- ✔ **The format and structure in which data is provided:** If your current data source complies with some type of industry standard and your potential new provider supports that standard, *in theory* you should have no changes. That's the theory, of course. Although most standards have options associated with them (ever wonder, then, why they're called standards?), you hope that changes are minimal.

- ✔ **The means of transportation:** No, you don't make a choice about whether tapes are shipped to you by Federal Express or the U.S. Postal Service. In this context, transportation refers to whether the data is shipped by tape (which format? which density?), by file transfer (which protocol? between which operating system platforms?), or over the Internet.

- ✔ **Data gaps:** Is *all* the data you get — every single element — provided by your new source? Are *range constraints* (which time periods are included, for example) the same?

- ✔ **New data:** Perhaps the reason you're considering switching is that the new external source can provide more data — perhaps much more — than your current source. Would this new data be of value to users of your warehouse, and, if so, how would it be used? How will it affect the size and performance of your data warehouse?

Don't underestimate the complexity of switching from an existing provider of external data to another. As with anything else in computing (your applications, your hardware — you name it), change can be beneficial, but surprises are almost always waiting for you. Carefully plan any changes to external data as though they were development projects in their own right. It's better to overplan than to be stuck in a situation in which you've canceled a contract with an existing provider, no more data is forthcoming, and your switch to the new provider is running months behind schedule.

Chapter 18

Data Warehousing and the Rest of Your Information Systems

A Data Warehouse Does Not Stand Alone

The nature of a data warehouse (that it is composed primarily, or exclusively, of data that comes from elsewhere — the secondhand data phenomenon) means that it cannot stand alone as an independent entity within your organization. Here are some examples of the interrelationship you have to deal with:

✔ New data must be sought for evolving business needs that must be satisfied by adding functionality to the data warehouse. In turn, all transformation, movement, quality assurance, and extraction procedures back to the data sources must be reviewed and modified.

✔ Changes to an application that provides data to a warehouse will likely affect the contents of the data warehouse and how data moves along the path to the warehouse.

In short, a data warehouse is part of a *system* (more likely to be fairly complex than relatively simple) of interacting components that must be reviewed from end to end every time change occurs anywhere in the system.

The Infrastructure Challenge

The phenomenal growth of distributed computing (client/server, Internet and intranet, and data warehousing) has resulted in a fundamental shift in the way applications are constructed. In the old days of mainframes and minicomputers, the *infrastructure* (operating systems, databases and file systems, communications and transaction managers) was contained largely within a single physical system. With distributed computing now the dominant model (even mainframes and minicomputers are usually part of a larger distributed environment), the infrastructure is spread over many different platforms across your enterprise.

The significance of distributed infrastructures can be summed up this way: When you develop any application or system, either data warehousing or a more traditional transaction-processing application, you have significant dependencies on pieces of the overall environment over which you have no *direct* control. Here are some data warehousing-specific examples:

✔ You design a data warehouse that, based on business requirements and applications' data availability policies, must have approximately 25 gigabytes of new and updated data extracted from various sources each Sunday evening and sent over the network to the hardware platform on which the data warehouse is running.

Your corporate networking infrastructure is still, unfortunately, based on 4-megabits-per-second token-ring technology. After additional analysis, the network can't come close to supporting the throughput necessary to move the data into your warehouse in the available time window.

✔ During the data warehousing project's scope phase, you determine that a "push" strategy (see Chapter 23) to update the data warehouse is the most appropriate model to follow. To implement a push strategy, though, each source application must be modified to include code that detects when data must be pushed (sent) to the data warehouse.

The legacy applications selected to provide data to the warehouse are, unfortunately, so difficult to understand that a policy of making no changes unless absolutely necessary is in effect for each of them.

✔ You decide to pursue a relational OLAP (or ROLAP, as described in Chapter 10) solution and run a series of benchmarks against three relational DBMS (RDBMS) products to see which one best supports informational and decision support processing (rather than transaction processing).

The product that performed most poorly in your benchmarks is, unfortunately, also your corporate standard, and any relational database installed anywhere in your company must be of this variety, no matter how it will be used.

Thinking conceptually (not worrying about implementation details) in the early stages of a data warehousing project or any other application development effort is not only acceptable but also good systems development practice. At some point, however, you must consider hardware, software, and other types of real-world constraints. Before you begin construction, be sure to consider everything that can affect your designs and plans for your data warehouse.

Strategic Initiatives: Watch Out!

Old-timers who have been in the information systems business for a while (from about the mid-1980s or earlier) have seen many strategic technology initiatives come — and go. Consider the following fictional situation:

✔ The vice president of Information Systems, impressed by claims of automatic application-generation directly from process and data designs, mandates that every application in the company will be developed using a computer-aided software engineering (CASE) tool. Every existing application will also be reverse-engineered back into the design stage, and all maintenance to those applications now must occur starting with the designs. The great CASE strategic initiative has begun!

✔ The chief information officer, captivated by claims of vastly reduced maintenance and operations costs, issues this proclamation: "Within three years, we will migrate all mainframe applications to client/server platforms and, once and for all, be rid of these costly mainframes." The great client/server migration strategic initiative has begun!

✔ The director of information technology, suddenly aware that an extremely serious Year 2000 problem is lurking throughout the company's legacy applications, attends a few seminars, talks to a consulting firm, and issues this declaration: "From now until January 1, 2000, everything we do will be oriented toward fixing all the Year 2000 sensitivity hiding in our applications — and everything else is on hold." The great Year 2000 fix-'em-up-and-move-'em-out strategic initiative has begun!

I'm not making light of the Year 2000 problem or oppressively high hardware maintenance costs or software productivity problems that might have caused a three-year backlog in application development requests. These situations, and many others like them, have been (and in most cases are still) real problems.

What often happens in response to these problems is that someone near the top, instead of proceeding cautiously, by first trying out a solution or two before making a total commitment to a particular path, selects a particular approach as the answer. Slogan-laden coffee mugs soon show up all over the place, motivational posters are plastered all over the hallway and cafeteria walls, and cynicism and sarcastic remarks flow in response to the first round of setbacks.

What do all these systems issues have to do with data warehousing? Simply this: After you develop and deploy a data warehouse, the warehouse and those who use it are susceptible to any of these types of strategic initiatives that pop up in your organization. You may even face these situations:

- ✔ Your data warehousing project or continued maintenance of an existing data warehouse is suffering from unanticipated budget cuts as funding is shifted toward the Year 2000 effort or the development of a company-wide global intranet or retrofitting every application that exists with a web front end or whatever strategic initiative pulls the funding away.

- ✔ Your data warehousing project is halted in the middle of development and you have to start over because of, for example, a new initiative to migrate all servers to Microsoft Windows NT and because your warehouse will be hosted on a UNIX system.

- ✔ Every extract program eventually has to change because of a massive migration initiative that affects every one of your data warehouse's sources.

Keep your eyes and ears open. As soon as you hear the first murmurs of anything that sounds vaguely like a strategic initiative, try to determine its potential effect on your data warehouse, no matter whether it's being developed or is already deployed. Participate in meetings; raise issues to your boss; be involved! (It sounds like a campaign to get people to vote, doesn't it?)

Internal Standards and How They Affect Your Data Warehousing Environment

You've found it — the perfect ROLAP desktop tool. It does everything!

You have one problem, though: The tool runs only on Windows NT, and your organization has selected Windows 95 as its standard desktop operating system for all users. Only a year earlier, more than 5,000 PCs were painfully migrated from Windows 3.1 to Windows 95, and nothing other than Windows 95 is now supported.

Welcome to the wonderful world of internal technology standards. Internal standards aren't a bad idea; in today's world of distributed computing, in fact, they're necessary to support connectivity and interoperability across an organization, particularly far-flung ones such as global multinational companies.

Internal standards simply mean that, as you develop a data warehouse, you aren't free to do whatever you want, even if it's the right choice.

Suppose that you decide that it makes sense in your environment to run standard reports from a data warehousing report server (refer to Chapter 9) and have them available for the numerous users who regularly need that information. After checking out various options, you decide that the logical choice is to post the reports on an intranet and let people access them through a web browser.

This solution has one problem, though: None of the company's desktops is fitted with a web browser. The corporate standard desktop, as controlled by the IT department, prohibits any type of browser to be deployed.

Although the no-browser scenario may seem unrealistic now that browser software is showing up all over the place in corporations, it was extremely real only a year or so ago. You can't develop a data warehousing environment in a vacuum, oblivious to what will and won't be supported in your organization. Check out the standards early in your development process. That step may save you a great deal of backtracking.

Dealing with Conflict: Special Challenges to Your Data Warehousing Environment

Not everyone you come in contact with, or depend on, will agree with you about the importance of your data warehousing project. Many of them, in fact, may think that it's little more than a downright nuisance. Some may take it a step further and think that you came up with this little data warehousing scheme solely to make their professional lives miserable.

Why? Consider these factors:

- ✔ Because every application from which you plan to extract data, no matter how unintrusively, is affected by your data warehousing project, the staff members who support those applications and their databases (or files) are also affected.

- ✔ The network administration staff, already struggling with a major company-wide intranet initiative, now must help you figure out whether enough network bandwidth is available to support your regular data extract, movement, and loading procedures.

- ✔ The database administration group, the people who handle all database structure creation and modification, are appalled that you want to frequently make changes to your data warehouse's database definitions, by yourself, without their involvement.

✔ The business organization whose members today use data extracts along the lines of "They aren't perfect, but they give us mostly what we need" (as discussed in Chapter 21) are now suddenly being told that their report-writing tools are being taken away. To get their regular reports, they must learn how to use the OLAP tool being deployed with the data warehouse.

To say it in plain language, more than a few people may be less than enthusiastic about your data warehousing project (and won't be disappointed if your project is a miserable failure).

You need these people — make no mistake about it. Here's how to handle these situations:

✔ **Take the "I feel your pain" approach.** Never treat these people as though they're members of your personal support staff for your project or, in the case of users, as though you're doing them a great favor by developing a data warehouse for their use. Talk to these folks, take the time to understand their concerns, and work with someone to find an amicable solution when the concerns are valid (when a database administrator's workday gets extended by 50 percent for the next three months, for example, because of the effect of your new data mart project).

✔ **Address problems and conflicts as soon as you're aware of them.** Don't let situations fester — that's just asking for trouble. Talk to someone; call a group meeting; elevate an issue that just can't be resolved — just do something!

✔ **Don't make unreasonable requests.** If the normal turnaround time for putting in a database structure change request is two hours in a development environment, don't pout or cause problems because you can't get changes done in a half-hour. Although the situation may not be perfect, it could be worse.

✔ **Explain yourself.** Don't assume that everyone understands data warehousing concepts, let alone the myriad of technology and implementation options.

✔ **Never be arrogant.** Don't have the attitude that "data warehousing is where it's at today," especially with the people responsible for supporting the production applications. They hate that attitude, and you will feel the effect of their wrath. Instead, understand — and communicate to others — your belief that data warehousing is *one part* of an effective, state-of-the-art information management solution.

Chapter 19

The View from the Executive Boardroom

I'll try to say this gently and not upset you too much (it has to be said):

Executive management doesn't care one iota about data warehousing.

"Oh, sure," you may think, "This guy doesn't know what he's talking about. Why, just last week, both our chief operating officer and chief financial officer said that the two data warehousing projects that are under way are two of the most important IT initiatives in the corporation. How could anyone have the audacity to say that executive management doesn't care about data warehousing?"

They don't. It's that simple. What they do care about is the business value a successful data warehousing project delivers. To be blunt, if your company had done a better job in the past of implementing and managing its information systems and applications, it wouldn't need data warehousing projects, at least the way you're probably doing them or are about to do them (such as copying massive amounts of — mostly — poor-quality data into another database or trying your best to clean up that data or handling ridiculous situations such as product codes sorted alphabetically in one application and numerically in another).

Just try to pontificate to executive management about the wonders of data warehousing. As soon as you explain what you need to do, you already have two strikes against you.

Although this description is somewhat harsh, the plain truth is that the folks at the top don't care about the mechanics of data warehousing, the methodology you follow, or even the principles of OLAP and data mining.

What *do* they care about? The answer is the principle of return on investment, or ROI. ROI includes both tangible benefits (expenses avoided or additional revenue generated as a result of the investment made in data warehousing, for example) and intangible benefits, which are more difficult to quantify because they may not have a near-term monetary result.

What Does Top Management Need to Know?

Somewhere in your organizational hierarchy, somebody has control over budgeted funds that can be allocated to your data warehousing project or to another project elsewhere in the organization or to purchase capital equipment (more computers, for example) or to pay for some other purpose.

That person has to be sold on the business value that a successful data warehousing implementation and deployment will deliver.

And so does that person's boss. And that next person's boss and the next person's boss and all the way up the hierarchy until someone whose job title has the words *chief* and *officer* in it is also sold on the business value of data warehousing. Whether that person is the chief operating officer or the chief financial officer or even the chief executive officer, all these folks have a common thread: Someone at or near the top must believe that a substantial return on investment will come from successful data warehousing in your company.

All the job titles in the preceding paragraph are from the business side of your organization. Although it's important from the IT side for the chief information officer or the chief technology officer to be 100 percent behind both the principles of data warehousing and the investment in your organization's data warehousing projects, *IT support is not enough.*

Again, executives up the organizational hierarchy on the business side don't have to know about the mechanics behind data warehousing. Some of them may have attended conferences where data warehousing was discussed or read about the subject. (Subliminal suggestion: Every executive should read *Data Warehousing For Dummies.*) They may even be grounded in its fundamentals.

Tell them this

Here's all that most executives need to know about data warehousing. When you're pitching a data warehousing project, work the following two statements into your presentation:

- ✔ "We have data all over the place on a bunch of different machines, and, frankly, we can't get at any of it. Oh, yeah, much of it is inconsistent too."

- ✔ "You know those reports you and your staff are always complaining about, the ones that always show up too late every quarter to be of any value? And the ones that have incorrect data, and no one uses them anyway? How would you like to fix that problem once and for all, with technology that really works?"

In these two statements, you have addressed both the technology side and the business value side of data warehousing. The first statement, the data warehousing side, addresses the reality that the company doesn't have one big data bank in which every piece of information is carefully catalogued and organized and available to everyone in your company who needs it.

(Don't laugh. You may be surprised at how many people without an IT background think that corporate systems are much better than they really are. These folks probably get this idea from movies and novels in which you can use a few keystrokes to access, in just seconds, every piece of information about an individual — for evil purposes, of course — or change it or even delete it, all in a flawlessly seamless way. Hah!)

A good dose of reality about the state of corporate data assets is usually a good topic to mention to justify why a project will take more than a weekend to complete.

The second statement addresses the question, "Why bother to do anything with that dispersed, inconsistent data — why not just ignore it?"

You can talk all you want about EIS and data mining. You can show slides and demos that depict drill-down and other OLAP principles. You can go on and on about being predictive, not reactive. I've never seen anything work better, however, to explain what a data warehouse can do than to put the business-value discussion in the context of what is almost always a "point of pain" in an organization: dealing with those convoluted reports that are always late, inaccurate, and worthless.

I strongly believe in the hypothesis that every business manager has between four and seven "attention points" that are used to help run an organization's operations and make decisions. In business life, the traditional way many managers address these points has been to use reports (usually one or two for each attention point) for analyzing information and making decisions.

In many settings, any information-driven analysis and decision making (rather than seat-of-the-pants decision making) boils down to the use of reports. That's right — reports. Reports are a concept that most managers and executives can understand, and they're the way to go when you're trying to "sell" data warehousing.

Here's a quick quiz: What's a recommended way to sell the concept of data warehousing, and your project in particular, to executive management? As a much better, much more timely way to generate reports. (I figured that the point in the preceding paragraph came across — I just wanted to make sure.)

Keep selling the data warehousing project

Anyone who has been involved in any type of application development effort, whether from the corporate side or the consulting side or the vendor side, knows that continued funding is almost always a question mark. No matter how enthusiastic the support is at the beginning of the project; no matter how many statements have been made that "this project is the most important one in the corporation today"; and no matter what the budgeted funds are, budget cuts or shifting priorities can always disrupt a project.

Therefore, from the earliest possible opportunity in the project (90 days at most; 60 days is even better), something tangible *must* be available for real-life use by the highest-ranking business executive who holds the funding strings for your project. Be sure to

- Provide a set of reports that you know will help this person perform analysis and make decisions. (**Hint:** Just ask.)
- Use real, not fake, data (even a small amount).
- Solicit feedback about usability, later steps, and everything else you can think of to ensure that the executive fully believes in your project and (unless something out-of-the-ordinary happens) will continue the funding until the project is completed.

Data Warehousing and the Business Trends Bandwagon

Business process reengineering, total quality management, Japanese-style management, and managing in one-minute increments.

I entered the business world in the late 1970s; in a little less than 20 years, a number of trends and fads have come and gone. First the book arrives, and then the seminars and consulting engagements with extremely high daily fees, and then more books by others trying to jump on the bandwagon. In some cases, these events are even followed by the "Uh-oh, I guess we were wrong" books and seminars and the damage-control consulting engagements with extremely high daily fees.

Okay, maybe that description is a little cynical. Or maybe I'm just envious and bitter because none of my books has ever started a major business or management fad.

Now that the data warehousing era is here, the next generation of business and management trends (you had better believe that a next generation will come along) may have a little more substance — a little more information — you can use to determine whether a trend is a step in the positive direction or just another fad that will eventually be as useful as a snowmobile in Phoenix.

If you've done your data warehousing correctly and have access to a large amount of corporate business intelligence, you can get the numbers to see whether your company has a problem in whatever area a trendy business approach may address. You can also perform a what-if analysis *before* you spend a gazillion dollars on consulting fees (and disrupt your business processes and organization) to implement whatever is being sold as the answer.

Suppose that data warehousing were as mature in the early 1990s as it is today and your organization had successfully implemented a data warehousing environment. Your profits are down, sales are flat, and the boom days your company experienced in the 1980s are gone. Along comes a consulting firm pushing this new idea of business process reengineering as the answer to all your corporate woes. You engage a team of consultants to study your business processes and to make recommendations for improvement. If your team of consultants is anything like many others, it spends a large amount of your money and then makes a standard recommendation: Fire many of your employees and let the consulting company employees outsource the work they leave behind.

(Oops, cynicism creeps in again.)

Before taking such a drastic step, as many organizations did, you could use information from your data warehouse to perform extensive analysis on the effect of such a drastic measure. Using what-if analysis with data pulled from the data warehouse, you may determine that the purported benefits and cost savings from the move just don't exist. Would this be a smart move?

Before following any business trends, try to figure out whether they have any substance. In most situations, it's nearly impossible to determine that information without looking into real corporate data, such as current sales and how they're likely to be affected by a recommended set of actions; current expenses across departments and how those expenses would be affected by proposed budget cuts and staff recommendations; and how those cuts may affect sales and marketing.

Data Warehousing in a Cross-Company Setting

Data warehousing is usually a private affair. Even when external data about your competitors is part of your environment, as described in Chapter 17, it's still your company's data warehouse, built for your company's benefit and use.

An interesting trend — one that's surely noticeable at the executive board-room level primarily because those folks are steering corporations in this direction — is to have multicompany cooperation. Two or three pharmaceutical companies may share the research-and-development expenses on a new generation of drug products, or two manufacturing companies may work together in a partnership to develop a product. A commercial bank and a brokerage institution may work together to offer jointly a series of financial products to the mass market, with the bank administering some products and the brokerage administering others.

Whatever the specifics of the industry and the situation, your company has a good chance of being involved in a multicompany partnership in which cross-company cooperation and sharing of information is a key part of success.

To that end, an interesting spin on the theme of data warehousing as a breaker of barriers is to have a multicompany data warehouse dedicated to more efficient analytical and information-delivery capabilities in support of a joint effort between your two companies.

As you may guess, a multicompany data warehouse is a slightly more complex creature than one dedicated to the support of a single company. Although you experience all the wonderful challenges of data extraction and transformation, tool selection, performance support, and other aspects of data warehousing, you also have to consider these issues:

✔ **Corporate standards:** Two (or more) sets of corporate standards will affect how your data warehouse and its tools are deployed. For example, one company may be a Windows 95 desktop/Windows NT server environment, and another may be a Windows 3.1 desktop/UNIX server. Whose standards will be used, and what is the effect on the other company's users?

✔ **Proprietary and sensitive data:** The business case for the multi-company data warehouse, and the accompanying functionality and data necessary to support the data warehouse's business mission, may mean that sales history information is made available for predictive sales forecasting. Sales history information involves a breakdown by region, territory, and possibly even customer. What are the effects of revealing customer lists, and strengths and weaknesses in various regions, to a partner that's also a competitor?

✔ **Security concerns:** In addition to data security issues, any linkage between two environments is likely to open up one environment to any security weaknesses in the other, such as unauthorized outside access and hacking.

✔ **Support costs:** Which organization has primary support responsibility for the data warehouse? Does it bear the full burden of support costs, or will those costs be shared? If so, how are support costs calculated, and how are they billed and paid?

✔ **Development methodology:** One organization may develop its data warehousing applications and environments in one way, and the other organization in a different way. Who controls the development processes? Are individuals from the other organization expected to learn and use the other's methods and techniques?

✔ **Dispute resolution:** Resolving any type of dispute in which parties are from different companies is always an interesting challenge.

✔ **Ongoing enhancements:** What cross-company management structure must be put in place to prioritize and approve enhancements to the environment?

Chapter 20

Surviving in the Computer Industry (And Handling Vendors)

. . . .

In This Chapter

▶ Beware: Hype ahead!

▶ A smart shopper's guide to conferences and trade shows

▶ A smart shopper's guide to data warehousing vendors

▶ A look ahead at data warehousing and mainstream information technologies

. . . .

*O*kay, if you think that I've been cynical in other chapters, all I can say is wait until you finish this chapter because you haven't seen anything yet!

Help — I'm Up to My Armpits in Hype!

The name of the game in data warehousing since the early 1990s has been hype. Lots of hype. Massive amounts of hype. Hype. Hype! HYPE!

Whew — I had to get that out of my system. I'm serious, though. Whether you're talking about OLAP tools, the ROLAP-versus-MOLAP wars, middleware tools, or any other aspect of data warehousing, separating merit from empty promise, fact from fiction, in the wonderful world of data warehousing has been exceedingly difficult.

Though data warehousing has proven to have more substance and to provide more value than many of its predecessors on the hype hit parade, the discipline has, in my opinion, been somewhat compromised by the usual bag of tricks on the part of, let's say the shiftier side of some product and service providers (vendors and consultants).

Although I'm not one to point fingers, anyone who has been to a data warehousing trade show or sat through a couple of product demonstrations (and then tried to implement a real-world data warehousing environment using products that just didn't work as promised) knows what I'm talking about. A world of difference exists between looking at a few glossy brochures before watching an oversimplified drill-down demonstration and facing real-world problems as you try to implement a data warehouse (for example, struggling with desktop configuration issues and performance and response-time problems).

Hype: Is it all part of the game?

I remember back in the early 1980s, when the then new Ada programming language was the answer to everyone's software development woes, especially for military and government systems. Ada was supposed to solve everything. It was the language of the future, built especially to overcome all the shortcomings of every other programming language in existence at that time.

I remember in the mid-1980s, when computer-aided software engineering (CASE) tools were touted as the answer to software-development woes. You drew your data models and process flows using the tools, provided and — presto — out came a complete application, ready to go. *This* was productivity, brought to you by the wonderful world of CASE.

I remember back in the late 1980s and early 1990s, when enterprise computing architectures such as the IBM SAA, the Digital Equipment NAS, and nearly a dozen others from different hardware vendors were the answer to the problems and challenges of distributed heterogeneous (multivendor) computing. You just wrote all your applications to use the application programming tap-dance interfaces (APIs) for this set of standards, and, before you knew it, you had a seamlessly integrated enterprise across multiple platforms.

I also remember (I could go on for a while on this theme, but I won't) the promise of artificial intelligence (AI) and expert systems shells in the mid- and late 1980s. A little forward chaining here, a little backward chaining there, throw in a neural network, and — poof — a "thinking" application was created to aid your decision making.

The list goes on, including first-generation client/server computing (remember the promise that you could save millions of dollars in maintenance costs as compared to your mainframe?) and specific change-the-industry standards efforts that no longer exist, such as Unix International and the Distributed Management Environment (DME) standard from the Open Software Foundation.

The common theme was highly touted silver-bullet solutions from vendors, sometimes one and sometimes a pack of them operating in a consortium, that provided significantly less benefit to you (and often no benefit) despite the thousands — sometimes tens or hundreds of thousands — of dollars you spent on their products and services.

Here are some data warehousing facts of life:

- ✔ Vendors are in the business of making money by selling products.

- ✔ Vendors' sales representatives make money if they sell products to you and others. If they don't sell those products, they don't make money and can even lose their jobs.

- ✔ Data warehousing consultants would love to tell you everything you have to know to successfully develop a data warehouse in your organization and maybe would even want to help you develop it. A prerequisite, though, is that they regale you with the wonders of data warehousing and the fabulous benefits you can gain and, oh, yeah, with the reasons that they're the ones you should listen to and employ on your project.

- ✔ Within every IT discipline (data warehousing is no exception), stories get old, and you're bombarded with products with this theme: "Okay, maybe the old version didn't work quite the way you wanted it to, or maybe it wasn't as scalable as you needed it to be, but guess what? Our *new* version has all these new features."

The challenge you face is in dealing with these issues in a productive, nonconfrontational manner without being steered down a path that doesn't make sense for you. In the following section, I tell you how.

How to Be a Smart Shopper at Conferences and Trade Shows

Make no mistake about it: You can gain tremendous value from attending any type of conference or trade show, including those oriented toward data warehousing. Vendors tout and demonstrate their latest products, you get to hear real-life case studies and stories about successful data warehousing implementations, and you can learn from consultants and others who can provide unique insight into up-and-coming problems you're likely to face.

When you attend a data warehousing event, though, you must behave as though you're shopping for a car or other expensive personal item:

- ✔ Do your homework before you attend.
- ✔ Ask lots of questions.
- ✔ Be skeptical.
- ✔ Don't get rushed into a purchase.

The short version: Be a smart shopper.

Do your homework first

When you register for a data warehousing trade show or conference, you typically do so from a printed brochure (or, increasingly, from a schedule on the Internet) that gives you a complete list of vendors who will attend, consultants and other speakers who will give presentations and their respective topics, special sessions and seminars, and hospitality suites and other services you can use to spend more time researching your specific data warehousing needs.

Plan your *entire* agenda well in advance of the event. Most conferences have a number of parallel session tracks, with anywhere from two to five simultaneous lectures and presentations. After reviewing the entire agenda for each day, mark for each time block the topic that's most interesting or pertinent to you. Don't be distracted by the headings given to tracks, such as systems track or OLAP track: Plan your schedule by *topic*.

If you're attending an event with other people from your organization, split up whenever possible and cover as many sessions as you can.

Ask lots of questions

Asking questions at presentations and during demonstrations at vendor booths is not only permissible, it's also encouraged. After all, you're there to learn as much as possible about specific techniques, experiences, and products. Don't use your question-asking time, however, to do any of the following:

- ✔ Show off how much you know (or think you know) about a particular subject.

- ✔ Pointedly contradict or embarrass a speaker, especially on matters of philosophy that have no right or wrong answers and are just different ways of doing things.

- ✔ Do or say anything that reflects negatively on your company (which is probably displayed prominently on your name badge).

Although these statements may seem somewhat silly, you probably have had the experience of attending a session that's continually disrupted by an audience member who argues with the presenter and who seems to be doing little other than trying to draw attention to himself. Don't be one of those people.

Be skeptical

Wait a minute. I just said that contradicting a speaker or presenter is considered to be in poor taste. How, then, could I turn around and advise you to be skeptical?

Simple. First, and foremost, be skeptical. When you hear about "revolutionary new features" or "order-of-magnitude increases in performance over our previous product version" or anything else that sounds a little too hype-tinged, say to yourself: "How could this be? What has changed so dramatically in the past few months that suddenly all these wonderful new capabilities are available?"

Next, ask questions privately or in small groups, not in a large forum in which a speaker may feel defensive. If you see something that seems too good to be true during a demonstration, ask the presenter *after* the session is over. If the waiting line is too long, go back later; that person, or someone else, will still be there. An even better idea is to ask several people at a vendor's booth the same question on different days and see whether the responses you get are consistent.

Although your questions may be somewhat general at first, try to present a specific, real-life example from your environment as the context for digging into whether a feature or capability would truly benefit your data warehousing project. You may say something like this, for example: "We looked at Version 1.1 of your product six months ago and ran some tests against a demo copy to check on performance. Although we were okay with 25 gigabytes of data, as soon as we went above that number, volume performance was terrible, even though we had only two fact tables and four dimensions. You mentioned that response time with 75 gigabytes in the new version is as good as we used to get with 25 gigabytes. Please tell me what has changed in the new version to make performance so much better."

Don't get rushed into a purchase

You may be faced occasionally with a limited-time-only offer of a steep discount on a product, but only if you order before the end of the trade show.

Never buy a data warehousing product at a trade show. Okay, you may buy a book (such as this one, if you're thumbing through it while standing in a trade show booth) or another low-priced item, but never an OLAP tool, middleware product, data quality assurance tool, or, certainly, a database management system.

Use a conference or trade show as a fact-finding mission. Collect the glossy brochures and white papers. Take home the conference proceedings with the presentation slides, but don't buy on impulse.

Dealing with Data Warehousing Product Vendors

The same basic guidelines of being a smart shopper apply when you deal with data warehousing product vendors:

- ✔ Do your homework.
- ✔ Ask lots of questions.
- ✔ Be skeptical.
- ✔ Take your time before committing to purchasing products.

The one-on-one nature of the vendor–customer relationship is somewhat different from the contact interaction that occurs at a conference or trade show. On the positive side, you (and your data warehousing needs) can get much more attention from a vendor when you're meeting in your office to discuss your data warehousing project and that vendor's sales representative is trying to make a sale to you, compared to the trade show cast-the-net approach, when a vendor tries to reach as many new prospects as possible.

On the negative side, though, the vendor's sales rep can focus tactics specifically on you and others in your organization, and you must be particularly cautious and on your toes regarding the sales techniques being used.

A product sales representative is not in the business of solving your business problem through a cost-effective, timely data warehousing solution. Although that person (and, in a larger sense, the product company as a whole) would want very much for you to be successful in your data warehousing endeavors (particularly so that your success story becomes a reference for them), never forget that their product sales and revenue take precedence over your budget and schedule.

Check out the product and the company before you begin discussions

Any category of data warehousing product (such as OLAP tools, data mining tools, basic reporting and querying tools, database engines, extraction products, data quality tools, and data warehouse administration and management tools) has lots of different products. Each vendor who makes one or more of those data warehousing products wants to involve you in a one-on-one discussion with a sales representative.

To be blunt, your time is a valuable commodity. Even if you weren't dealing with project schedule pressures, you and others in your organization should give only a finite amount of time to vendor meetings.

Do your homework first at trade shows and conferences (and, as noted, even before you go to the trade shows). See what user interfaces look most appealing, and study performance and response-time statistics (as many as are available) for database volumes similar to what your environment will have. Don't just lug around those glossy brochures you pick up at the trade show booths — *read* them.

Next, get on the Internet and check out vendor Web sites. Use an Internet search engine to retrieve product reviews, analyst comments, news releases, and anything else you can find about the vendor's company (history, financial strength, and what others say about them, for example) and the products in which you're interested.

Request or download a demonstration copy of the product, if one is available.

Then it's time to talk to a sales representative in person, assuming that everything seems okay so far.

Take the lead during the meeting

Before a vendor sales representative sets foot inside your office, make absolutely clear what you expect to cover during that one- or two-hour initial meeting. You should do at least the following:

- ✔ Hear a presentation of no more than ten minutes about the company's history and background and the background of the products you're discussing.

- ✔ See an initial, end-to-end (or as close as possible) demonstration of a product's capabilities. The demonstration should last no more than a half-hour.

- ✔ Have a list of specific questions. They should cover features and capabilities, product installation base (how many copies have been sold and used and at how many companies), new version enhancements and features, and product architecture (interfaces, different platforms supported and differences across platforms, and scalability). Again, these questions should be specific to your environment and data warehousing project.

During discussions before the in-person meeting, give some of, but not all, the questions to the vendor representative. State that those items are important to you and that you want to discuss them during your meeting. You can gauge vendor responsiveness by how well your prepared questions are answered and also compare them to the responses to your impromptu questions. With the latter, you can gauge how well vendors know their own products and how well they react to unanticipated questions and challenges (rather than just hear scripted responses).

Be skeptical — again

Now it's time for down-to-earth, open discussions with your product vendors (not held in a crowded booth at a trade show). If you have heard certain things about a product that concern you (product scalability above a certain number of users, for example), ask! Demand proof (reference sites, discussions with a development manager, and hands-on testing in your organization, for example) of anything and everything that concerns you.

Be a cautious buyer

No matter how attractive a product looks, take your time in committing to a purchase. It's software, not a one-of-a-kind work of art. You have no reason to hurry, even when your data warehousing project has an aggressive schedule.

Always test-drive software under your environment's conditions:

- ✔ Use your data.
- ✔ See how many attempts it takes to install the software correctly.
- ✔ Determine the responsiveness of the vendor's support staff.
- ✔ See what works as advertised — and what doesn't.
- ✔ Ask what your users think about the product's usability.
- ✔ Find out how stable the software is. Does it cause your client and/or server systems to crash or lock up? If so, how frequently?
- ✔ Find out what performance is like in your environment.

Sometimes a desktop product (an OLAP tool, for example) is suitable for only a certain portion of your user base. Perhaps only a small number of power users would use that tool and the rest of the user community would use a basic reporting tool or, for the first iteration of the data warehouse, no tool. Perhaps casual users would use a standard browser to access standard reports posted on the company intranet. In these situations, never let a vendor pressure you into purchasing more copies of a product than you need. You can always buy more, if necessary. The last thing you want is a bunch of shelfware sitting around and taking up disk space.

A Look Ahead: Mainstream Technologies and Vendors

As data warehousing and traditional computing technologies converge, it's a whole new ball game as you try to sift through vendors claims and promises, from both traditional data warehousing vendors, who are already trying to make their products' respective capabilities "go enterprise" (be able to work in large, enterprise-wide global settings) and others, who see the lucrative data warehousing market as an area into which they can expand.

Beware! I've already seen more than a few 1980s-era marketing messages from the distributed database world make a comeback:

✔ "This product provides transparent access to any data in any database anywhere."

✔ "Put one subject area into this data mart and another subject into a second data mart, and — presto! — you can join them whenever you need to and treat the two data marts as one logical data warehouse."

Although I'm not one to scoff automatically at everything I hear about new and improved product capabilities, much of what's showing up lately as capabilities designed to address shortcomings in first-generation data warehousing has a feel (to me, anyway) of "been there, done that."

The proof is in the pudding. (I have no idea what that saying means, and I don't think that it applies to data warehousing. It just seemed like the right thing to say.) Dealing with vendor promises and claims (and the consequences of product, shall we say, characteristics that you wish you had known about before you bought them) will become even more of a burden as the extract-and-copy-and-copy-again first-generation data warehousing morphs into all the things discussed in Part VI. That part of the book describes topics such as near-real time updates to the data warehouse, the access of data at its point of origin rather than from the database into which it's copied, and the inclusion of multimedia in your data warehouse.

Chapter 21

Existing Sort-of Data Warehouses: Upgrade or Replace?

. . . .

In This Chapter

▶ Taking a complete inventory of extract files across your organization

▶ Deciding what to do with each extract file

▶ Mastering the complexities of migrating extract files to a real data warehouse

▶ Recognizing that taking away user functionality is (almost) never acceptable

. . . .

*A*bout two years ago, I began working on a data warehousing project with a fairly large bank. I was working with the retail part of the bank, in which individual consumer (credit card, lease, and mortgage) loans were handled. (The wholesale side handled large commercial loans and other financial transactions with companies.)

I set up a kickoff meeting with the project's sponsor, who outlined all the (numerous) initiatives the project encompassed. We put together a time line of which areas to tackle first and which ones would follow and then set up a series of meetings with different managers and technologists in the various business groups in the bank's retail organization.

The first meeting was held with a group responsible for analyzing how the bank's customers handled their payments for consumer loans: how many paid on time, paid only the minimum amount due each month, and defaulted on or missed payments, for example. This group's goal was to manage the bank's risk against its entire portfolio of loans and to perform statistical analysis in an attempt to predict where problems might occur. To accomplish this goal, the group would look at historical payment patterns and perform trend analysis and other statistical functions.

The meeting began with the project sponsor explaining what the group was planning for the bank: Build a data warehouse to support risk management for consumer loans in addition to other functions handled by other departments. We spent the rest of the meeting with the loan payment analysts describing how they did their analysis, what data they used and where it came from, and other pertinent information.

A few days later, I was speaking with the manager of the group, who had been in the meeting. He said, "You know, I don't understand this data warehousing thing. We already pull key data elements from our production systems into a flat file — I personally hand-picked which elements we need — and we've been doing this type of analysis for about two years. Tell me again, what additional benefit will I get from a data warehouse?"

To complicate matters, the second group meeting was with another organization responsible for analyzing credit bureau scores for the bank's customers. This group would periodically receive, from a provider of external data (refer to Chapter 17), credit bureau data about anyone who had any type of line of credit (including a bank card) or loan.

This meeting began much like the first one, except that the project's sponsor wasn't there and I was facing the group alone. At their request, I explained the principles of data warehousing and how data would be pulled from various sources and made available for analysis. Next, they took turns explaining to me how they performed statistical analysis with their own data extracts that merged data from different sources and analyzed bankruptcies, delinquencies, and lots of other measures in concert with the credit bureau data.

Again, the request was made: "Explain again what new functionality a data warehouse will give me."

The real answer to this question, posed from both groups, was, "In your particular situation, not much." Doing the tap dance of a good data warehousing consultant, I explained the big picture: It wasn't just their own respective groups but also many other groups on the retail side of the bank where that same information was necessary. The data in its current form just wasn't available or wasn't in a flexible enough form to be used in other ways (OLAP, for example) than the statistical processes that were being used.

Honestly, each of these individuals who asked "What do I gain from this?" was exactly right. Neither organization had its own data warehouse or was doing its processing against a data mart extracted from some larger organizational data warehouse. What they *were* doing, however small-time it was, was well suited for their respective needs. Their business needs didn't call for OLAP-style functionality and other 1990s-era business intelligence capabilities. Summarized data? "Sorry, no can do." These folks needed detail-level data for their statistical analysis. Drill-down? "Not interested, thanks anyway for asking." All they needed to do their jobs was statistical processing, and mainframe SAS did that just fine, thank you.

Note: Other groups on the retail side of the bank did need to do drill-down analysis by region against summarized data. To their managers and analysts, the idea of a data warehouse supported by OLAP tools was an enticing, high-value proposition because they didn't have anything similar at the time.

Here's the dichotomy:

- **Data analysis "have-nots":** Organizations and individuals who have few (and more likely no) capabilities to do the type of analysis that can bring about information-driven decision-making.

- **Data analysis "haves":** Organizations and individuals who may not have a data warehouse up and running but are doing something with data they're getting from somewhere. In many cases, it's suiting their business needs just fine.

The following section describes the latter group.

What's Out There?

Your organization has overwhelmingly favorable odds of having at least one sort-of data warehouse used to provide informational (reports) and, sometimes, analytical capabilities to one or more groups of users. The odds are also good that the term *extract file* is used to describe this type of environment because it's populated by extracts of data from production systems rather than by users being forced to execute their queries or receive their reports from the operational production databases or files. Still interested in playing the odds? Here are a few more:

- Although the extracted data is almost always housed in a single file or database, a merge process is probably combining extracted data from more than one application source.

- Only selected elements, not all elements from all tables or files, from each data source are usually extracted and copied to the extract file.

- Some sort of data quality assurance process is usually going on at each step of the way, from initial extract to loading into the extract file.

- Some power users probably can execute queries or create statistical programs (in SAS or SPSS, for example) against the data, but many users aren't likely to touch the data directly. Instead, they're probably regular recipients of reports generated either automatically or in response to their requests.

Sure sounds like a data warehouse, doesn't it?

Why aren't extract files considered to be data warehouses?

They are, sort of. Chapter 1 describes the historical roots of data warehousing in the 1970s. Extract files, whether in the 1970s or 1980s or still in existence today, exist for the same basic reasons that a full-fledged data warehouse, or a data mart, does: to provide information delivery despite a variety of barriers, such as hard-to-understand data structures, "don't touch the production system" rules, and the lack of multifile or multi-database cross-reference.

Some data warehousing proponents would argue that combining and reconfiguring data simply for the purpose of generating reports or to perform statistical analysis is hardly a data warehouse in the modern (1990s) sense of the term. Extract files aren't equipped with OLAP capabilities, they would argue: no drill-down or data pivoting, for example.

I would argue that if you separate the data warehouse side (what it takes to gather, move, and reconfigure data from one or more sources) from the business intelligence side (what you do with the data after you have it available), the picture becomes much more clear. Extract files, or whatever you want to call them, are very much part of the barrier-breaking philosophy of a data warehouse. Many of them are file-based rather than built

on databases, and they aren't likely to be flexible in support of ad hoc querying and dimensional analysis. In a real sense, however, these environments serve the purpose of warehousing data for subsequent use.

To many users, OLAP capabilities such as drill-down and data pivoting have little or no use, at least not in the context of their current job definitions. The users' jobs call for functionality that can be delivered from these extract files and the static reports and statistical analysis accomplished with that data.

I'm not saying that all data warehousing initiatives should be scrapped in lieu of continuing to run on top of existing extract files. I am pointing out, though, that for as much interest as data warehousing has generated since the early 1990s, the premise, if not the means and tools, for a large segment of the business community is the same old story.

The moral of the story: Don't go into an organization that effectively uses data through extract files and expound on the wonders of data warehousing. Instead, as discussed later in this chapter, be cautious about proposing any data warehousing solution that can be viewed as a step backward. If you do that, you're in for a long, bumpy ride.

The first step: Cataloguing the extract files, who uses them, and why

Before you even begin to consider what to do about the extract files and other types of sort-of data warehouse environments that exist, you must find them. It isn't easy, considering the homegrown nature of these environments.

Here's a hint: Follow the reports. Through group work sessions and individual meetings, determine and catalog the reports that are used throughout the organization you're working with to build a data warehouse. Some of them are likely to be coming directly from the production applications and their respective databases and files. For now, don't worry about them. (Keep track of them, though, because they're an excellent starting point when you start the "what data do we need?" analysis for determining what should be in the data warehouse.) Other reports are by definition coming from data extracted from one or more applications and stored somewhere. Those reports are the ones to concentrate on now.

Using the set of reports as your starting point, first determine who is using them and who is responsible for generating them. The reason that the users are important is that it's not unusual for reports to be generated, perhaps for many years, that are no longer used. In these situations, you're halfway home toward eliminating this don't-really-use-it functionality from your data warehousing environment (and managing its complexity).

The people responsible for generating the reports are important people to know. They're the ones who probably can tell you where the data is coming from, what the processes are to prepare and load that data before the reports are run, and what the issues and problems are with data availability and integrity.

Sometimes no single individual knows the entire end-to-end sequence of steps used to extract data, prepare and organize that data, and run the reports, especially when these processes cross organizational boundaries. (For example, the IT organization handles the initial extraction of the data and some rudimentary quality assurance, and the business organization handles the merge processes and runs the reports.) In these situations, get all these people in the same room to discuss and agree on how things work. You can avoid spending a great deal of time playing "he said, she said" with people who, frankly, you're probably aggravating with your constant questions and requests for meetings.

Eventually, through diligence, you get a complete picture of who is using which data, who is responsible for making that data available, and what's going on behind the scenes to make it all happen.

Don't forget the "why" part of the picture: why (for what business purposes) extract files are being used. You have to find out anyway, as part of your requirements analysis. While you're checking out what's going on today, ask questions while you have the users' attention. It saves you time in the long run.

And then, the review

Do not skip this section. If you do, serious problems lie ahead.

After you have created your catalog of information, you *must* embark on a candid, no-holds-barred review process with each organization using extract files. Although this process is ideally part of the data warehousing project's scope (Chapter 13 discusses how to choose a methodology), schedule conflicts and timing constraints may require additional meetings, preferably as early in the process as possible.

Your goal is to determine the true business value obtained from using these extract files and to determine what additional business value may be obtained. You have to take this approach with the extract file users: "Forget this data warehousing stuff — let's talk about your extracts." They're already likely to feel threatened that their capabilities are about to be taken away by the evil data warehousing empire (as discussed later in this chapter, in the section "Beware: Don't Take Away Valued Functionality").

As the data warehousing project moves forward, you want to figure out what part of the existing environment is worth salvaging (not only functionality but also steps and processes, as discussed in the section just mentioned).

Decisions, Decisions

Your diligence has now ferreted out a complete inventory of extract files filling the role of prehistoric data warehouse, each one most likely serving a single organization's needs. Next, you and the business users have reached consensus about what is good about each file, what needs to be improved, and other aspects.

Now, it's decision time.

Although it may come as a surprise to you, you have no reason not to build a data warehousing environment to contain one or more existing extract files. The key is the word *environment*. Although a single, monolithic data warehouse probably would have difficulty interacting with these extract files, an environment constructed in a mixed-mode, component-oriented manner (as described in Chapter 13) can encompass a component or two that are a bit long in the tooth.

Each extract file must be put to a test, with one of these three answers:

- ✔ Discard it.
- ✔ Replace it.
- ✔ Retain it, possibly with some upgrades or enhancements.

Choice 1: Get rid of it

If, and only if, you have universal agreement from every corner of the organization that an extract file has absolutely no use (for example, no one looks anymore at the reports that are generated; no one has updated the data-extraction and -input processes, even though source applications have changed; and the system is generally doing little other than wasting disk space), an obvious choice is to dump the file without any type of replacement or upgrade.

Although some individual data elements may eventually find their way into the data warehouse, they have *no* business value in the current setting (data organized in a specific way).

Be brave: Throw it out.

Choice 2: Replace it

Suppose that an extract file is being used, but, honestly, it's somewhat cumbersome and difficult to use. Not all the necessary information is available, changing the extraction processes to extend the list of attributes is too difficult, and it meets only about 50 percent (or less) of the users' needs.

The choice is easy:

1. **Retain the functionality users want that already exists in the extract files as part of your data warehousing environment.**

2. **Create designs and plans for the functionality that is necessary but is not in the extract files.**

3. **Replace the extract file by folding the existing functionality into the data warehouse along with the newly designed features and getting rid of the old, antiquated environment.**

Choice 3: Retain it

Ah, but what if these conditions exist:

- ✔ The extract file is a relatively recent addition to that organization's capabilities (within the past three or four years, for example).
- ✔ The data is stored not in a flat file but rather in a relational database.
- ✔ The data quality is excellent.
- ✔ Users are equipped with basic reporting tools and are doing some degree of ad hoc querying on their own.
- ✔ The environment generally doesn't look too bad.

(A grandmotherly saying is appropriate here: "Your data warehouse should look and feel so good when it's that age.")

You should strongly consider retaining this type of environment. Although you may want to consider upgrading it a little (you can read more about that process in the following section), you definitely shouldn't throw it out and try to replace it.

What kind of upgrades may be appropriate? How about these:

- ✔ Add data elements closely related to ones which already exist (their point of origin is the same application file or database, for example) that people in other organizations may use.
- ✔ Do a little performance tuning to increase response time if a larger group of users will access the database.
- ✔ Increase the frequency of updates, and restock if business needs dictate doing so.
- ✔ Equip users with new tools in addition to their existing ones to expand their horizons in data analysis and use.
- ✔ Add — only if you're daring — a new subject area or two to this environment to provide an even richer set of data for analytical purposes. Be careful to avoid disrupting existing functionality.

If you're considering adding new subject areas to your extract, look at an extract file that's worth salvaging as your '67 Corvette that needs a little work and has been garaged for a while. Although you can always sell the car and buy a new one, when you step back and consider all your options, it's probably less expensive to invest in the required maintenance. Besides, you're already familiar with (in tune with) the car. It may not be new, and it doesn't have all kinds of advanced computer controls and antilock braking; it may not have a back seat or a rear window; but it still gets you where you want to go. ("Yeah, we're going to Surf City, gonna have some fun. . . .")

Caution: Migration Is Not Development — It's Much More Difficult

When you select Door #2 (replacement) in the preceding section, you face a *migration* situation: moving functionality and data from an existing environment to a new one.

Because I cannot possibly describe in detail in just a few short paragraphs all the complexities of migration and how to deal with them, I just hit the highlights in this section.

Unlike a development project in which no functionality exists, a migration project requires that you not only develop and deploy capabilities in a new environment but also retire that same functionality from the system being replaced. You have to consider these issues:

- ✔ **Cut-over requirements:** For example, what functionality moves, in how many phases, and when it occurs

- ✔ **Your fall-back plans:** For example, what happens if the new system doesn't work

- ✔ **Additional staff requirements:** Potentially to support two environments simultaneously if you have a multiphase migration plan and training requirements in new technologies and products, for example

- ✔ **User training in the new tools and contents:** What new data is available and how it can (and should) be used

The good news is that the process of migrating an informational and analytical environment, such as an extract file and the processes used to populate it, is significantly less complex in most cases than doing the same with a transaction-processing system that's mission-critical to your organization, such as the customer order-entry system or the payroll system.

Don't overlook the complexities of migration, however, even when a data warehouse is a target.

More about migration

Here are a couple of books with more information about migration strategies and techniques that can help smooth your move from extract files to a data warehousing environment:

Transitioning to Open Systems, by Steven Shaffer and me (Morgan Kaufmann Publishers, 1995). Although the book is a bit of overkill for data warehousing migration, it briefly describes how to select your target architecture, tie the architecture back to your business vision and mission, and related subjects.

Migrating Legacy Systems: Gateways, Interfaces, and the Incremental Approach, by Michael Brodie and Michael Stonebraker (Morgan Kaufmann Publishers, 1995). Although this book also probably has more details than you need for a data warehousing migration, it's comprehensive nonetheless.

Beware: Don't Take Away Valued Functionality

If you decide to pursue a replacement–migration strategy for your existing extracts, please pay careful attention to this section. (Don't say that I didn't warn you.) One of the worst things you can do (something that causes users to snarl every time your name is mentioned) is to implement a newfangled, much-improved, all-kinds-of-gadgets data warehouse and, at the same time, take away functionality and capabilities from the users of existing extract files.

Oh, sure, you may have a certain feature on your Phase II list and another one on the maybe-next-year-if-we-get-funding list. Go back to the beginning of this chapter, though: Average business users don't care whether answers are provided by a data warehouse with all the bells and whistles or a plain-vanilla extract file. They care only about reports, statistical analysis, or whatever else has to be done. Keep in mind that functionality in this context may equate to certain data, such as the facts used to support decision-making or provide analytical capabilities. Your new data warehousing environment may have several reporting and OLAP tools that support querying, generate reports, or perform statistical analysis, just like the old environment did. If data that was in the old extract files is no longer available, however, because it's not in the data warehouse, you've done it — you've taken away functionality.

Not every data element has to be propagated into the data warehouse or every report automatically generated using the new tools. The discussion earlier in this chapter about getting down and dirty with users about what business value truly exists comes into play here. Don't spend time and effort moving data and functionality that isn't used; at the same time, you *must* be sure that necessary capabilities aren't taken away.

Chapter 22

Working with Data Warehousing Consultants

*L*et me begin this chapter with a disclaimer: I'm a data warehousing consultant.

By the time you reach the end of this chapter, you'll probably agree that I treat fairly the subject of whether you need data warehousing consultants. You won't see any subliminal advertising (call Alan) anywhere in this (use Alan for your data warehouse) chapter.

The reason I discuss this subject is simple: You'll most likely need consultants for your data warehousing project, and I give you as unbiased a perspective on this subject as I can.

Do You Really Need Consultants to Help Build a Data Warehouse?

The answer in a word: probably.

It's not that people from within your organization aren't capable of working with data warehousing technology or completing a project without outside help. A simple fact of corporate IT life in the 1990s overwhelms factors such as capabilities and knowledge: We're in a consulting-driven era, plain and simple.

I should note that I've written four editions of a computer-consulting book since the early 1980s, and the skyrocketing demand in the 1990s for outside consulting expertise in nearly every medium- to large-size organization has been truly remarkable. The reason for the increased demand for consulting services is partly the convergence of two major trends:

✔ **The increasing pace of technological change:** Client/server computing, the Internet, and improvements in relational database capabilities are some examples.

✔ **The aftereffects of the U.S. economic recession in the early 1990s:** Although some areas were hit harder than others, companies across the board were hit hard by downsizing, reengineering, and the rest of the stuff most of us went through not long ago. Even though economic recovery took hold and is still flourishing, corporate IT organizations are still operating under the "stay lean and mean" philosophy.

The combination of these two trends means that an overwhelming majority of new systems development, including data warehousing, is being done at least in part by outside consulting organizations.

You can always fight the trend and try to do in-house data warehouse development, and you can easily be successful. Your internal IT staff is probably spread fairly thinly across a multitude of initiatives (can you say Year 2000?), however, and applying for personnel requisitions for a major hiring plan is just plain out of style in most corporations. (Can you say outsourcing?)

I wholeheartedly encourage you to try to accomplish your data warehousing initiatives through the use of in-house staff, either exclusively or at least with the majority of your team members being employees of your organization. If your organization is like most others, though, your data warehousing fate rests solely on how well you identify and use outside data warehousing consulting expertise.

Watch Out, Though!

If you've ever worked with IT consultants (data warehousing specialists), you realize that not all consultants are equally skilled, equally dedicated, or equipped with the same, shall we say, degree of ethics.

Before getting into the aspects of individual consultants and the roles they can play on your data warehousing team, let me distinguish between different *types* of consultants and their relevance to your project.

A large part of the growth in consulting services in the 1990s has been in the area of consulting formally known as *staff supplement,* and less formally known as *body shopping.* A number of consulting companies have been successful in creating a collection of individuals (sometimes employees of the company, sometimes independent consultants, and sometimes both) and placing these individuals, one or two at a time, in organizations looking to fill a personnel gap here and there.

To be fair, many consulting companies that perform primarily staff supplement work put together small-scale project teams of four or five people (rather than provide a person here and there) when they have an opportunity to do an entire client project. These firms typically steer away from project-oriented work, however, because placing individuals in staffing supplement positions is, to be blunt, a relatively low-risk way to build a company (as discussed next).

If your organization has an ongoing data warehousing initiative staffed primarily by internal IT members but your team has a few open slots, you may best be served by working with a staff-supplement-oriented consulting company to find the one or two missing links on your project team.

Be careful, though: If you're paying good money (and you will, believe me) for the services of these individuals, be prepared to complete a thorough interview process to ensure that they're not only technically qualified but also a good cultural fit for working on-site within your organization. When a consulting company uses subcontractors, they're likely to have little or no history. They may have been chosen for your project based solely on a few keywords that showed up on a résumé database search. Make sure that you carefully determine whether these people are the right fit for your data warehousing project.

The other side of consulting, the part dominated by large systems integrators, is oriented primarily toward project work rather than staffing services. Many of these firms eschew staffing work and engage a client only (or primarily) if they have control over a project's methodology, the resources assigned to the project (even those from your own company), and the format of deliverables.

Although this rigid stance may sound harsh at first ("Do it my way or else, even though you're paying me"), a sound theory is behind it. Some firms are so experienced at putting together successful project teams and performing in a certain, methodology-driven manner that to do otherwise is riskier to a client's project than if they continually adapt their processes and techniques for each client.

If you're a data warehousing consultant

This chapter is oriented primarily toward the user community and how the people in it may find and retain you (or your consulting brethren) for their data warehousing projects. If you're a data warehousing consultant, though, here are some tidbits of advice:

✔ **Stay on top of all the changes taking place in the field of data warehousing.** Have you heard of hybrid OLAP? What are your thoughts about data mining? Is it for real? What are the new products in the middleware extraction and transformation game? Although you never know everything that goes on in this or any other technology area, you have to avoid getting caught by surprise during an interview or business development session if you're asked your opinion about a new product or architectural trend.

✔ **Remember that it's not only technology skills that make a successful data warehousing consultant but also business skills.**

Although I don't believe in the industry-expert approach to data warehousing implementation, you must have a set of core knowledge about business to be able to ask the right questions during the scope process or to create, for example, a definition for a sales-and-marketing fact table.

✔ **Be flexible.** Be able to work as a hands-on technologist (performing source systems analysis or data modeling, for example), a data warehousing architect or advice-oriented consultant, a project manager, or other types of roles. This flexibility helps you stay billable (whether you're independent or working for a consulting company) and generally helps make you a better consultant by giving you a broader perspective of both data warehousing and the consulting profession than if you continually play the same role in one engagement after another.

In the area of data warehousing consulting, it's almost comforting to work with a firm that has these qualities:

✔ A successful track record of data warehouse implementations with a variety of technologies (not just ROLAP or MOLAP — both, for example)

✔ Insight into the direction of data warehousing technology and architecture as they apply to your business problem rather than a canned solution ("We've always done it this way") that may not be a good fit for you

✔ A commitment to the success of your project by taking on full responsibility for all aspects of implementation rather than a supply of technologists who don't assume responsibility for project management and direction

In many situations, the lines between consulting companies — the different types of firms, and even firms within the same category (staffing-oriented or project-oriented) — are somewhat blurry. The purpose of this section is not to steer you in one direction but rather to point out that a data warehousing consultant from one type of environment may be a good fit for your particular needs — or maybe not. Similarly, a particular consulting firm may best serve your needs, depending on how you want to proceed with your data warehousing project (such as how many, if any, internal people will work on it). Or perhaps that consulting organization, regardless of its data warehousing expertise, isn't a good fit for the particular implementation model you're pursuing.

Here's the key to avoiding mistakes: Before you talk with any consulting firms or individuals about your data warehousing needs, have a good idea first about what type of model you're most likely to pursue (internal management of the project rather than management by the consulting organization). This way, you can better determine not only the technical capabilities but also the cultural fit that best meets your needs, deliverable dates, and budget.

A Final Word about Data Warehousing Consultants

Although it's important for both individual consultants and consulting companies to check references and technical and business qualifications, such as product and industry experience, following your instincts is also a good idea. Data warehousing technology is changing so rapidly that you may do more harm than good if you insist on using a consultant (or a company) who has experience with specific products, who has previously implemented a data warehouse in your industry, or who otherwise fits a checklist of qualifications.

Someone who lacks experience in a particular industry or in the use of a certain product but who otherwise impresses you as an insightful, hard worker who can get the job done is certainly worth considering. You may want, for example, to see the person in action for perhaps a week or two, as part of a team doing the data warehousing scope. Don't get caught up in the laundry list mode of finding and retaining consulting assistance.

Part VI
Data Warehousing in the Not-too-Distant Future

The 5th Wave   By Rich Tennant

"We're researching molecular/digital technology that moves massive amounts of information across binary pathways that interact with free-agent programs capable of making decisions and performing logical tasks. We see applications in really high-end doorbells."

In this part . . .

Data warehousing is changing — right before your eyes.

By the year 2000, you're likely to implement a data warehouse in a way that's much different from the way it's done today. You'll make the leap from today's first generation of data warehousing to a new generation of technologies and architectures.

Be prepared: Read this part of the book to see what's coming soon and what these new data warehousing models mean to you.

Chapter 23

The Operational Data Store ("I Need Information Now!")

Because the idea behind the operational data store (ODS) is relatively new in the world of data warehousing, this area doesn't have much agreement, including about what an ODS is.

Some definitions of an ODS make it sound like a classical data warehouse, with periodic (batch) inputs from various operational sources into the ODS, except that the new inputs overwrite existing data. In a bank, for example, an ODS (by this definition) has, at any given time, one account balance for each checking account, courtesy of the checking account system, and one balance for each savings account, as provided by the savings account system. The account balances are sent from the various systems periodically (such as at the end of each day), and an ODS user can then look in one place to see each bank customer's complete profile (such as the customer's basic information and balance information for each type of account).

If you want to call an environment such as this one an ODS, by all means, go right ahead. (Oooh — sarcasm.) Terminology aside, this example is just a batch-oriented data warehousing environment doing an update-and-replace operation on each piece of data that resides there (and, of course, adding new data as applicable) instead of keeping a running history of whatever measures are stored there. This so-called ODS is not challenging to implement, and almost everything discussed to this point in this book can be applied here (for example, the batch-oriented middleware tools and services described in Chapter 7 and reporting and OLAP tools).

My version of an ODS is a little more architecturally challenging and, for purposes of this chapter, somewhat more forward-looking. It uses an end-to-end approach that requires applications to be *warehouse-enabled* (sensitive to the realization that they will provide data to a data warehouse). Warehouse-enabled applications support a push architecture and enable an informational database to be refreshed in real-time.

Although the premise of breaking down application and system barriers is very much in concert with what you do with a data warehouse, you have one major problem: The pace of updates into your informational and analytical environment is much too slow if you use classical data warehousing and its batch-oriented processes for extracting and moving data.

Forget about terminology and buzzwords. Focus instead on the architectural and time-oriented differences between what's described in this chapter and everything you've learned about data warehousing.

Then, it will all be clear.

The ODS Defined

Here's my definition of an *ODS* (it's a long one, but I make it clear momentarily): an informational and analytical environment that reflects at any point the current operational state of its subject matter, even though data that makes up that operational state is managed in different applications elsewhere in the enterprise. Here's what it means:

- **"Informational and analytical environment":** The user interface and behavior of an ODS look and feel like a data warehouse. That is, an ODS user has a querying and reporting tool, an OLAP tool, or possibly an EIS tool through which information and analysis are requested and delivered. (Data mining doesn't apply to an ODS environment, in case you were wondering.)

- **"Reflects at any time the current operational state":** Okay, quick — sit down at your query tool and ask a question of the ODS. The answer you get back must reflect data as it's *currently* stored in whatever operational system it came from. If an update occurs in an operational system to a customer's checking account balance, the ODS must make that same change in real-time or almost real-time (*very* quickly). In almost all situations, therefore, extracting batch-oriented data for inclusion in an ODS doesn't work.

- **"Subject matter":** As with a data warehouse, you should create an ODS with a specific business mission in mind for a manageable set of subject areas.

Can an ODS contain historical data?

Why not? Some folks declare that an ODS can't contain historical data — only the current values for all its data elements. They say that if the environment has historical data, it's a data warehouse, not an ODS.

I disagree. I worked not long ago on a banking client's ODS that fit all the real-time update requirements from various data sources, pushed out via messaging, as described later in this chapter. The client requested that the ODS have some summarization tables because its customers occasionally ask for

historical information, such as, "What was the total interest paid on all loans of all types in the preceding three quarters?" The client's objective was to have a single place for its users to access not only all the various operational data points, such as the current outstanding balance on various credit instruments, but also the answers to these historically-oriented questions.

So what's wrong with a little history stored in some summarization tables in the ODS? I say "nothing."

> ✔ **"Data managed in different applications elsewhere in the enterprise":**
> An ODS is not a single unified database (a *big* one) that a number of
> applications use. Rather, it's a separate database that receives informa-
> tion from various sources with appropriate transformations, quality
> assurance, and other processes.

An ODS Example

Suppose that you work in a large, global financial company that provides a variety of services to elite companies and individuals across the world. Your company has grown to its current form as a result of a series of mergers and acquisitions throughout the 1980s and 1990s. The trend in recent years toward a convergence of banking and securities services has given your company an opportunity to become a full-service provider to your customers.

Your company's average customer is likely to participate in many (perhaps all) of these types of activities:

✔ Traditional stock brokering (buying and selling shares of stocks, including margin account activity)

✔ Fixed income investments (corporate and governmental bonds)

✔ Options trading accounts, including risk arbitrage

✔ Cash asset management

✔ Short-term loans and other debt instruments

✔ Intermediate- and longer-term loans and other debt instruments

✔ Venture capital investments

You want your customers to use your company as one-stop shopping for anything involving large sums of money.

The complications

Your company's situation is a little complicated, however, particularly in these two areas:

✔ The mergers and acquisitions have left your IT infrastructure with a large number of *silo* applications (applications that aren't integrated with one another, even though they probably should be), none of which has been successfully integrated with the others. One system handles stock trading for U.S. stocks, for example, and another handles stock market activity from non-U.S. global exchanges. In addition, separate systems handle fixed-income activity, all debt activity in the United States, all short-term debt in Europe, and intermediate- and long-term European debt. And the list goes on.

✔ The definition of a customer is somewhat hazy. Individuals set up corporations and partnerships through which they make investments or secure loans for business deals. Your corporate customers may be subsidiaries of other corporations, who may also be a customer of yours.

The problem is that your business practices call for all credit activity with every customer to pass through a series of quality assurance checks before being approved:

✔ Every customer of yours, whether an individual or a company, has several ceilings on debt activity. One ceiling is an amount of total outstanding debt at any given time. Until this first-level ceiling is reached, a customer can, without human intervention, automatically take out a new loan or act against a credit line, buy stocks on margin, or perform any other type of activity that increases debt.

✔ Every customer can exceed the first-level ceiling, to a second ceiling amount, after receiving approval from one of your company's executives.

✔ For an executive to approve credit activity past the first ceiling to the second, a series of measures must be checked: For example, a certain asset balance must be in place; the customer may not have reduced total assets on hand in all accounts of all types (such as cash, stocks, and bonds) by more than 15 percent in the preceding 30 days; and the bank has maximum amounts for total debt in each country, adjusted by assets held in each country.

✔ To help control risk, your company tracks the relationships between all your customers to get a real picture of a customer's financial state. For example, an individual may control a series of corporations, each of which is treated as an individual customer with its own asset and debt activity, in addition to that of the individual's own accounts. When your company's executives approve any additional beyond-the-first-ceiling debt, however (for a real estate partnership which involves that individual, for example), they must assess an overall picture of what's going on with that individual's activity to avoid too much risk exposure in case of financial problems.

Although the quality assurance checks just described are conceptually straightforward, they're obviously extremely complex to implement, for one simple reason: Data is needed from systems all over your enterprise, from many different systems, to feed into those checks. This data includes information such as all the asset activity, all the debt activity and current loans outstanding, and information about which loans were just paid down earlier in the day.

One approach you can try is to provide your company's executives (the ones who have to make the loan-approval decisions) with interfaces into every system in which necessary data may be found. Users then can run a long series of queries (if they can even be supported), pull out the appropriate values, paste them into a spreadsheet program, and make the decision.

This approach has two problems, however: The chance for human error is high, and the pace at which this type of activity must occur is okay only during "ordinary" times. During a time of financial crisis, however, when many or most of your firm's customers are buying and selling stocks, covering margins, buying and selling options and trying to handle their hedge accounts, executing against credit lines, and doing all kinds of other activities very quickly, your company's employees will never be able to keep up.

The ODS solution

The ODS comes to the rescue. Figure 23-1 illustrates a conceptual architecture by which you implement an ODS to meet your business missions. First, the ODS provides a consolidated picture of a client's balances for automatic loan processing under the first ceiling. Next, the ODS enables executives to make yes–no decisions about loan requests up to the second ceiling.

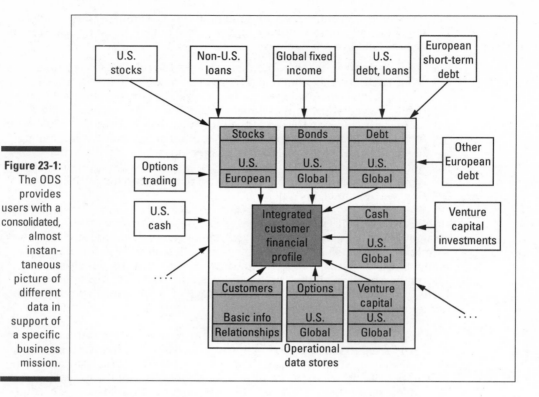

Figure 23-1:
The ODS
provides
users with a
consolidated,
almost
instan-
taneous
picture of
different
data in
support of
a specific
business
mission.

To get a better look at the data flows within the ODS environment, see Figure 23-2, in which updates to one of the data sources (the system to handle U.S. debt) propagate into the ODS environment.

The following steps indicate what occurs in the ODS environment:

1. A customer makes a regularly scheduled loan payment that's processed by the system that handles payments on U.S. loans and lines of credit.

2. The loan payment application updates its database to reflect the payment.

3. The loan payment application then *immediately* pushes the updated data to the ODS.

4. The ODS receives the update and processes it, updating its database contents (in this example, reducing the customer's total outstanding debt amount).

5. The ODS performs any internal processing, consolidation, alerts, or other necessary functions.

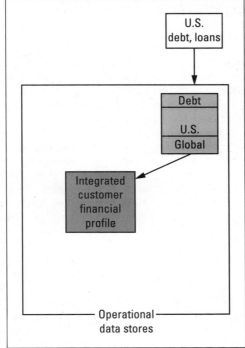

Figure 23-2:
The ODS
has to
reflect the
state of
data
throughout
the
enterprise
as quickly
as possible.

An environment such as this one can, if everything is architected properly, provide a picture of all relevant data from all over the place — now — in support of the firm's risk-management mission.

You *must* validate the need for real-time updates into your ODS because these updates are complex to create, as described in the following section. Constantly challenge assumptions, and ask questions: "What happens if you have to wait until the end of the day? What if updates were twice a day? Every hour?" Be absolutely certain that the mission dictates this approach because it takes longer (and is more expensive) than a data warehouse.

ODS Architectural Challenges

This section describes the architectural challenges of an ODS (and how to overcome them) from an end-to-end, source-application-to-ODS perspective.

The basics: Warehouse-enabled applications

The key to implementing an ODS is to have warehouse-enabled applications. I don't think that it's possible to implement an ODS with real-time propagation of data from the various sources by using classical, non-intrusive data warehousing techniques, such as leaving the source systems alone and periodically pulling data from the databases and files.

To implement an ODS, the source systems must be *warehouse-enabled*. Somewhere in the application (or the surrounding environment), the application must be equipped with logic which is aware that just because, for example, a customer loan payment has been processed and an update successfully made to the application's database, more remains to be done (specifically, making sure that the update is sent out into the ODS environment).

The mechanics of making a system warehouse-enabled vary widely depending on the characteristics of each system. A relatively modern client/server application that has a database with *stored procedures* (database-managed procedural logic) can be equipped, in a relatively straightforward manner, with stored procedures triggered by database updates. Each stored procedure is then responsible for using messaging or another technique (described later in this chapter) to propagate that update out to the ODS environment.

A mainframe legacy application is usually more difficult to handle. It can be modified, for example, to interface with a product such as the IBM MQSeries messaging system to enable messages to be sent between queues on different platforms. (For more information about MQSeries, point your Web browser to www.software.ibm.com/ts/mqseries/.) Or a database and files can be monitored for activity and data intercepted and sent to the ODS.

To support instantaneous data propagation into an ODS environment, the source applications and systems must be involved in order to minimize as much as possible the time lag between source update and ODS update.

Messaging

The preceding section refers to messaging as a mechanism for moving data from one environment to another. Regardless of the products and technologies you use, you should take a look at cross-system messaging architectures.

Messaging is typically an *asynchronous* means of communications from one environment to another. The source of the message (in this case, the application in which an update is being made) can continue with its own work without having to hook up with the recipient of the message. The messaging system and its associated *protocols* (a means of acknowledging the receipt of a message or detecting any associated problems) handle verification and validation services. Messaging and asynchronous communications give you a great deal of flexibility in architecting distributed environments in which you must send data back and forth across systems quickly and can't afford to tie up any one system while it waits for another to do whatever is necessary with the message.

Feedback loops

One of the main challenges you face in an ODS environment isn't as much in the technical arena (which is challenging enough!) as in business processes and how they may have to change.

Consider the example from Figures 23-1 and 23-2. Suppose that the two different source applications that handle customer credit-line payments have also traditionally been the place where new loans were approved or where a customer was permitted to act on an established line of credit.

According to the guidelines and business rules (the reason for the ODS in the first place), loan approval can't happen in those applications. Why? Because the loan system doesn't have access to all the necessary information (such as cash and other asset balances, loan activity handled by other systems, and the relationship among various customer partnerships and corporations) to make the decision according to the business rules.

You can handle this type of problem in one of two ways. The first approach is to remove that type of functionality from the source application or at least block it from being able to be used. After the ODS is in place, users of the ODS make all the yes–no loan decisions according to the business rules.

This approach is generally recommended: Make business decisions using environment support wherever it exists (in this case, in the ODS).

If organizational politics and other considerations come into play, however, you may have to take an alternative approach. Assume that your firm's chief credit officer insists that all U.S. and global loan decisions remain with credit officers using the respective systems they've been using for the past five years.

In this situation, you can enhance the enterprise with feedback loops *from* the ODS *to* one or more of the data sources, as shown in Figure 23-3. This scenario operates as follows:

1. As described earlier in this chapter, all data sources propagate all relevant updates into the ODS environment from their respective databases and files as soon as they occur.

2. The ODS still provides a consolidated picture of the state of each customer, and other nonloan decisions and information are handled through the ODS.

3. A request to act on a line of credit or take out a new loan, however, is entered into one of the three systems that handle loan processing (U.S., European short-term, and other European).

4. Each of those applications makes a request to the ODS for "advice" for that customer, and the ODS provides, based on its internal business rules, a yes–no answer about the loan in a message (as indicated by the heavier arrows in the figure).

5. The credit officer, using the regular system, either books a loan or declines it.

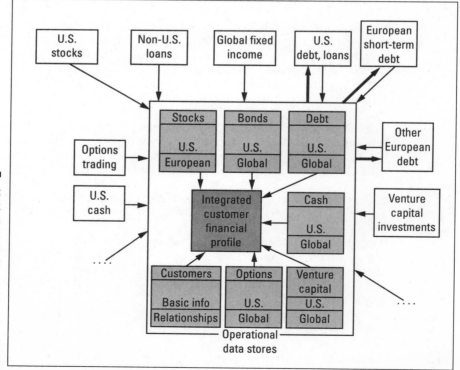

Figure 23-3:
A feedback loop sends consolidated data from the ODS, or an ODS-produced decision, back to a source application.

Feedback loops are complicated! They cause increased network traffic, and they introduce another set of cross-application, cross-system dependencies. Don't implement them in an ODS environment unless you have to.

Data message hubs

Suppose that your environment has a number of feedback loops and several different operational data stores. Suppose also that it has a great deal of source-to-source-to-source data movement: One application sends information to another application, and that application sends the information on to several other applications.

The result is typically a spider's web of communication lines that are complex to manage and maintain. An alternative approach is to implement a *data message hub* architecture (also called a *data message broker*), in which fewer hubs (perhaps only one) serve as a collection and distribution point for messages across your enterprise. Each application then *publishes* (makes available) a certain set of messages and also *subscribes* to (accesses) others that may come from other applications. Each hub keeps a list of which applications are subscribing to which messages and, after receiving any message, distributes it to the appropriate destinations.

Object-oriented technology, particularly the use of *object request brokers,* is an up-and-coming way to implement a data message hub architecture.

Chapter 24

Show Me the Pictures: Incorporating Multimedia

. . . .

In This Chapter

▶ Recognizing that today's data warehousing is limited to traditional data types

▶ Understanding that traditional data types are not enough

▶ Looking at business intelligence in an increasingly multimedia world

▶ Examining scenarios for multimedia business intelligence

. . . .

> *1f a picture paints a thousand words,*
> *then why am I stuck with tabular data?*
> *I want to access images*
> *And possibly video too.*

(Apologies to David Gates and Bread — really.)

Traditional Data Warehousing Means Analyzing Traditional Data Types

Unless you've used an extraordinary, state-of-the-art data warehouse, your business intelligence functionality has probably been limited to these types of data:

- ✔ **Numeric:** Integers and decimal numbers

- ✔ **Character:** Typically fixed-length alphanumeric information that's rarely more than about 100 characters per occurrence

- ✔ **Dates:** Either actual dates or, more likely, ranges of dates (such as a month and year for which product sales are grouped and stored)

That's about it.

To be fair, data warehousing in its original incarnation, as a storage place for information drawn from legacy applications to support reporting and analysis, hasn't needed anything other than these traditional data types.

As Bob Dylan might say, however, "The times, they are a-changin'."

"It's a Multimedia World, after All. . . ."

I have one word for you: Plastics.

Oh, wait. That was *The Graduate*. Now I remember the word:

Internet!

Fire up your web browser. Spend a few hours poking around the Internet, checking out all kinds of cool sites. (If you're at work and your boss walks in, point to this chapter and say that you're doing data warehousing research — honest!)

You can find images, video and audio clips, entry forms for filling out information to submit to a site's database, tabular results based on requests you may make — almost anything.

The lines between *structured data* (traditional data types that computer applications have been using for years) and *unstructured data* (such as multimedia documents) have blurred. It used to be that if you wanted to create a multimedia environment that included both structured and unstructured data, you loosely followed these steps:

1. Build a relational database for your structured data.

2. Use a document-management system or an image-management system for your unstructured data.

3. To handle logical links across environments, set aside in each relational database row one or more columns that point to related documents or images, as appropriate.

These environments were relatively awkward and prone to problems, such as software upgrades to one system having an adverse effect on the other (links that break, for example).

Data warehousing? Don't even try it. It has been difficult enough dealing with all the cross-source discrepancies and problems. Worry only about those areas for now, and get the warehouse up and running.

How Will Multimedia Business Intelligence Work?

Suppose that you're using a multimedia-enabled data warehousing environment to do comparative analysis between services offered by your company (a bank) and your competitors' corresponding offerings.

You run some basic reports and a few queries (refer to Chapter 9) to check out market share, portfolio performance, and other measures. Or, for more advanced analysis, you use an OLAP tool (refer to Chapter 10) to perform all kinds of drill-down analysis on the data, in an attempt to fully understand the intricacies of your company's performance with respect to your competitors.

Sometimes, though, the answers aren't in the numbers. Suppose that you've noticed a sudden increase in account closures at your bank during the past two months. What's going on?

The premise of business intelligence is exactly as the term reads: Getting as much intelligence as possible, from as many sources as possible, to help you understand what's going on and act on it. Under this broad definition, intelligence can easily include the following types of information not found in (or accessible through) a traditional data warehouse:

- A competitor's local newspaper advertisement offering no-fee checking for one year and an extra 1.5 percent earned on money-market deposits if a potential customer shows a bank statement indicating that an account at your bank has been closed

- A videotape of local television advertising with that competitor's same offer

- A link to each of your competitors' Web sites, where you can analyze the types of electronic banking services they offer

- A transcript of an interview with a regional economic expert stating that your bank is a prime takeover target and probably won't be in business under its current name at the same time next year

In this simple example, because the items occur locally or regionally, you may believe that you can access all this information from a multimedia-enabled data warehouse. ("A good banking analyst probably knows all this stuff anyway," right?)

Think about this example on a global scale, however. Are you wondering why your company's sales are slipping in Sweden? Wouldn't it be helpful to have these types of capabilities for a globally competitive situation?

I once created for a client in the chemical industry the architecture for a quasidata warehouse environment (*quasi* because it had only a single source of data but a huge amount of historical information that had to be brought into the new system).

About 80 percent of the historical information was on paper, and the client was considering eventually entering it into a document-management system. For budgetary reasons, the project phase I was involved in dealt only with the conversion of traditional historical data (character, numeric, and date information) and mapping and transformation of the new incoming data. The documents would be handled later.

It's relatively easy, however, to imagine an environment in which all this data, which dealt with the same subject matter, could be treated equally. If the data were on paper, it could be scanned in as an image, indexed by keyword, and made accessible through the same environment as the traditional data. The client's business intelligence would be tremendously increased by having access to this information. (The client agreed that the information was valuable — it just didn't know what to do with it.)

An Alternative Path: From Unstructured Information to Structured Data

The example in the preceding section demonstrates an approach of putting structured data first, in which a business analyst uses data warehousing as a gateway into appropriate unstructured supporting information.

You can just as easily take the opposite path toward a unified approach to business intelligence. Suppose that you're browsing the Internet or the company intranet and a product diagram or blueprint or some other type of image or document catches your attention. Each piece of unstructured information can just as easily provide a path for you to access an OLAP-generated report posted on the company intranet (which can, in turn, have links to point you toward other structured or unstructured information).

The structured and unstructured data barriers are breaking down quickly, as are the pathways across those softened barriers. If your work processes are traditionally collaborative in nature, performing tasks such as workflow or image management, they just as easily can be augmented to point you toward data warehousing capabilities that provide you with additional value. In contrast, the reports and query results you get and use as part of traditional analytical processing can serve as a pathway into a world of multimedia information that can supplement the data you typically handle.

Chapter 25

Virtual Data Warehousing: Hype or Trend?

Here's an analogy I've heard used to describe the idea of data warehousing and data marts.

"Your applications are manufacturers of data, and you're the consumer. Although you can run around to all these different manufacturers and pick out a few items from the first one and a few more from the second one, that would take a great deal of time and effort.

"What these manufacturers do is ship the data they've manufactured to a data warehouse, which is sort of like a wholesaler. Although you can shop for your data directly at the wholesaler's location, it's hard to find stuff there, and the wholesaler doesn't like consumers who don't 'buy in bulk.'

"So the data warehouse (the wholesaler) ships some of its contents (maybe sprucing up the data a little) to data marts, which are really retailers. That's where you have the best chance of finding the data you need, after it has been manufactured and shipped and is ready for sale."

It's not a bad analogy in that it applies a concept almost everyone is familiar with (manufacturing, distributing, and buying products) to source-to-target movement within a data warehousing environment.

One problem, however, is becoming somewhat significant.

Whereas produce and clothes and other products are physical in nature and must move to a retail outlet for people to be able to purchase them (unless shoppers want to physically go to a wholesaler or even back to the manufacturer), data is not physical, at least not in the same sense. If you had the right tools, could you access data back at its source — the application (or the manufacturer)? Certainly!

The problem has been that the right tools haven't existed. No, even that's not quite correct. Although tools have been available to provide this type of in-place access, the challenges have been more in the area of the corporate infrastructure (particularly networking bandwidth and the resulting throughput) and immature base technologies for handling cross-system data access in a timely, efficient manner.

That's all about to change, however.

Looking at the Basics of Virtual Data Warehousing

This section discusses the background of virtual data warehousing: its roots, how it has evolved, and the challenges that still exist.

Background

To best understand the idea of virtual data warehousing, think back to the second half of the 1980s, when DBMS vendors were trying to implement distributed database management systems. (This subject is discussed in Chapter 1, in the context of distributed database technology as a predecessor to the data warehousing revolution of the early 1990s.) One of the most significant stumbling blocks (a showstopper!) with distributed DBMS technology was that multisite update operations, particularly with the networking technology of the time, couldn't work in the real world because of woefully inadequate performance.

Around 1990, some of the distributed DBMS technology was being applied in a read-only manner: Information was pulled from a variety of source databases and mapped and transformed, and then the result was presented to a user. The process was similar to data warehousing, with the middleware functions (extraction, mapping, transformation, and movement, as described in Chapter 7) handled on a just-in-time basis without all the preloading.

About this time, first-generation data warehousing (again, built on batch-oriented copying and preloading of data into a separate database) began to catch on, and read-only distributed database models faded into the background.

Market repositioning

Around 1995, though, some of these vendors (who still had products to provide this read-only, just-in time functionality) began repositioning their software as *virtual data warehousing* tools. The fundamental premise was that sometimes it just doesn't make sense to copy and manipulate a bunch of data just in case someone needs it. Why not access data directly from the source on an as-needed basis?

Challenges

Alas, accessing data over a network at its source has proved to be the least challenging of the problems in trying to provide, essentially, in-place data warehousing. The same challenges faced in any data warehousing environment (such as dealing with data quality, deciding what types of transformations must occur, and choosing how to handle those transformations when different sources are inconsistent) are still present. Just because you can get to data at its source, in almost any database or file structure, doesn't mean that it provides the necessary business intelligence when it's in your hands.

Examining Why Traditional Virtual Data Warehousing Doesn't Work

The trend in bottom-up data mart construction is, in reality, a method of developing a *component-based* data warehouse. Rather than have a single database into which all data is fed (and that's your data warehouse), a series of components each handles a particular set of functions (such as answering specific business questions) or certain subjects. Together, these data marts (components) comprise a data warehousing *environment*.

This is the basis for virtual data warehousing.

The architecture

Figure 25-1 shows an environment in which individual components are created within the data warehousing environment in a bottom-up manner. Instead of the components being combined into one large database (and all the data being copied again), a data warehousing environment is created in which each component's contents can be accessed from a client's desktop tool as though they were all stored together, even though they're not.

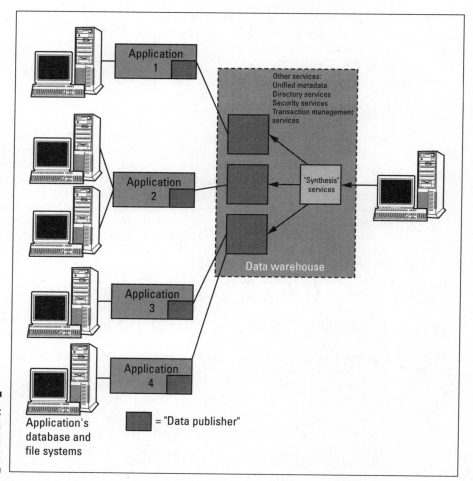

Figure 25-1:
Virtual data
warehousing
in practice.

Think about how you use a web browser on your desktop. You either click a link or type a specific URL, and the environment, working behind the scenes, takes you to the right place for the content you asked for. Now imagine the Internet running *much* faster. When you go to various sites, you're not "bringing back" ads for the latest four-wheel drive you've been coveting or sports scores or Dilbert cartoons or whatever else it is you do on the Internet. You're bringing back pieces of data that are then combined, as explained in the following section, and sent back to your browser. *That* is virtual data warehousing. It's just like the Internet!

I highly recommended that you not build a virtual data warehousing environment to access source data directly, in its native format. As mentioned earlier in this chapter, your challenge is not how to join cross-platform databases (combining IMS data with DB2 data, for example) and handling those types of system-level transformation. Your major challenge is in the area of the quality of the data and other aspects.

Each application should therefore be warehouse-enabled (refer to Chapter 23) and contain a *data publisher* that's responsible for all the middleware services, such as extraction and quality assurance, as specified in the environment's business rules. The data publisher could conceivably operate almost in real-time mode, as it would have to do in an operational data store (again, refer to Chapter 23), or it could function in a periodic (batch-oriented) mode if instantaneous updates aren't required. The data publisher would be a mini-middleware product embedded in the application (or a service accessed by the application).

When you think of virtual data warehousing, replace the question "Can I get to the data?" with the question "Can I get to *usable* data?" The data publisher plays an important role and should not be neglected.

Data architecture is another area you cannot neglect. Just because you're developing components in a bottom-up manner and they're being accessed in place rather than being copied into a larger data warehouse database doesn't mean that you can neglect this function. Suppose that one component stores customer IDs as a five-digit number after transformation occurs and contains only customers who made purchases within the past six months. Suppose also that another component contains all customers who have ever bought your company's products and uses a seven-character alphanumeric identifier. In this situation, you may have the same type of data mismatch problems as though you're accessing data directly from the sources. Although differences are permissible between component contents, you must understand and manage the differences so that you don't impede the business intelligence mission.

The synthesis service

Unlike traditional Internet usage, for example, where each hit returns information that probably won't have to be correlated with information from other hits, a virtual data warehouse may have to combine facts from one component with facts from another. (Figure 25-1 shows a synthesis service component within the virtual data warehouse.)

You could push synthesis service functionality into the client tools. Considering the trend of thinning out client software and running a great deal of functionality through a web browser, however, this approach would be counter to architectural direction.

If the data warehousing environment, which "knows" that it's virtually (remotely) accessing data from multiple sources, has a component that handles the synthesis of results from the other components, the responsibility for consolidating these independent results sets can be offloaded from the client tool.

Or, with the trend toward applets, perhaps the data warehousing environment can send a synthesis service applet to a client's web-enabled tool to perform results synthesis on the client side. It would take advantage of desktop processing without the downside of client-side storage and maintenance of the service's instructions. That's something to watch for.

Other services

The virtual data warehousing environment should include services that may typically be handled within the single database in a centralized environment. These true middleware services complement the traditional data warehousing middleware, such as extraction and transformation:

- ✔ **A unified metadata service:** Users see a single logical view of the environment's contents without having to know the location and particulars of each component.

- ✔ **A directory service:** Individual components can be found within the environment even if they're relocated or otherwise modified.

- ✔ **Security services:** These services handle permissions, authentication, and other security needs in a distributed environment.

- ✔ **Transaction-management services:** In addition to the synthesis service, which is a type of transaction-management function, these services provide routing, load balancing, conflict resolution, and other functions necessary to ensure data integrity. (Yes, these services are also necessary even in a supposedly read-only environment.)

Facing the Infrastructure Challenge

Wow! Virtual data warehousing sounds like a fairly neat, state-of-the-art idea. How come it isn't more widespread?

The answer, in a word, is infrastructure. Although you can talk all you want about emerging networking and communications technologies and the tremendous throughput we all will have someday, most corporations are still several generations behind the state of the art in their networking infrastructure. They're struggling to deal with the major investment required for what is essentially the Internet and Distributed Computing Age.

Virtual data warehousing requires significant throughput of data in what is often an unpredictable manner. (This statement usually causes a network administrator to shudder and then break down and cry.) The irony is that a virtual data warehousing environment almost assuredly requires, over time, significantly less data movement across the enterprise than traditional data warehousing with its philosophy of copying millions (perhaps billions) of bytes, just in case someone wants to ask a question possibly requiring that data.

Traditional data warehousing has the advantage, however, of working the clock (as they say in football) by scheduling large-scale batch loads for either system downtimes or at least relatively light operational loads, using offline data-transfer means (tape, for example) rather than network file transfers and other tricks of the trade.

Until an organization's communications infrastructure can pump the data through, virtual data warehousing probably will remain on the fringes, just out of reach.

Making Virtual Data Warehousing a Reality in Your Organization

If you're interested in virtual data warehousing as an architecture of the future, here's a list of what you have to do:

✔ **Supercharge your networking infrastructure.** Yes, it's expensive, but you gotta do what you gotta do.

✔ **Stop thinking about data warehousing in centralized terms.** Think distributed. Free your mind!

✔ **Insist that any new application developed for your organization, no matter who does it, is warehouse-enabled.** Although the application doesn't necessarily have to pump out data in real-time to an ODS (though if you need an ODS, that would probably be a good idea), it should be capable of doing the necessary data publishing service functions.

✔ **Think enterprise!** Just because you're dealing with bottom-up component development doesn't mean that you're developing a stand-alone piece of data. The last thing you want to wind up with is an "islands of data mart" problem to replace the "islands of data" situation you've been dealing with your entire career. (I *know* that you have because we all have.) In a traditional data warehousing environment, you're forced to deal with these enterprise-scale data architecture issues. Don't let your foray into virtual data warehousing undermine all the good that has taken place in your organization in dealing with this problem.

Part VII
The Part of Tens

The 5th Wave

By Rich Tennant

WHILE SEEKING HER PC-BASED RECIPE INDEX, DEBBY INADVERTENTLY LOADS A CAD PROGRAM. INSTEAD OF MAKING CHERRIES JUBILEE, SHE BUILDS A SUBOCEANIC DIVING PROBE.

In this part . . .

1 f you want easy-to-access, succinct advice about many different data warehousing topics, this part of the book is for you.

Chapter 26

Ten Vital "Deliverables" for the End of Your Project Scope

*T*he first phase of your data warehousing project should be its *scope,* in which you discuss and finalize these elements:

  ✔ The functionality your data warehouse will provide

  ✔ The data necessary to support that functionality

  ✔ The sources you have to access to obtain that data

  ✔ Your next steps

Following the completion of the project scope, you move directly into the design phase.

Wait — not so fast!

This chapter presents a checklist of "deliverables" you *absolutely* must produce by the end of the scope phase, before moving into the design phase. Some of these elements are tangible, such as a design-phase project plan; others, such as consensus about the mission, are intangible. The intangible deliverables are just as important and essential as the tangible ones; make sure that you take care of *all* these elements.

A Complete, Prioritized List of Functionality to Be Provided

One of the biggest mistakes you can make during your project scope is to concentrate solely on data needs and neglect functionality. You *must* focus on functionality as a framework in which you can determine *real* data needs, not just the ones that are good to have.

Furthermore, you must prioritize this list of functionality because you're likely to implement your data warehouse's features in several different *iterations* (back-to-back mini-projects that each add new capabilities). You must identify the most important functionality, therefore, for early implementation.

You need the data requirements too, of course. After you identify the functionality, the data follows in a fairly natural way.

A Complete List of All Candidate Data Sources

Even though you don't start digging into your data sources until the design phase begins, you must have a list of (and, preferably, some basic information about) all the data sources that will provide data to your warehouse. Without this complete list, creating your design phase project plan is almost impossible, as discussed in the following section.

A Design-Phase Project Plan

When you know the project's functionality and its data needs and you've identified its data sources, you have a darn good framework for setting up your project plan — a *detailed* project plan — for the design phase of your project. While you're still working on and finalizing its scope, put together the project plan for team review; this way, you can catch and handle any surprises or problems early, before you begin the design phase.

The Names and Respective Roles of Your Design-Phase Project Team

You gotta have your team lined up! Although your team may not be the same one that just went through the scope phase and may change even more as you move into construction of the data warehouse (after the design phase), you need team members' names, roles, skill levels, and availability, such as their vacation and training plans and whether they're available 100 percent of the time.

A Complete Budgetary Estimate

After you complete each phase, which tells you what you need to know for the following phase, you then can create project plans, set your budget, and line up your team, for example.

As you probably know, however, corporate life isn't quite that simple. The phrase *budgetary estimate* strikes fear in most data warehouse implementers because you're told, "Yeah, yeah, I know about your phased methodology and all that, but how much will this whole thing cost me?"

Whether you like it or not, many projects are make-or-break early in their life cycle (during the scope phase) based on whether their executive sponsor has the funds to see the project to completion. Corporate leaders believe that they shouldn't waste funds on projects that will survive, for example, only through the design phase and part of the construction phase — but maybe not all the way to the end of construction. (That belief is based on a great deal of logic because the performance of managers and executives is often measured on the tangible benefits they deliver to their organization.)

You have to listen to your "gut feeling," therefore — based on what you've learned during the scope phase — and call on all your past experience, play all kinds of what-if scenarios, and come up with a general range for the *probable* total cost of the data warehouse. Even if you have not been specifically requested to provide this information, at least have it prepared, just in case — you won't be sorry.

Consensus about the Mission

The mission of the data warehouse is more than just focusing on various points of functionality; it's basically the answer to the question (as discussed in Chapter 1), "Why bother creating the data warehouse?"

The mission must have universal consensus among your organization's business community (or as close to it as possible). Without it, organizational politics usually overcome any progress you make down the development road, and your data warehousing project gets pulled into a quagmire that looks like something from a prime-time network soap opera. (Remember *Dynasty,* from the good old days of the 1980s?)

Risk Assessment and a Plan to Manage Risk

Suppose that you've spent two or three weeks (or however long the project scope is) discussing and picking apart functionality and the data necessary to support it. You've discussed data sources and have heard a little about the level of difficulty in extracting information from each one. You've listened to team members and now have a good idea about their respective positions, agendas, and other attributes. Now you have an idea about what will occur during the design phase.

So how risky is this project? You have to catalog all these tangible and intangible factors, look at their potential effect, and then identify ways to manage and control any risk that exists.

Then you're ready to proceed.

A Gap Analysis

So what's missing? What data sources have you identified even though you weren't able to find anyone who knows anything about them? What organization's scheduling conflicts kept its members from participating in the scope phase (but you were directed to proceed anyway)? Are you uncertain whether their business requirements have been handled adequately? What data has been identified as absolutely critical for the data warehouse but apparently isn't stored anywhere in the enterprise?

These and other missing elements must be collected and reported as a *gap analysis* along with a plan to handle these issues.

Tentative Executive-Level Support

The executive sponsor from the business side (the person controlling the funding who represents the data warehousing project to the company's executive board) must be "onboard" with what's going on with the project. This statement is true for not just the upcoming design phase but also for the entire project.

You should try to have a conversation in which the executive sponsor makes a commitment to you that unless something out of the ordinary occurs, the project will be supported to its completion. This conversation should take place near the end of the project scope phase, when you have tangible results to indicate the project's viability.

Logistical Requirements and Support Plans

Few things are more frustrating in a development effort of any kind as entering a phase of activity in which you need office space, computers, software, and other support tools. The worst part is when you not only don't have them but also don't know when, or whether, you ever will.

Use the time during the scope phase to line up everything you need. You don't want the design-phase clock to start ticking without having everything you need in place or a *guarantee* that everything will be in place when you need it.

Chapter 27

Ten Questions to Consider When You're Selecting User Tools

*F*ew things are more frustrating than successfully building a data warehouse and then having it rendered unusable by less-than-satisfactory user tools. This chapter presents some questions to consider when you're evaluating tools you're considering purchasing.

Can Users Easily Build Their Own Query and Report Screens?

In most data warehousing environments, a substantial number of report and query screens and templates are common to a significant portion of the user community, and the development team builds these capabilities for the users. At the same time, though, to avoid creating a backlog of requests that the support staff cannot easily handle, users *must* be able to create and use their own queries and reports.

While you're evaluating a tool, find two users who have no experience in user reporting and querying products and a third user who has used another product but not the one you're considering. A few days before you run your usability test, give the tutorial documentation (the written version) to only one of the users with no experience. Then have all three people try to solve two or three business problems of varying difficulty by creating a query or report with the tool. See how they do!

Can a User Stop a Runaway Query or Report?

Almost every user tool occasionally submits a query (or performs some other type of operation, such as running a report) that keeps going, and going, and going. . . .

A user tool *must* give users a way to stop this type of query or report gracefully, without doing any of the following:

- ✔ Locking up the user's desktop PC and forcing him or her to have to turn it off or reboot
- ✔ Interfering with other users' work (by having to halt the database server and restart it, for example)
- ✔ Otherwise causing a disruption in business as usual

Check out each product, and make sure that *any* user can stop the runaway query or report from a desktop PC.

How Does Performance Differ with Varying Amounts of Data?

You may have determined during the project scope that your data warehouse will start with 5 gigabytes of data, for example, and grow to 50 gigabytes during the next two years. It pays to know, however, how each tool will perform with not only the initial 5 gigabytes and the eventual target but also with 100 or even 200 gigabytes, just in case.

In case of what? Here are just a few possibilities:

- ✔ New data sources no one could foresee during the project scope
- ✔ A decision to add an increased level of detail to the data
- ✔ A decision not to delete old data but rather to keep it in the data warehouse

If your data warehouse will never approach terabyte-size (a trillion bytes of data), don't worry about how a tool performs with that much data — it's irrelevant. What's more significant is whether the tool will perform as well (or nearly as well) with 50 gigabytes of data as it does with its initial 5 gigabytes.

 Performance is not a tool-only situation; it also depends on the DBMS you use, how you design your database, and many other factors. Ask your questions in an environment as close as possible to what is available during production.

Can Users Access Different Databases?

I'm talking about different databases of information from the same tool, not necessarily different DBMS products. For example, a user may access the regular data mart stored on a local Windows NT server for most queries and reports and, by using the same tool, have access to this information:

- ✔ Another department's data mart, for occasional queries
- ✔ The organization's main data warehouse
- ✔ An external data provider over the Internet

The main point is that users should *not* have to switch tools to perform similar functions (basic querying and reporting or OLAP, for example) against different data sources.

Can Data Definitions Be Easily Changed?

Although the process of getting the first set of data definitions up and running is fairly easy in most user tools, how about when modifications have to be made?

✔ How easy is it to update your entire user community's data definitions, and how long does it take? (Do you have 100 users? One thousand? Five thousand?)

✔ What has to happen to modify queries and reports which use data that no longer exists or data that has had its structure (its data type and size, for example) modified?

✔ What happens to scripts and programs that are part of the tool?

Does the Tool Fit into Your Organization's Standard Desktop Configuration?

If you've ever dealt with oh-so-crowded PC desktops (crowded with a bunch of software programs, not papers and coffee cups), the term *DLL clash* is probably familiar to you. (DLL means *dynamic link library*.)

Considering that most organizations have internal standards for their client PCs, the process of figuring out how well a tool fits into your standard configuration should be straightforward. Assuming that the product runs on your desktop operating system (always a showstopper if it doesn't), you should consider these issues:

✔ How well the connectivity and interoperability software you need (such as ODBC, or *Open Database Connectivity,* drivers) work

✔ Whether the software should be loaded in any special order

✔ When you have choices about where certain components of a tool can reside (on each client, for example, or located once on each server), the recommended configuration and, in your environment, whether any problems exist

Whatever it takes, find the most obvious PC geek in your organization — the one who reads *Byte* magazine and four or five others from cover to cover each month and who has an elegantly framed picture of Bill Gates in a place of honor at home. Have that person check out configuration issues for each tool you're evaluating.

How Does Performance Change with a Large Number of Users?

You have to know how performance changes when the number of users increases. Although you should see little or no performance effect if a tool's environment is designed correctly and efficiently, you want to make sure.

What Online Help and Assistance Is Available, and How Good Is It?

Are wizards available? A tutorial? Context-sensitive help? Templates for queries and reports that can be used?

Does the Tool Support Interfaces to Other Products?

Here's something that's unlikely to change for many years: The desktop analysis tool of choice is the handy-dandy, trusted spreadsheet program. Although some OLAP products feature direct interfaces from their database into a spreadsheet (typically Microsoft Excel), even if you will use a product's reporting and querying capabilities, users should always be able to bring data back and pop it into Excel for more analysis, manipulation, or whatever they want to do.

Reports generally should be capable of being included in word-processing documents or graphics and presentation programs (for example, Microsoft Word and PowerPoint, respectively), into a personal database (such as Microsoft Access), and, of course, into a spreadsheet.

What Happens When You Pull the Plug?

Go ahead — try it. In the middle of a query or report, turn off your PC and see what happens. You want to ensure not only that users can restart a desktop PC without any leftover configuration problems (for example, temporary files and workspace errors that prevent additional work from being done until they're cleaned up) but also that the interruption doesn't affect your warehouse's database (and any intermediate servers).

Chapter 28

Ten Secrets to Managing a Project Successfully

*B*eing a successful data warehouse project manager means that you have to do more — much more — than simply create project plans and ask team members to turn in weekly status reports. This chapter presents the secrets to success.

Tell It Like It Is

It doesn't matter whether you're working with users, executive sponsors, consultants, vendors, team members, or anyone else. The most important thing you can do to set the groundwork for successfully managing a data warehousing project is to speak your mind in a completely honest manner.

You don't have to be abrupt or rude or have the attitude of "It's my way or no way." You should follow these guidelines, however:

- When problems occur, don't bury them or pretend that they don't exist. Other people know about the problems, so deal with them aggressively.

- Don't be afraid to tell an executive sponsor that your project will be adversely affected by those out-of-the-blue budget cuts or the absence of those three team members who have been reassigned for "just a little while."

- Don't hesitate to tell a vendor when a product isn't performing as promised and to demand that something be done about it.

The key: Communicate quickly and openly and with integrity. You won't be sorry.

Put the Right People in the Right Roles

The right person in the right role is an important key to project success.

You have to recognize that the best database designer may be somewhat challenged when it comes to working with front-end OLAP or data mining tools. The person who can do whiz-bang tasks with a particular OLAP tool may be a lousy facilitator and should, during the scope phase of a project (refer to Chapter 13), either sit silently in the back of the room or just not even be there.

Be a Tough but Fair Negotiator

Budget cuts, pressures to compress the development schedule, vendor support, working with the corporate infrastructure group to line up installation and rollout support — all these issues, and many more, usually are the responsibility of the project manager. The manager must ensure that these tasks, which all involve negotiation, take place. After you "tell it like it is," as discussed at the beginning of this chapter, you establish the groundwork for tough, fair negotiations that are grounded in reality, not in emotion or speculation. Don't be afraid to negotiate from this basis: "If X happens, Y will be the result."

Deal Carefully with Product Vendors

Be careful when you gather information from vendors and other sources, as described in Chapter 20, and when you question a vendor about a product, as explained in Chapter 33. Recognize that vendors want to sell you products, not solve your business problems. Although it's great when they can do both, your priorities are not the vendors' priorities.

It's *your* project. Don't be pushed into making product decisions that aren't in your best interest.

Watch the Project Plan

Although I firmly believe that being a good project manager means more than just tracking how the project schedule is going, you can't ignore the project plan.

If you're not interested in gathering team members' regular submissions to help keep your project plan up to date, add to your team a project-control staff member who has the specific task of managing the project plan. Work with a local college or university to get a work-study or cooperative education (co-op) student; it's a cost-effective way to handle this important task.

Don't Micromanage

Everyone has a particular management style. Some people focus on delegating tasks, and others are more hands-on. If you're the type who likes to handle most things yourself, the advice in this section is for you.

Don't *micromanage*, or insist on knowing every little detail about every task that everyone is doing. (That panicky, out-of-control feeling will go away.) Even on smaller projects, trust your developers and analysts to know their jobs. Check in on them to see how they're doing, and make sure that they're progressing on schedule. Let them do their jobs, though, especially on larger projects. You have enough to worry about as a project manager; don't take on additional worries that team members usually can resolve for you.

Use a Project Notebook

Start off every project with a comprehensive project notebook that you distribute to every member of your extended team (not only the developers and key users but also the executive sponsors). The notebook should have these items:

- ✔ Copies of key memos
- ✔ A description of earlier work done on the data warehousing project (prototypes, for example)
- ✔ A summary of discussions you've already had with vendors
- ✔ High-level statements of requirements
- ✔ Whatever else is necessary to ensure that the notebook represents the *complete* picture of what you're trying to accomplish

Even if your organization has a fantastic *intranet* (an Internet environment inside the company) or a widely used Lotus Notes (or other type of group-ware) environment, hand out printed, bound notebooks. You can't assume that everything you need is available in electronic form (it usually isn't) or that every person who needs to use the project notebook uses a computer with equivalent enthusiasm (they don't). Be sure to have enough copies of a printed notebook available at your kickoff meeting so that no one gets left out.

Don't Overlook the Effect of Organizational Culture

Suppose that you work for a consulting firm whose employees typically work 50 or 60 hours each week on projects. You're assigned to be the project manager for a client's data warehousing effort and will manage a team composed of four members from your company and four from the client's. You develop an aggressive (but realistic) project plan, based on the client's budget and time constraints, that will likely involve some late-night and weekend work. (That concept is nothing new to your company's employees.)

Suppose, however, that your client's employees won't even consider working more than 40 hours a week. Now what?

Although you can factor this attitude into the workload of the client's team members as best you can, you have to consider other factors too:

✔ If your client insists on having responsibility for database builds and rebuilds, who will handle those tasks if they have to be done over the weekend or late at night during a critical stage of development?

✔ When the unavoidable project hiccups occur (and you had better believe that they will), will your client's team members be as likely as your firm's team members to give a little more effort?

Don't overlook the impact of organizational culture on the project you're managing, especially if you're an outsider (a consultant, for example, or someone from another company who's working on a joint cross-company data warehousing project).

Don't Forget about Deployment and Operations

Design and development are difficult enough for a data warehouse (or any environment, for that matter). Don't overlook how the results of your work will function in the real world, with real users. Make sure that your project plan allows time for lining up support after the data warehouse "goes live."

Take a Breather Occasionally

Insist that everyone leave early on Friday after a particularly hard week. Don't sneer and scowl when team members tell you that they want to go to the company picnic when you're a day or two behind schedule with three weeks to go.

It's only work. By taking an occasional breather, you (and your team members) become reinvigorated, and productivity increases. It's well worth your while to take off a weekend here and there or to spend slightly fewer hours working overtime.

Chapter 29

Ten Sources of Up-to-Date Information about Data Warehousing

In This Chapter

▶ Specialized data warehousing Web sites

▶ Industry analysts' Web sites

▶ Product vendors' Web sites

*Y*ou probably won't be surprised to hear that the term *up to date* means "go look on the Internet." It's worth your time to check out the Web sites in this chapter.

The Data Warehousing Institute

www.dw-institute.com

At the Data Warehousing Institute's comprehensive site, you can find these items:

✔ Press releases

✔ Upcoming events

✔ White papers, including links to white papers at other sites

✔ Case studies

✔ A directory of vendors

✔ Best practices (learn about how others have succeeded in various data warehousing categories)

The Data Warehousing Information Center

> `pwp.starnetinc.com/larryg/index.html`

At the Data Warehousing Information Center, you can learn about data warehousing and decision-support technology, find links to a variety of other sites, and provide the site's operator, Larry Greenfield, of LGI Systems, Inc., a place for "rants and raves" (his words) about data warehousing and decision support.

The site has tables of various tool categories and products in those categories, along with links to the vendors' respective sites. It also has links to white papers, articles, periodicals, conferences, and many other services.

The OLAP Report

> `www.olapreport.com`

The OLAP Report is published by Business Intelligence, Ltd., a subscription service. This Web site has information available for nonsubscribers, including

- A glossary
- A paper about the origins of OLAP
- Market analysis

Subscribers have access to product reviews, case studies and other types of analysis, and other material.

Datamation

> `www.datamation.com/PlugIn/workbench/olap/olap.htm`

The Datamation site has articles, interviews, white papers, and resources about OLAP.

data-warehouse.com

`www.data-warehouse.com`

The site has a variety of information about data warehousing, including company success stories, articles, and discussion forums.

Data Warehousing on the World Wide Web

`www.datawarehousing.com`

This site (that's its name in the heading) documents information on the Internet that's related to data warehousing. The site is sponsored by Data Mirror and has links to companies, papers and articles, directories, and list servers (with subscription information).

The International Data Warehousing Association

`www.idwa.org`

The International Data Warehousing Association Web site features online conferences and other material available to the general public, in addition to reference pages and newsletter articles available only to members.

Industry Analysts' Web Sites

You can get information about data warehousing, and the IT industry in general, from sites run by some of the leading industry analysts:

- ✔ **META Group:** `www.metagroup.com`
- ✔ **Gartner Group:** `www.gartner.com/default.html`
- ✔ **International Data Corporation (IDC) Research:** `www.idcresearch.com`
- ✔ **Forrester Research:** `www.forrester.com`

Cambridge Technology Partners

`www.ctp.com`

Okay, although it's sort of a shameless plug, the Web site for Cambridge Technology Partners (my employer) has links to data warehousing pages for information about technology, tutorials, white papers and position papers, methodology, and other data warehousing information.

Product Vendors' Web Sites

Hundreds, if not thousands, of these sites exist. Although the vendors are dedicated to selling their respective products, lots of their sites have white papers, late-breaking news about their products and features, and other worthwhile material.

In addition to using a search engine to find these sites, many of the Web sites listed in this chapter have links to vendor sites.

Chapter 30

Ten Mandatory Skills for a Data Warehousing Consultant

A good data warehousing consultant has certain abilities in dealing with people and a knowledge of various aspects of data warehousing. This chapter lets you in on a few tips.

Broad Vision

Even a data warehousing consultant who is an expert in a particular area (star schema design in a relational database in support of OLAP functionality, for example) should have a broad vision in at least these areas:

- ✔ Overall end-to-end data warehousing architecture, from tools to middleware

- ✔ An understanding of client/server and web-based computing architectures

- ✔ Skills in digging through data sources to see what's *really* there

Because the components of a data warehousing environment are interrelated, a consultant must be able to not only provide technical expertise in one or two areas of a project but also see the big picture.

Deep Technical Expertise in One or Two Areas

If you're going to pay the big bucks for a consultant who claims to be a data warehousing expert, that person must a true expert. More specifically, a consultant should be able to claim, proudly *and accurately,* to be the *best* in one or two areas (database design and front-end tools, for example).

Communications Skills

"Um, well, you know, I think that, uh, that requirement the guy in back mentioned, like, last week, right? You know, like, what were we talking about?"

Although a consultant's written and verbal grammar doesn't have to be perfect (an occasional dangling modifier is okay), even the most technically astute consultant must be able to convey ideas and understand what others are communicating. It's critical!

The Ability to Analyze Data Sources

A consultant should *never* design the necessary transformations for a data warehouse (refer to Chapter 7) solely by using listings of data structures and definitions provided by the keepers of an application or the IT department. A consultant must be able to dig into source databases, even if it's only in a secondary role. For example, even a consultant who isn't the primary source data analyst may have to figure out why the OLAP tool returns strange results.

The Ability to Distinguish between Requirements and Wishes

A consultant's ability to distinguish between user requirements and wishes is important primarily in working on the scope (the first phase) of a data warehousing project. A disparate group of users is likely to bombard you with cries of "I need this!" and "I want that!" During crunch time, good facilitation and negotiation skills are essential when functionality has to be cut from the list or at least deferred until the next version of the data warehouse.

Conflict-Resolution Skills

No matter what role a consultant plays, from project manager to data analyst to quality assurance (QA) specialist, that person is an outsider to the members of an organization — and someone from the client company is almost always resentful of the outsider's "intrusion." A consultant on a data warehousing project (or any other project, for that matter) must identify these situations early and do the best possible job of diffusing any conflict that threatens to destroy a project.

Shameless plug: If you're a consultant, you can learn all about how to gain these skills, and much more, in *How to Be a Successful Computer Consultant,* Fourth Edition (available from McGraw-Hill Book Company in late 1997). It's the first book I ever wrote, back in 1985, and it's still going strong!

An Early-Warning System

A consultant should also act as an early-warning system to identify and report problems to you, the client, so that you can deal with them. The consultant shouldn't be a snitch or a "rat," but should be more than just a nose-to-the-grindstone technician. Because this person is an outsider and not involved (you hope!) in your internal organizational politics, he or she should have some freedom to notify you of problems.

A consultant whose organization has problems (another consultant who isn't performing up to par, for example) may not feel free to let you know about problems. That's where your company's people should also act as an early-warning sign for the consulting organization's staff members. (That's why conflict-resolution skills are so important!)

General Systems and Application Development Knowledge

As data warehousing and mainstream computing continue to converge, an increasing number of warehouses will be built using distributed objects; the use of messaging and other data-movement technologies for near-real-time business intelligence will increase; and lots of other capabilities that weren't part of your typical first-generation data warehousing environment will develop. A consultant with strong skills should have at least a working knowledge of these areas, in addition to basic programming skills and other abilities.

The Know-How to Find Up-to-Date Information

From data warehousing product bug fixes to information about the latest architectural trends, a good consultant knows how to find up-to-date information quickly — in time to be put to good use on your data warehousing project.

A Hypefree Vocabulary

Because it's almost impossible to avoid catchy buzzwords (can you say data mart?) in the data warehousing world, don't hold it against a consultant (or anyone else) who uses these phrases. I'm generally wary of consultants who sound like they went to a trade show and met up with the data warehousing pod people: "Don't be afraid. Join us for some neural network data mining that uses subject-oriented data to give you predictive pattern recognition — we are your friends!"

Chapter 31

Ten Signs of a Data Warehousing Project in Trouble

The obvious way to tell that your data warehousing project is in trouble is when you don't have anything to show for your efforts and you thought that you would. You should try to get some indication that trouble is brewing, however, *before* you reach that point. This chapter presents ten early warning signs.

The Project's Scope Phase Ends with No General Consensus

The allotted time for the scope phase of your data warehousing project ends (usually two or three weeks and a little longer for larger projects), and the members of your constituency are unhappy. They're still grumbling and disagreeing about the project's direction and its potential business value (or lack thereof), the relative priorities of capabilities and how they map to various project phases, and other points of contention.

You're in trouble.

The Mission Statement Gets Questioned after the Scope Phase Ends

You're three weeks into the design phase, following a four-week scope. You're in an all-morning status meeting with the IT and business organization executive sponsors and four key managers from the business groups who will be the data warehouse's main users.

Just before a coffee break, one of the managers says, "You know that mission statement we talked about on the second day of the project? I want to talk about that some more because I have some problems with it."

You're in trouble.

Tools Are Selected without Adequate Research

A project decision-maker looks around the room in disgust, sighs deeply, and says, "Look, we just don't have time to check out these tools because the schedule is too tight. That vendor who was in here yesterday — what was that company's name again? You know, the ones with the product that — I can't remember all the details. Anyway, I liked their demo. We'll buy that tool."

You're *probably* in trouble.

People Get Pulled from Your Team for "Just a Few Days"

"I'm going to borrow Mary, John, and Sue Ellen for a couple of days because we have something important over in the shoelace plastic-tips division that must get done as soon as possible. Anyway, I think that it will be for only a few days. Try to stay on schedule."

You're in trouble.

You're Overruled When You Attempt to Handle Scope Creep

You're in the last week of the design phase, and a business unit manager sits down across from you in the cafeteria. Between mouthfuls of Chef's Daily Surprise, he tells you about "these one or two things I just thought of that would make this data warehouse thing work much better." You politely explain the concept of scope creep in the context of "Wait until the %$#^@ next phase of the data warehouse!" (except that you're more diplomatic about it). Then, two days later, the manager's boss (who also happens to be your boss) sends an e-mail message directing you to "add those one or two things to the features list, but don't let them affect the schedule."

You're in trouble.

Your Executive Sponsor Leaves the Company

You've done a fantastic job of selling the business value of your data warehousing project to executive management, and everything is rolling along nicely. Suddenly, two days after a stunning announcement of disappointing quarterly sales and earnings, the executive sponsor from the business side of the organization resigns. Your project is now without an executive sponsor.

You *may* be in trouble: Work fast, and don't look back.

You Overhear, "This Will Never Work, but I'm Not Saying Anything"

Everyone in the company is supportive of your data warehousing project. You're pushing the cutting edge of technology, and everyone on your team is enthused. Their weekly status reports even reflect the progress they're making. The project's chief architect assures you that the more you get into the project, the more everyone is convinced that sound technical decisions have been made.

Then, in the cafeteria, you overhear two of the more senior developers discussing the project. One says, "There's no way that this thing can work. Performance is terrible, and half the time the same query against the same data returns different results! But I'm not going to be the one to bring it up!"

You're in trouble.

You Find a Major "Uh-Oh" in One of the Products You're Using

Despite your best efforts at product evaluation, something has slipped through the cracks, and a major feature simply doesn't work. Although one workaround is available, it's a major hit against performance. The vendor's representatives slyly say, "Well, we had heard that it may be a problem. Our development organization is looking into it and will probably make a patch available in the next month or so."

You're in trouble.

The IT Organization Responsible for Supporting the Project Pulls Its Support

Your development group is in charge of most of the data warehousing development, including the OLAP and reporting front ends and the database definitions. The IT organization, though, is responsible for creating the databases and performing the loading routines; performing the backup and restore procedures; and taking care of many of the project's other infrastructure elements.

Because of higher priorities, the IT organization pulls the people responsible for supporting your project, and their manager promises to "look into another answer." She says, "Maybe we'll hire a couple of contractors, but I won't be able to look into that until next week."

You're in trouble.

Resignations Begin

Resignations are a sure sign that major problems lie ahead. Even people who are unhappy with a company often give in to loyalty or a sense of duty and stick around until the completion of a project. (Or maybe they just want the résumé fodder.)

When a number of people resign in the middle of a project, however, you're in trouble.

Chapter 32

Ten Signs of a Successful Data Warehousing Project

As mentioned elsewhere in this book, just because everyone gathers in the company cafeteria for cake and plasters the walls with congratulatory banners doesn't mean that your data warehousing project was a success. Here's how to tell that you were *really* successful.

The Executive Sponsor Says, "This Thing Works — It Really Works!"

Suppose that a senior executive at your company makes it a point to find you and tell you that you did a great job *and* that you're a nice person *and* that the data warehouse you built and delivered really works and is being used. The executive even points out that the warehouse is delivering information that is being factored into boardroom-level decisions.

You've succeeded!

You Receive a Flood of Suggested Enhancements and Additional Capabilities

Sometimes, after the celebratory party in the cafeteria (can you tell that that's one of my favorite cynicism-tinged themes?), a data warehouse slowly fades away like an old soldier. (Quiz: Who used a similar phrase, to what audience, and in what year?)

Users and their managers may bang on your office door (or, more likely, invade your cubicle) wanting to show you memo pads with sketches of additional reports and queries they want and asking questions such as "How hard would it be to add this feature?"

You've succeeded!

User Group Meetings Are Almost Full

Your company should always organize a data warehouse user group in which issues such as training, enhancement requests, and tips and tricks for using query tools can be discussed and handled in a coordinated manner.

User group meetings that are often canceled because of a lack of interest are a good indication that few people are using the data warehouse. In contrast, regular user group meetings that are packed are a strong indication that . . . you've succeeded!

The User Base Keeps Growing and Growing and Growing

You start off with an initial user community of 50 business area analysts. Two months later, another 50 are added. During the next six months, an additional 150 users, including several in executive management, join the "family."

You've succeeded!

The Executive Sponsor Cheerfully Volunteers Your Company As a Reference Site

Your executive sponsor is so enamored with the data warehouse that management wants your company to serve as a reference for product vendors and for the outside consulting company that worked with you to build it.

You've succeeded!

The Company CEO Asks, "How Can I Get One of Those Things?"

The big cheese wants the OLAP tool (or at least an Executive Dashboard System) installed on the PC in the executive suite and requests a weekly hour-long private session with a member of the data warehousing support staff to answer specific questions.

You've succeeded!

The Response to Your Next Funding Request Is "Whatever You Need — It's Yours"

Corporations are notorious for this type of funding policy: "Don't tell us what you did yesterday. Tell us what you'll do tomorrow *if* we deem you worthy to send funding your way, and don't you dare fail to deliver because you and your résumé will be on the street faster than — ."

Sorry, I digress. Anyway, suppose that your data warehouse is so popular and held in such high esteem that you're given a "blank check" for your next project.

You've succeeded!

You Get Promoted — and So Do Some of Your Team Members

Nothing says lovin' in the corporate world like flowers — and a promotion. Suppose that the job you did on your data warehouse leads directly to a promotion for you *and* for other members of your team.

You've succeeded!

You Achieve Celebrity Status in the Company

Company employees stop you in the hallway or invite you to lunch to ask your opinion about technology, development methods, and all sorts of other subjects. Although you're not quite at the level of rock star or professional athlete, with groupies and all, diners in the cafeteria point toward your table and whisper, "That's the one!"

You've succeeded!

You Get Your Picture on the Cover of Rolling Stone

It won't happen, but you would *know* that you've truly succeeded!

Chapter 33

Ten Subject Areas to Cover with Product Vendors

*V*endors. Can't live with 'em; can't — oh, never mind. I can't think of any particular witticism right now. Maybe I should have a contest: Whoever sends me the best conclusion to that phrase wins a mention in the Acknowledgments in a future, updated edition of *Data Warehousing For Dummies*. (You'll probably stay up nights working diligently on that one!)

Anyway, this chapter presents ten subject areas you should discuss with *any* data warehousing product vendor, no matter which product category (OLAP tool, middleware tool, or DBMS, for example) you're considering buying. I've also listed the specific question or questions you may want to ask. You'll probably notice that all these questions are somewhat odd because they have little to do with product features and how they work; if you do a good job of hands-on evaluation of the products, you can figure out how the features will work. Although the questions are more along the lines of "Let's figure out your company's character," in my opinion, they're *extremely* important.

The Product's Chief Architect

Who is your product's chief architect, and what is this person's background?

Most companies have a single individual who is primarily responsible for crafting and setting a product's technical direction. This person is often *not* the same as the "company visionary," who may be, after all, the CEO with a business background who has seen a market need and is now trying to fill it.

The person you're asking about is the one whose imprint is all over the product. Learn as much as you can about this person's background and experience and other information.

 If the current chief architect is not the original chief architect, ask what happened to that person. It's not a good sign when a person who probably had a decent compensation package and attractive stock options is no longer with a company, especially a relatively new one.

The Development Team

How big is your development team, and how does it compare with last year's?

Here are some guidelines to consider when you ask this question:

- A relatively small development staff (for example, five or six people for a commercial product) may indicate skimpy quality assurance (QA) and product testing. It may also indicate that the vendor (or its financial backers) is taking a wait-and-see attitude toward the product before pumping in more funds. You may also see other signs that a less-than-full-scale, bet-the-company commitment is being made to the product.

- A development team that's the same size or — worse — smaller than it was a year earlier most likely indicates internal concern about the product's market viability.

- A development team that's significantly larger than it was a year earlier indicates enthusiasm for the product's chances and viability in the marketplace.

Customer Feedback

How have you addressed the top three customer complaints about the preceding version of this product?

Vendors have customer-support service organizations and call centers and should know the answer to this question. (If they don't, consider it a bad sign.)

You should determine whether customer complaints occur in clusters according to specific feature, performance, connectivity, or whatever — and then determine the company's reaction and responsiveness.

Employee Retention

How high was employee turnover in the past year?

Pay attention to this indicator of a company's internal mood, especially if it's a relatively young company that hasn't gone public yet. Few people leave a growing company in which a big payoff waits around the corner.

The Marketplace

Which one company do you see as your chief competitor?

A vendor usually targets one company as its chief competitor and strives to overtake it. Or, if a vendor is the industry leader, it may just try to stay ahead of the latest up-and-comer.

You can learn a great deal from the way this question is answered.

If a vendor responds, "We really don't have any competitors," it's either blissfully ignorant or arrogant. Either way, watch out!

Product Uniqueness

What are the three most significant innovations in your product?

In what is often described as a *commodity product marketplace,* vendors' products are pretty much the same in terms of features and capabilities. Competition is usually based on price and other basic attributes, or it can be positioned as a truly innovative product, worthy of market leadership — and a hefty price tag and significant support costs.

In the latter situation, ask this question to see what makes the vendor tick.

Clients

How many clients have bought this product, and how many can serve as references?

What kind of market share does this product have?

Of the companies who bought it, how many are happy enough to tell others about their wonderful decision?

Watch out for vendors who claim that their customers are happy but don't want to be identified because they're doing top-secret, strategic work. How could it be damaging for the world to know that a company purchased and is using a product if its application and business use isn't also revealed? If a product vendor avoids providing references, start asking questions!

The Future

What significant advances do you expect in this market segment this year, and what are you doing in each area?

Here's what you want to find out (but without asking the question this way): "Are you guys just standing still, milking money off this product, or are you continuing to improve it?"

Internet Approach

What is your strategy for Internet technologies?

Almost everyone has a Web enablement story. Ask the vendor for its version.

Integrity

Do you guarantee that your product will work as advertised?

Ah, a truly inspirational question. Gauging a vendor's response to this question tells you a great deal about the character of both the company and its sales representative. It also generally indicates whether you're in for a bumpy ride if you do business with these folks.

Index

(continued)

(continued)

(continued)

(continued)

(continued)